D1599425

American Covert Operations

American Covert Operations

A Guide to the Issues

J. Ransom Clark

Contemporary Military, Strategic, and Security Issues

PRAEGER™

An Imprint of ABC-CLIO, LLC
Santa Barbara, California • Denver, Colorado

Library of Congress Cataloging-in-Publication Data

Clark, J. Ransom.
  American covert operations: a guide to the issues / J. Ransom Clark.
    pages cm. — (Contemporary military, strategic, and security issues)
  Includes bibliographical references and index.
    ISBN 978-0-313-38328-1 (alk. paper) — ISBN 978-0-313-38329-8 (ebook)
  1. Special operations (Military science)—United States—History. 2. Intelligence
service—United States—History. I. Title.
    U262.C53 2015
    356'.16—dc23   2015005698

ISBN: 978-0-313-38328-1
EISBN: 978-0-313-38329-8

19 18 17 16 15   1 2 3 4 5

This book is also available on the World Wide Web as an eBook.
Visit www.abc-clio.com for details.

Praeger
An Imprint of ABC-CLIO, LLC

ABC-CLIO, LLC
130 Cremona Drive, P.O. Box 1911
Santa Barbara, California 93116-1911

This book is printed on acid-free paper (∞)

Manufactured in the United States of America

Contents

Preface

This work is designed to be an introduction to the concept and the practice in the United States of covert and special operations as tools of American presidents in conducting foreign and national security policy. It is also intended to serve as a guide to the substantial body of literature–both academic and official–on the subject. The hope is that discussion here will spark readers' interest in extending their knowledge and understanding of the role that covert and special activities have played in how the United States has interacted with the rest of the world over time as well as in some specific situations. Attention to the text, notes, and selected bibliography can send the reader off to check out the works of both critics of and apologists for the use of such operations. Every effort has been made to make clear that in the reality of the American political structure covert and special operations represent the translation of policy (or, some will argue, the lack thereof) into action.

The focus here is on placing the use by the government of the United States of covert and special operations into an historical and functional context. While acknowledging that the government's use of secret means remains a matter of controversy, this is not a catalogue of disastrous misdeeds or amazing successes. Outrage over decisions made and implemented is largely absent, although some acts in retrospect seem so incredibly ill-advised that some comment becomes necessary. The main issues attendant to the use of covert and special operations are explored in the broadest sense and as they arise naturally in the longitudinal narrative. Both the "what" and "why" of particular occurrences are presented; and when outcomes are assessed, it is within the context of their time and the objectives of choices made. The primary effort is directed toward chronicling on a selective basis how covert and special operations have continued to be present in American decision-making in war and peace from the nation's founding to the present—and are likely to remain so into the future.

Individual volumes of the *Foreign Relations of the United States* series from the U.S. Department of State, Office of the Historian, are referred to throughout the chapter endnotes as *FRUS*, [years covered], [volume number], [volume title], [document title], [document date], [document number]. *FRUS* materials are available at: http://history.state.gov/historicaldocuments.

All materials with an Internet address were accessed December 31, 2014.

The support from my wonderful wife, Helen Obenchain-Clark, over the lengthy period devoted to researching and writing this book was a necessary and critical component in finishing the project. The same is true for my long-suffering editor at ABC-CLIO/Praeger, Steve Catalano, whose patience must have been sorely tried but who did not let it show.

I dedicate this work to my four grandsons who have served one or more tours in Iraq and/or Afghanistan with the U.S. Army and Marine Corps. I am proud of and honor their service.

CHAPTER 1

Establishing Context

This initial chapter outlines the context, definitions, and general terminology that surround the subject of American covert and special operations. It "sets the stage" for the chronological presentation that follows by introducing the ideas and concepts that appear later in more highly developed form. Examples used to illustrate or add emphasis to the general points made here are drawn from more in-depth discussions in the relevant chapters.

The use of secret means to pursue perceived national interests has been practiced throughout human history. Thus, it should be no surprise that American leaders have turned to such means from the country's beginning. U.S. history is replete with uses of covert means in pursuit of national goals. At the country's beginning, the Continental Congress and its agents were actively involved in the covert financing of the war for independence; and George Washington participated in plans to kidnap not only the traitor Benedict Arnold but also a future British king.

In American history, initiation of covert operations in peacetime has, with a few exceptions, been the prerogative of the president, while wartime covert activities, especially the creation and use of specialized units, have rested primarily with the military command structure. Of course, the president is the commander in chief in peacetime and war. A close reading of the decision-making process during the Vietnam War clearly shows U.S. presidents involved in the conduct of both the conventional and unconventional aspects of the war. In recent years, we have seen officially unacknowledged attacks from unmanned aerial vehicles (UAVs) or drones used as a critical component of waging war against international terrorism, specifically al-Qaeda and its affiliates. Lethal attacks by drones against terrorist sites, groups, and individuals in war zones and beyond would not have occurred without the approval of Presidents George W. Bush and Barack Obama.

While using the same playbook, covert operations are generally viewed as a "civilian" activity and special operations as a "uniformed" activity. Nonetheless, there are numerous examples of ostensibly civilian operations that included military involvement. President Thomas Jefferson's clandestine envoy to North Africa raised a surrogate military force to overthrow the Pasha of Tripoli but was backed up by a handful of U.S. Marines and a Navy midshipman. James Madison had American gunboats waiting offshore during the incursion of a group of "volunteers" into Spanish-held northern Florida. The activities of the Office of Strategic Services (OSS) in World War II involved a mixture of civilian and military personnel and cultures. In both the Korean and Vietnam wars, some of the best-known leaders on the "civilian" side of covert operations were military officers on temporary assignment to the Central Intelligence Agency (CIA). Such seconding of military personnel to perform unconventional, military-like tasks in civilian attire blurs the civilian-military distinction. In 2001, a mix of CIA covert paramilitary officers and U.S. Special Operations Forces fueled the campaign that ousted the Taliban from Afghanistan. And more recently, the raid by Navy SEALs that killed Osama bin Laden was undertaken under the direction of then CIA director Leon Panetta. Thus, covert and special operations intersect and merge at times, becoming almost indistinguishable. This trend is especially evident in the post–September 11 (9/11) quasi-warlike environment.

What Are We Talking About?

Nineteenth-century Prussian military theorist Carl von Clausewitz argued, "[W]ar is not a mere act of policy but a true political instrument, a continuation of political activity by other means."[1] The political options available to a nation that desires to affect the behavior or attitude of another nation (or, increasingly, a nonnational actor) range from doing nothing to waging total war. In between, there are a number of political instruments that avoid doing nothing yet stop short of waging all-out war. These include one-on-one diplomacy, third-party or multinational negotiations, targeted trade barriers, economic boycott, broad multinational economic sanctions, and other acts that are completely open and visible to the targeted side. Nations may choose to adopt other less visible means of seeking to counter the actions of one or more nations or groups or to influence the direction (positively or negatively) that others may take. This is where the concept of covert operations—another set of political instruments for doing something rather than launching a full-scale war—comes into play.

In its simplest form, "covert" means hidden; and "secret" is a basic synonym. Thus, at its most elemental, a covert operation is one the instigator of which wants to keep hidden or secret from the intended target, as well as others—that is, hidden in its inception and execution; perhaps, hidden in its potential attribution; and, at times, even hidden in its result. The drive to influence others is the raw meat of politics, domestic and foreign. Governments are rarely fully forthcoming about the methods and goals of even their overt political activities, and covert operations give the appearance of being able to impact the affairs of others without necessarily being held accountable for actions or outcomes. In peacetime operations, the desire for deniability—we didn't do it!—is one of the basic reasons that covert operations remain a policy option for governments. The goal of a peacetime covert operation is to influence events or the actions of others without anyone knowing that such has occurred. In wartime, military-initiated covert operations may be less concerned with hiding who is behind an activity than with ensuring that the inception and execution of actions are conducted with the greatest secrecy in order to attain maximum surprise and impact.

Some Definitions

The U.S. military has probably gone the farthest in drawing some definitional lines across the broad area of covert and special operations. The 2012 version of the *Department of Defense Dictionary of Military and Associated Terms* defines covert operations as those operations that are "so planned and executed as to conceal the identity of or permit plausible denial by the sponsor." This is in contrast to "clandestine operations," in which "emphasis is placed on concealment of the operation rather than on concealment of the identity of the sponsor." Within these definitions, special operations can be both covert and clandestine and are defined as:

> Operations requiring unique modes of employment, tactical techniques, equipment and training often conducted in hostile, denied, or politically sensitive environments and characterized by one or more of the following: time sensitive, clandestine, low visibility, conducted with and/or through indigenous forces, requiring regional expertise, and/or a high degree of risk.[2]

It is interesting that this definition eliminates specific verbiage that was in the dictionary's 2005 version. It substitutes "time sensitive" for "covert" where it previously noted that special operations "often require covert, clandestine, or low-visibility capabilities." Also omitted are the earlier references to (1) operations being carried out "in conjunction with . . . other government agencies," (2) the use of not only indigenous but also surrogate forces in operations, and (3) Special Operations Forces being dependent on "indigenous assets."[3] These changes may have been made to counter concerns about the use of military personnel in circumstances that would require the president to report to Congress on a particular activity if the CIA was performing it.

The definitional picture is clouded by the institutionalization of the term "covert action," a practice that began following World War II. That term is narrower in its definition than the broader "covert operations" formulation. "Covert action" describes a set of policy options, generally associated with the CIA, specifically designed to give the appearance of being overt and indigenous to the target area and in which the role of the United States would not be obvious and, in fact, could be denied. (See sidebar, *Official Definition of Covert Action.*) However, this goal of attaining "deniability" has become increasingly problematical since virtually instantaneous communication from almost anywhere has increased dramatically. Whether a large-scale covert operation can be kept secret is very much in doubt today. During the intervention by the United States in Laos in the 1960s and early 1970s, the North Vietnamese certainly were aware of the U.S. support for Hmong tribesmen, while the main Western media of the day chose to underreport or misreport that conflict in favor of blanket coverage of events in Vietnam. On the other hand, the "covert" aid to Afghans fighting the Soviet forces in the 1980s was anything but covert in that it was well known that the United States was furnishing arms and other aid to the Mujahedeen. Similarly, the use of drone aircraft to attack terrorists in such locales as Yemen and East Africa is regularly reported by the U.S. and world media. In fact, the New America Foundation maintains a public database of U.S. drone strikes in Pakistan and Yemen from 2004 to the present.[4]

Official Definition of Covert Action

The Intelligence Authorization Act of 1991, Pub. L. 102–88, 105 Stat. 429 (Aug. 14, 1991), Section 503 (c)(4)(e), defines covert action as "an activity or activities of the United States Government to influence political, economic, or military conditions abroad, where it is intended that the role of the United States Government will not be apparent or acknowledged publicly, but does not include: (1) activities the primary purpose of which is to acquire intelligence, traditional counterintelligence activities, traditional activities to improve or maintain the operational security of United States Government programs, or administrative activities; (2) traditional diplomatic or military activities or routine support to such activities; (3) traditional law enforcement activities conducted by United States Government law enforcement agencies or routine support to such activities; or (4) activities to provide routine support to the overt activities . . . of other United States Government agencies abroad."

Both deniability and operational secrecy of covert and special operations are also influenced by the roles played by the U.S. Congress and its members in performing that institution's responsibility for oversight of government operations. As early as 1812, Congressional concerns about the looming war with Britain forced President Madison to disavow his covert support for an effort to wrest Florida from Spain. In 1846, there were many heated words in the House of Representatives directed at former president John Tyler and his secretary of state, Daniel Webster, over a domestic covert operation that facilitated the conclusion of a treaty with Britain in 1842, settling a dispute over the boundary line between Maine and Canada. However, it is after World War II, when the administration of President Harry Truman began the institutionalization of intelligence and covert activities, that the relationship between Congress and the president came under increasing stress. For a number of years, Congress generally allowed wide presidential latitude in covert operations, with after-the-fact discussion and/or criticism of presidential decisions. From the mid-1970s and increasingly after the Iran-Contra scandal in the 1980s, Congress had substantial success in requiring presidents to provide at least notification to the relevant congressional committees (or a limited number of congressional leaders) of projected covert operations being run by the CIA. However, there is no requirement for notification of Congress of activities undertaken by the Pentagon under the special operations rubric.

A Typology of Covert Operations

Americans neither invented nor are the sole practitioners of covert and special operations. In fact, they have been practiced for a long time. As one historian of ancient intelligence activities points out, "the historical record suggests that very few societies . . . could pass up the opportunity of using such useful and flexible tools when overt military operations were either impractical or impossible."[5] In more modern times, the language may be different, but the meaning—and the practice—is the same. For instance, the British refer to "special political action," while the Russians use the term "active measures."

Covert and special operations are generic terms that taken together provide a "big tent" for a number of activities by which national policy is carried out with varying levels of secrecy and varying degrees of intrusion into the affairs of others. From the instigator's point of view, covert and special operations may range along a spectrum of actions—from relatively low-risk, low-profile activities based on indirect persuasion to high-risk, high-profile ventures involving the direct use of military force. Because they are perceived as increasing flexibility within policy choices, covert operations are sometimes referred to as the "third option" or the "quiet option." However, there are numerous instances (old and new) where "quiet" is not the description of how a particular operation actually played out.

Covert and special operations can be categorized into five basic types— propaganda, political action, cyberwar (the newest addition to the list), paramilitary activities, and unconventional military operations. However, all or a mixture of the forms may exist in a given situation.

Propaganda

Propaganda sits at the low-risk, low-profile end of the covert operations spectrum. Despite the tendency of people to react negatively to the use of the term, "propaganda" is not per se a bad thing. That is, it does not have to be—and the best propaganda usually is not—false information. Basically, it amounts to little more than seeking to influence the thinking or attitude of a target audience toward some subject. Democratic governments use propaganda for civic purposes, as in "Register to Vote" or "Eat more Vegetables and Fruits" campaigns. From 1953 to 1999, the United States engaged in open or "white" propaganda through the United States Information Agency (USIA). Via films, print publications, and television and radio programs, USIA's propaganda about American society sought to show the advantages of democracy over communism.

Propaganda is a minimally invasive form of interference in the affairs of others. A covert propaganda campaign might involve nothing more than hiring a journalist with access to the media in a target country to publish articles supporting U.S.-backed policies or challenging some position of the local government. Benjamin Franklin, the Continental Congress's representative in France during the Revolutionary War, had a Dutch journalist on the payroll, who placed pro-American articles in European newspapers. This was in addition to the Continental Congress's funding of a pro-American newspaper in Quebec. During the American Civil War, Confederate representatives in Europe conducted a wide-ranging propaganda campaign in an effort to counteract the strong aversion of many Europeans to slavery. As new information media came into existence, they, too, became vehicles for the dissemination of propaganda. One of the early acts of the U.S. military government in Germany at the end of World War II was to launch a radio station in Berlin (Radio in the American Sector or RIAS) as a means for challenging communist propaganda. Covert broadcasting also played an important role in the Cold War with the CIA's funding of Radio Free Europe and Radio Liberty.

Propaganda can be used as the main focus of a covert effort, or it may be an ancillary aspect in a broader range of activities. Propaganda campaigns are rarely one-shot affairs, as changing attitudes across a population usually requires repetition for reinforcement. Nor are propaganda campaigns spur-of-the-moment happenings. Campaigns of any sort require purpose and preparation, followed by continuing attention and guidance to make sure that the original purpose is being met. Moving a propaganda campaign forward requires people ("assets") who are both capable of understanding what needs to be done and able to make it happen. The assets needed to make an operation work should be in place (and tested) prior to launching the operation.

After an item of propaganda is placed in a newspaper, it is hoped that it will be repeated by other news media. Foreign wire services are an especially desirable ancillary target for further dissemination. However, wider distribution also creates the potential for "blowback," where U.S. media report the planted information to U.S. audiences. U.S. intelligence services are prohibited from propagandizing the American public, but there is little doubt that "blowback" happens. It is reasonable to expect that as the subject matter of planted overseas propaganda increases in importance ("news worthiness") so does the likelihood that it may show up on a major U.S. news service and in daily newspapers or television news broadcasts.

At the opposite end of the propaganda spectrum from "white" propaganda, where the source or sponsor of the material is openly identified (as in "Voice of America" radio broadcasts), are other forms of propaganda, collectively referred to as "black" propaganda. This propaganda presents itself as originating with a source other than the actual source. It may be factually truthful, but does not have to be. In fact, it can be utter fabrication in its sponsor, content, and stated purpose. Black propaganda might include a claim by a dissident radio station that it is emanating from within the target territory, although it is actually in another country. During World War II, the Morale Operations (MO) Branch of the OSS used black radio broadcasts in the Italian campaign and, after D-Day, directly targeted German soldiers and the general population. After the Allied armies had freed Paris, MO went on the air with *Volkssender Drei*, purporting to be the voice of the German Freedom Party and claiming that local anti-Nazi partisans located in Germany's Alpine region were operating it.[6]

One form of black propaganda, called *dezinformatsiya* or disinformation, was an effective weapon for the Soviet Union during the Cold War. False stories generated years ago by Soviet disinformation specialists continue to resonate in certain parts of the world. The effort to spread the idea that AIDS was created in a U.S. government laboratory is still believed (or at least repeated) in third world and Western media, as is the equally fabricated canard that the CIA had a hand in the assassination of President John F. Kennedy.[7] Black propaganda can also play an integral role in military operations designed to deceive an enemy. The Allies' subterfuge by which the Germans became convinced that the Allied landing in 1944 would occur elsewhere than Normandy was a classic deception effort. The deception focused on manipulating Hitler's perception of the situation by providing false but corroborating information across a range of information resources.

Political Action

The kinds of politically based activities that constitute political action involve a level of aggressiveness beyond the creation and dissemination of propaganda. The degree of invasiveness in the affairs of others will vary according to the means being employed, but political actions will usually stop short of the direct use of force. Essentially, political actions involve the use of political means to seek to influence, change, or reinforce the political direction or stance of the government of another country.

The decision to engage in a political action will necessitate choosing among several techniques. Many political actions involve assisting individuals and/or groups to do something that they want to do but lack the resources to accomplish. The central element in the decision-making process of the supplier of the assistance is whether the receiving group's goals are consistent with the supplier's own interests. The United States has on multiple occasions provided funding and advice for the election campaigns of individuals or parties in order to forestall the taking over of a government by a group perceived as hostile to U.S. interests—for example, Italy in 1948 and Chile in 1964. Quiet monetary subsidies have been extended to labor, cultural, social, intellectual, and other kinds of national and international civic engagement organizations in their competition with groups hostile to U.S policy goals—such as, subsidies to the National Student Association post–World War II. At times, covert campaigns designed to affect a country's economic machinery have been launched in an effort to create adverse economic conditions within that country—as in Cuba after 1959. The United States has also aided in planning, preparing, or otherwise supporting coups by internal forces to remove a sitting government—examples include Hawaii in 1893 and Iran in 1953.

All types of covert political actions are controversial to various degrees. This is in essence the "Should we or shouldn't we" debate. However, the area that is most hotly disputed involves the direct application of violence—assassination. There is no widely accepted legal definition of assassination, and the difference between how such acts are viewed in wartime and peacetime further complicates the issue. The targeted killing or assassination of a military leader during wartime is accepted as a completely legitimate activity. The planned ambush and shooting down in April 1943 of the airplane carrying the commander in chief of the Japanese Combined Fleet (and architect of the attack on Pearl Harbor), Admiral Isoroku Yamamoto, is accepted as an action against a valid military target. On the other hand, assassination during peacetime has been generally interpreted to mean the killing of a specific individual for political reasons, an act that has been almost universally condemned for centuries. Nevertheless, the United States has on several occasions plotted to assassinate a foreign leader. The best documented (and most outrageous) of such efforts may be those targeting Cuban leader Fidel Castro. From 1961 to 1965, CIA personnel, acting they believed on the desires of President John Kennedy as transmitted to them by Justice Secretary Robert Kennedy, used American underworld figures and anti-Castro Cubans in a series of plots (none obviously successful) to kill the Cuban leader.[8] In the intervening years, the line dividing how wartime and peacetime assassinations are viewed has been blurred by armed conflicts that fall into the ill-defined "other than war" category, into which counterterrorism operations appear to belong. The use of missile-firing drones to target terrorist sites, groups, and individuals, including in some instances U.S. citizens, has introduced a new, technologically advanced twist to discussions about what constitutes assassination when such lethal activities occur away from the battlefield.

Cyberwar

The techniques included in the term *information warfare* a few years ago have now been expanded to encompass the concept of "cyberwar." Because of its newness in our thought processes and because much about it remains shrouded in secrecy, there is no standard definition of cyberwar. However, the definition used by the Rand Corporation works well:

> Cyber warfare involves the actions by a nation-state or international organization to attack and attempt to damage another nation's computers or information networks through, for example, computer viruses or denial-of-service attacks.[9]

The widespread availability of new communications technologies represents an additional option in the toolbox of covert and special operations and a threat to the potential cyberwar targets in this country. One astute commentator argues that the United States dived headlong into the cyberwarfare arena without an accompanying strategy (offensive or defensive), creating a new military command (U.S. Cyber Command or USCYBERCOM) in 2009 "to use information technology and the Internet as a weapon."[10] Like covert and special operations generally, cyberwarfare has a range of uses that reach from the minimally invasive to the highly invasive and highly disruptive. In an approach certainly more personal than dropping propaganda leaflets from airplanes, it has been widely reported that prior to the beginning of the

2003 U.S. attack on Iraq, the U.S. military hacked into the Iraqi Defense Ministry's e-mail system and sent Iraqi military officers e-mails urging them to abandon Saddam Hussein's regime. More recently, the Stuxnet computer virus/worm (and follow-on derivatives), widely argued to be the covert creation of either the U.S. or Israeli intelligence services, shut down a key group of Iranian nuclear centrifuges believed to be used to make bomb-grade uranium fuel. There is high expectation that the use of covert cyberattacks will continue to increase in number and sophistication into the future.

Paramilitary

Higher up the covert action spectrum from propaganda, political action, and cyberwar in terms of the level of violence—and in the level of difficulty in maintaining secrecy and deniability—are paramilitary operations. The larger these kinds of activities are, the less likely they can remain covert. At most, large-scale paramilitary activities might be "officially unacknowledged."

CIA Career Opportunities

The basic nature of covert paramilitary operations can be discerned from the CIA's listing of career opportunities: "Minimum requirements for Paramilitary Operations Officers include a bachelor's degree, military special operations or combat arms experience (ground, air or maritime), as well as combat leadership experience. Previous foreign travel and foreign language proficiency is highly valued."

Source: https://www.cia.gov/careers/opportunities/clandestine/paramilitary-operations-officer-specialized-skills-officer.html.

What, then, constitutes a paramilitary operation? The Defense Department defines paramilitary forces as "[f]orces or groups distinct from the regular armed forces of any country, but resembling them in organization, equipment, training or mission."[11] (See sidebar, *CIA Career Opportunities*.) In essence, these are military-type actions using ostensibly nonmilitary personnel (but not necessarily lacking military background). A covert paramilitary operation conducted by the CIA might involve:

- CIA officers—usually a limited number of individuals most of whom have military experience and often have served specifically with special operations units;
- U.S. military personnel seconded to the CIA by their individual services and who are particularly active in the training stage but also may engage in planning operations;

- contract employees hired for their individual skills (such as aircraft maintenance) for a specific activity or a set term as opposed to traditional employees who can be expected to remain continually employed and to move from project to project; and/or
- foreign national personnel who have been trained or are in some way supported by the CIA and who are engaged in military-like activities outside the traditional command structure of their national military organizations.

The supported forces may be operating within their home country or may be expatriate forces operating from a third country. The foreign national or surrogate force is the actual fighting element in this arrangement, with training, arms, supplies, and other equipment being supplied directly from the CIA or through arrangements with the U.S. military. Only a limited number of American personnel are involved and are not part of the fighting force except when forced to do so by circumstances. A military-managed covert paramilitary operation will look much the same except the Americans involved will be predominantly uniformed personnel, with the occasional civilian usually in an advisory capacity. American officers and noncommissioned officers may on occasion be allowed to lead foreign military or paramilitary units in combat situations. This occurred in Vietnam in the mid-1960s when U.S. military personnel of Military Assistance Command Vietnam's (MACV) covert arm, the Studies and Observation Group (SOG), led reconnaissance teams drawn from the South Vietnamese Special Forces across the border into Laos.

Covert paramilitary operations will usually have at their core a political objective, although they may appear to be focused on military objectives. An operation might involve the creation, training, use, or support of an indigenous, irregular military force for waging guerrilla warfare against an occupying power or a repressive regime. In this sense, the supported paramilitary force can be either a resistance movement (the French Maquis in World War II) or engaged in an insurgency (the ill-fated Cuban force that landed at the Bay of Pigs in 1961). In situations such as the OSS's teaming with the Kachin and other tribes in Burma in World War II and the CIA's involvement with the Hmong in Laos in the 1960s and 1970s, the supported groups were minorities intent on maintaining both their lands and way of life against an invading force. Paramilitary forces may undertake harassment and hit-and-run attacks against their opponents' regular forces; sabotage and demolition of military and economic facilities; parachute, cross-border, or maritime insertion of agents or supplies for supported groups; and the collection of intelligence for the planning or support of further operations. Other American paramilitary activities have included the provision of covert advice and assistance on counterinsurgency matters to governments under stress from antigovernment, guerrilla forces. The mission of Air Force lieutenant colonel (later major general) Edward G. Lansdale to the Philippine government in the 1950s to defeat the insurgency of the Hukbalahap or People's Liberation Army is one such operation. In addition, the intelligence assistance provided to a country or group under the auspices of a covert political action operation can begin to leak into the paramilitary realm, since training to resist an insurgency can change into helping plan or even participating in operations against those forces.

Discussions following World War II about the continuing need for paramilitary capabilities focused on such matters as support to underground resistance movements, guerrilla liberation groups, and indigenous anticommunist movements. But much of that discussion and subsequent decision-making drew heavily (perhaps too heavily) from OSS's experiences in World War II. The OSS's unconventional war mission included the Jedburgh teams, which worked with the anti-Nazi resistance in Europe, and Detachment 101 in Burma, which teamed with indigenous tribes to fight the Japanese. Efforts from the 1940s into the 1960s to create anticommunist resistance movements in Albania, Poland, the Soviet Union, North Korea, China, and North Vietnam, absent any viable internal resistance movement, did not yield the same successes that characterized paramilitary tactics in World War II.

Following the September 11, 2001 (9/11) terrorist attacks on the United States, a campaign of covert paramilitary and special operations has been an integral part of America's counterterrorism response during the administrations of both George W. Bush and Barack Obama. The *New York Times* has described this campaign as a "shadow war against Al Qaeda and its allies." (See sidebar, *The Shadow War*.)

The Shadow War

"In roughly a dozen countries—from the deserts of North Africa, to the mountains of Pakistan, to former Soviet republics crippled by ethnic and religious strife—the United States has significantly increased military and intelligence operations, pursuing the enemy using robotic drones and commando teams, paying contractors to spy and training local operatives to chase terrorists."

Source: Scott Shane, Mark Mazzetti, and Robert F. Worth, "A Secret Assault on Terror Widens on Two Continents," *New York Times*, August 15, 2010, p. A1.

That shadow war began when a CIA paramilitary team landed in Afghanistan two weeks after the 9/11 attacks. The CIA team linked up with the Afghan Northern Alliance and worked in tandem with follow-on uniformed special operations personnel and the U.S. Air Force and Navy to provide the

Alliance and the disparate groups allied with it with the firepower needed to drive the Taliban leaders and the al-Qaeda terrorists out of Kabul and into the mountains between Afghanistan and Pakistan.

When the United States and its allies invaded Iraq in March 2003, paramilitary and special operations personnel from both the CIA and the military's Joint Special Operations Command (JSOC) were on the ground in various parts of the country. In some cases, they were working directly with disaffected groups, particularly the Kurds in northern Iraq.[12] After the attention of the policy makers turned back to the situation in Afghanistan, the war there took on an especially intense paramilitary and special operations side. The CIA reportedly funds and controls a 3,000-man paramilitary force of local Afghans called Counterterrorism Pursuit Teams. The force is supposedly used to conduct covert paramilitary operations in Afghanistan and the tribal areas of Pakistan against al-Qaeda and Taliban targets.[13]

Since the covert paramilitary function was assigned to the CIA after World War II, voices have argued that such a role properly belongs to the military services. However, in the late 1940s, a military establishment in the throes of major postwar downsizing had no interest in adding any form of unconventional forces to its dwindling rosters. The military's antipathy to paramilitary and special operations activities continued well into the 1990s. That did not mean, however, the debate has been settled; and the proposal to turn paramilitary responsibilities over to the Pentagon has cropped up multiple times over the years. Included among the numerous recommendations of *The Report of the National Commission on Terrorist Attacks Upon the United States* (the 9/11 Commission), issued on July 22, 2004, was one to transfer "[l]ead responsibility for directing and executing paramilitary operations . . . to the Defense Department." There "it should be consolidated with the capabilities for training, direction, and execution of such operations already being developed in the Special Operations Command."[14] Nonetheless, events since 2004 indicate that the purely paramilitary function may continue to rest with the CIA. This is true even though the military services have seemingly discovered that their special operations forces are especially important in dealing with the fragmented threat posed by international terrorists and, therefore, deserving of greater attention than has previously been the case.

Unconventional Military Operations

What is under consideration when discussing covert operations run by the military are essentially those associated with specially organized task groups or units. The close coordination that has in recent times seemingly characterized the relationship between the CIA and the military in the conduct of covert operations is illustrated by the SEALs' raid in Abbottabad, Pakistan, on May 1, 2011, which killed Osama bin Laden. The raid was conducted as a covert operation under the overall direction of then CIA director Leon Panetta but using U.S. uniformed troops that are part of the JSOC. Although it did not interfere with the successful conclusion of the operation, the crash of one of the Black Hawk helicopters used in the raid helped to turn what was intended to be a covert operation into a highly public news story. However, the fact that bin Laden was finally run to ground was probably too significant to have remained secret for very long.

Creation and use of specialized forces in times of difficulties is nothing new in American history. They even predate the founding of the country, reaching back to the Ranger companies raised by Major Robert Rogers to fight on the British side in the French and Indian War (1754–1763). The kinds of stealthy, hit-and-run tactics employed by Rogers were also the forte of Francis Marion, South Carolina's "Swamp Fox," and his men during the Revolutionary War. Horse-mounted raider forces waged unconventional warfare on both sides in the American Civil War. In the wars in the American West following the Civil War, the U.S. Army created special units called Indian Scouts, which were comprised of members of the local Native American tribes. Their role was to apply local-area knowledge to aiding the cavalry in tracking hostile tribes. It is such local-area expertise that modern-day special operations forces seek to develop internally and procure through coordination with indigenous, surrogate forces.

Despite the earlier examples of the creation and use of unconventional forces, the U.S. military special forces of today are more direct descendants of the numerous elite forces created during World War II. Beyond the covert paramilitary activities of the OSS, the U.S. uniformed services deployed a large number of units specially trained to wage unconventional warfare. These military covert operatives plied their trade in all theaters of the war. Some of these units and their leaders became legendary in the annals of U.S. special operations.

After World War II, demobilization meant the end for most of the military's specialized units. Thus, when the North Koreans invaded South Korea in June 1950, the services had neither the troops nor the infrastructure in place to wage unconventional war. Before the war ground to a halt in 1953, however, the Army, Navy, and Air Force had all initiated covert and special operations. In a repetition of past decisions, most of the specialized forces developed in Korea were disbanded or rolled into existing conventional units. The most obvious of the continuing units was the 10th Special Forces Group (Airborne), established in June 1952 at Fort Bragg, North Carolina. This was the first formal and permanent unconventional warfare unit in U.S. military history. Some individuals deployed to Korea to work with partisan units being inserted behind North Korean lines, but the first real test for the Special Forces' unconventional skills came in Laos. From 1959, Special Forces personnel were part of a CIA covert operation to assist the Laotians in fighting indigenous and North Vietnamese communists. The covertness of the operation was emphasized by the deployment of military personnel in civilian clothing.

From the late 1950s, Army Special Forces teams became increasingly committed to counterinsurgency activities in South Vietnam. Initially, the teams worked with the CIA on developing the paramilitary potential of ethnic and religious minority groups, particularly tribal elements in the Central Highlands. After its formation in 1964, Studies and Observation Group (SOG), a joint special operations task force of the Military and Assistance Command, Vietnam (MACV), grew into a full-spectrum covert operation entity and assumed responsibility from the CIA for operations directed against North Vietnam. SOG ground reconnaissance teams consisting of U.S.-led indigenous personnel conducted cross-border operations in both Laos and Cambodia. Other SOG components were responsible for wide-ranging psychological/propaganda operations, for managing maritime operations against targets in North Vietnam, and for training and directing agents who were infiltrated via airdrops and over-the-beach insertions into North Vietnam. The Special Forces also carried out covert operations targeted on locating and rescuing captured U.S. military personnel. The best-known rescue mission was not an SOG operation. On November 20, 1970, the rescue force flew in helicopters from Thailand to the North Vietnamese prison compound at Son Tay less than 25 miles west of Hanoi. That the prisoners had been moved from this prison camp was disappointing, but the raid clearly illustrated the level of expertise that had been developed for special-task-oriented operations.[15]

In April 1980, the loss of the operational edge that special operations forces had built up in Vietnam was highlighted by the failure of the Iran hostage rescue mission (Operation EAGLE CLAW). In the aftermath of the Vietnam War, the traditional hostility of the conventional military establishment toward special operations had come to the fore and funding of special operations had been significantly reduced. A Special Operations Review Group found significant command-and-control problems with Operation EAGLE CLAW exacerbated by the ad hoc nature of the operation and excessive compartmentalization among the services. When the military found it impossible to reform itself in matters of interservice cooperation and encountered the same command-and-control problems during the 1983 invasion of Grenada (Operation URGENT FURY), Congress stepped in. The Cohen-Nunn Amendment to the 1987 Defense Authorization Act mandated the creation of a unified combatant command headed by a four-star general for all special operations forces. The U.S. Special Operations Command (USSOCOM) was formally activated on June 1, 1987.[16]

Although U.S. special operations personnel from several services participated in the military intervention in Panama in December 1989, the first real test for the newly formed USSOCOM came in the Middle East. Operations DESERT SHIELD and DESERT STORM brought a substantial deployment of unconventional warfare units and personnel. These forces undertook a wide range of covert and special operations before and during Operation DESERT STORM.[17] In October 1993, a mission by a special operations task force went badly awry in Somalia. The result was the so-called Battle of Mogadishu, the subject of the book *Black Hawk Down* and the movie adaptation of the same title. In the mid- and late-1990s, Army Special Forces and Navy SEALs deployed first to Bosnia and, then, to Kosovo in support of the NATO air campaign against Serbia. In Kosovo, special operations civil affairs units airlifted supplies to refugees and displaced persons; and psychological warfare personnel generated radio/television broadcasts and leaflet drops from dedicated aircraft. Special Forces teams also rescued the only two U.S. pilots downed during Operation ALLIED FORCE.[18]

Uniformed American special operations troops deployed to join the CIA paramilitary officers who had linked up with the Afghan Northern Alliance two weeks after the September 11, 2001, terrorist attacks. The capability of the special operators to call in U.S. Air Force precision-guided weapons and bombing attacks on the Taliban forces provided the Alliance and its partners the firepower to oust the Taliban from their hold on power in Kabul. While often viewed as a relatively conventional war, the invasion of Iraq (Operation IRAQI FREEDOM) in March 2003 also had a significant unconventional, special operations side. The effort began with the early infiltration into Iraq by the CIA and Special Operations Forces. Included in the missions for these forces was working with the Kurdish forces in northern Iraq to secure the airfield at Bashur. The special operators also worked closely with the Kurdish forces and the U.S. Air Force to rout the terrorist organization, Ansar al-Islam, from the group's stronghold on the Iraqi-Iranian border.[19]

The war against the remnants of the Taliban in Afghanistan became increasingly covert and special operations intensive. Special operations forces conducted night raids against suspected insurgents. These raids became increasingly unpopular among Afghans; and in April 2012, control of special operations missions, including night raids, was handed over to Afghan forces, with American troops to occupy only a supporting role.[20] At a minimum, however, that "supporting role" still involved "assisting" in conducting raids that target insurgent leaders. In addition, the role of special operations forces became even more prominent during the drawdown of conventional coalition forces from Afghanistan. Special operations teams deployed to the far reaches of the countryside where they trained Afghan commando forces and Afghan Local Police units.

Notes

1. Carl von Clausewitz, *On War*, trans. and eds. Michael Howard and Peter Paret (Princeton, NJ: Princeton University Press, 1976), p. 87.

2. United States Department of Defense, *DOD Dictionary of Military and Associated Terms*, Joint Publication 1–02 (Washington, DC: Department of Defense, November 8, 2010, amended through December 15, 2014), at: http://www.dtic.mil/doctrine/new_pubs/jp1_02.pdf (hereinafter *DOD Dictionary*).

3. United States Department of Defense, *Department of Defense Dictionary of Military and Associated Terms*, Joint Publication 1–02 (Washington, DC: Department of Defense, April 12, 2001, amended through August 31, 2005), I-1, at: http://www.bits.de/NRANEU/others/jp-doctrine/jp1_02(05).pdf.

4. See http://natsec.newamerica.net/about.

5. Rose Mary Sheldon, "The Ancient Imperative: Clandestine Operations and Covert Action," *International Journal of Intelligence and CounterIntelligence* 10, no. 3 (Fall 1997): 299.

6. On MO's radio operations targeting Germany, see Lawrence C. Soley, *Radio Warfare: OSS and CIA Subversive Propaganda* (New York: Praeger, 1989), pp. 123–55.

7. See Max Holland, "The Power of Disinformation: The Lie that Linked CIA to the Kennedy Assassination," *Studies in Intelligence* 11 (Fall–Winter 2001): 5–17. See also, U.S. Information Agency, *Soviet Active Measures in the "Post-Cold War" Era, 1988–1991* (Washington, DC: U.S. Information Agency, 1992), at: http://intellit.muskingum.edu/russia_folder/pcw_era/index.htm.

8. See U.S. Congress Senate Select Committee to Study Governmental Operations with Respect to Intelligence Activities [Church Committee], *Interim Report: Alleged Assassination Plots Involving Foreign Leaders*, 94th Congress, 1st session, S. Report No. 94–465 (Washington, DC: GPO, 1975), pp. 4–5, 71–180, at: http://www.intelligence.senate.gov/pdfs94th/94465.pdf.

9. Rand Corporation, "Cyber Warfare," at: http://www.rand.org/topics/cyber-warfare.html.

10. Richard A. Clarke and Robert K. Knake, *Cyber War: The Next Threat to National Security and What to Do about It* (New York: HarperCollins, 2010), pp. x–xi.

11. *DOD Dictionary*.

12. See Mike Tucker and Charles Faddis, *Operation Hotel California: The Clandestine War Inside Iraq* (Guildford, CT: Lyons Press, 2008).

13. Bob Woodward, *Obama's Wars* (New York: Simon & Schuster, 2010), pp. 8, 52, 59, 160, 170, 265, and 367.

14. National Commission on Terrorist Attacks Upon the United States, *The 9/11 Commission Report*, July 22, 2004, p. 415, at: http://www.9–11commission.gov/report/911Report.pdf.

15. General Manor provides a first-hand account of the Son Tay raid at http://www.sontayraider.com/history.htm.

16. See United States Department of Defense Special Operations Review Group, *Rescue Mission Report* [the Holloway Report] (Washington, DC: GPO, August 23, 1980) at: http://www2.gwu.edu/~nsarchiv/NSAEBB/NSAEBB63/doc8.pdf; and United States Special Operations Command, "Founding and Evolution of USSO-COM," in *United States Special Operations Command: History*, 6th ed. (March 31, 2008), at: http://www.socom.mil/Documents/history6thedition.pdf.

17. United States Department of Defense, *Conduct of the Persian Gulf Conflict: An Interim Report to Congress* (Washington, DC: GPO, July, 1991), pp. 5–1 to 5–6, at: http://www.dod.mil/pubs/foi/operation_and_plans/PersianGulfWar/305.pdf.

18. See Special Operations Association, *Special Operations Commemorative Book* (Nashville, TN: Turner Publishing Company, 2006), pp. 61–62.

19. See Catherine Dale, *Operation Iraqi Freedom: Strategies, Approaches, Results, and Issues for Congress* (Washington, DC: Congressional Research Service, Library of Congress, March 28, 2008), p. 19, at: http://www.fas.org/sgp/crs/mideast/RL34387.pdf; and Andrew Krepinevich, *Operation Iraqi Freedom: A First-Blush Assessment* (Washington, DC: Center for Strategic and Budgetary Assessments, 2003), pp. 18–19.

20. Alissa J. Rubin, "U.S. Transfers Control of Night Raids to Afghanistan," *New York Times*, April 8, 2012.

CHAPTER 2

From Revolution to World War II

The American Revolution

Covert operations were an integral part of the War of Independence.[1] On September 18, 1775, the Continental Congress established the Secret Committee, and charged it with covertly obtaining military supplies for the new nation. The Committee made its purchases through third parties, hiding its identity from suppliers who might not want to risk the wrath of Great Britain or did not want to do business with revolutionaries. Today, this tactic has a name—*plausible deniability*. To counter British control of ocean routes, the Secret Committee's ships bringing military supplies from distant ports conducted false-flag operations—they flew the flags of other nations. The Secret Committee also sold gunpowder to the Continental Congress's officially sanctioned covert navy—the privateers. The European powers had established a body of international law allowing the commissioning of individuals or groups to arm privately owned vessels and make war on an enemy's sea-borne commerce. Congress issued commissions—letters of marque and reprisal—to ships capable of attacking and capturing British merchant vessels and occasionally smaller Royal Navy ships. In one of the few significant naval engagements of the Revolutionary War, the privateer *Bonhomme Richard*, a renamed French ship donated by Louis XVI and commanded by Captain John Paul Jones, scored a victory in British waters in September 1799 over the British frigate *HMS Serapis*.[2]

On November 29, 1775, the Continental Congress created the Committee of Correspondence, which conducted many activities expected of an intelligence service. It used overseas agents, funded propaganda activities, and organized covert operations. In December, it met in Philadelphia with a French intelligence agent and began the negotiations that eventually brought the French into the war on the American side.

A number of Americans working in London and Paris played roles, first, in creating covert sources of military supplies and, later, in encouraging the French to join directly in the struggle. They included Arthur Lee, Silas Deane, and Benjamin Franklin. Without the support of French foreign minister Charles Gravier, Comte de Vergennes, and eventually of Louis XVI, what would have come from their efforts is arguable. The individual around whom much of the assistance revolved was the playwright Pierre Augustin Caron de Beaumarchais, author of *The Barber of Seville*. Beaumarchais had been involved in secret missions for Louis XV and Louis XVI; thus, when his sympathies were won over to the side of the British colonies, it was probably natural for him to come up with a covert scheme for aiding the Americans.

With loans from France and Spain, Beaumarchais established an ostensibly commercial trading company, *Roderique Hortalez et Cie*, which was in actuality a "black" operation through which covert assistance was channeled. While the French government did not share Beaumarchais's enthusiasm for the revolutionary cause, the company gave France an opportunity to cause trouble for Britain and to sell off some of the dated equipment in its arsenals. Artillery, gunpowder, muskets, blankets, clothing, tents, and other items were sold to Hortalez on credit. The company resold the merchandise to the Americans in exchange for trade goods, such as tobacco and cotton, which were marketed in Europe. The French government and private investors brought in to supply such articles as shoes and clothing were to be reimbursed for the original loan and the value of the supplies. Profits and losses belonged to the company. And there were losses, as the Continental Congress, for a number of reasons, including lack of funds and infighting within the Congress and among its representatives in Europe, failed to pay for what it was receiving. In the end, Beaumarchais was left empty-handed, a not uncommon outcome for middlemen in covert operations.[3] The clandestine French aid has been credited with enabling Washington to keep the Continental army in the field until the Americans could win their critical victory at Saratoga in October 1777.

In addition to help from the Spanish king, Carlos III, in funding Beaumarchais's covert supply operation, there was under-the-table assistance from Spanish-controlled territories. American traders picked up arms and ammunition from ports in Spain and the West Indies. The West Indies ports were used as bases by colonial privateers as they preyed on British merchant shipping. In the summer of 1776, the Spanish governor in New Orleans acceded to the urging of New Orleans businessman Oliver Pollock and delivered a substantial amount of gunpowder to American agents, and then allowed it to be transported up the Mississippi under protection of the Spanish flag. Other

Spanish aid moved from New Orleans to George Rogers Clark's river posts and to American-controlled ports for Washington's forces. Pollock financed much of the material flowing out of New Orleans by borrowing against his good name. His devotion to the cause brought bankruptcy.[4]

The Continental Congress in February 1776 approved a number of covert political and propaganda activities targeted on convincing Canadians to join the colonies in their struggle. It funded a pro-American newspaper in Quebec and sent a Catholic priest, Father John Carroll, to lobby for the American cause among Canadian clergy. Obviously, these covert efforts were not sufficient to shake Canada away from allegiance to the British throne.

Benjamin Franklin was on a committee appointed by Congress to develop a plan to encourage desertions among the Hessian mercenaries being hired by George III. A resolution offering land grants to deserters was translated into German and distributed covertly among the Hessian troops. Franklin was also involved in the forging of a letter that purported to be from a German prince to the commander of Hessian mercenaries in America. The letter argued that casualties among the German troops was much higher than the British were reporting, and that he was entitled to more "blood money," that is, the money paid to him for his men killed or wounded in British service, than he had received. The letter encouraged the officer to allow wounded soldiers to die, rather than save them to live on as cripples. As is often the case with propaganda, it is difficult to link results directly to the effort. Nonetheless, as many as 5,000–6,000 of the estimated 30,000 German soldiers that came to America to fight for the British may have deserted and taken up residence in the new country.[5]

As commander in chief of the Continental army, George Washington launched his share of secret operations. Washington was a master of the use of intelligence and deception in keeping his ragtag forces in the field, and he was open to unorthodox measures to achieve his goals. One such goal was to capture the traitor Benedict Arnold. Efforts to get the British to trade Arnold for the captured Major John André failed, so Washington's thoughts turned to a covert operation to seize Arnold and return him for American punishment. Over time, several plans were devised for kidnapping Arnold. For various reasons, none of them succeeded. In the end, the treasonous general would live out his life in England, hated on one side of the Atlantic and ignored on the other. Washington authorized at least one unsuccessful attempt to capture British generals Sir Henry Clinton and Baron Wilhelm von Knyphausen. Another proposal that was never implemented envisaged kidnapping King George III's son, Prince William Henry (the future William IV), during a visit as a naval officer to New York.[6]

Washington also organized America's first special operations unit— Knowlton's Rangers, named after their commander, Lieutenant Colonel

Thomas Knowlton. The role of the 120 handpicked volunteers was primarily armed reconnaissance in the no-man's land between the opposing forces. This was also the unit from which Nathan Hale volunteered for the spy mission that cost him his life. Knowlton's Rangers might have voiced a complaint heard by the specialized units that followed them: That generals tend to use them for whatever generals need at the moment, rather than for the special purposes for which they were created. Knowlton was killed in the Battle of Harlem Heights on September 16, 1776, when the Rangers were committed to battle on the British flank as light infantry. Revolutionary America also conducted effective use of covert warfare, especially in the southern colonies. Francis Marion (the "Swamp Fox") and Thomas Sumter (the "Carolina Gamecock") led the best known of these partisan groups. Marion and Sumter employed classic guerrilla tactics, with the civilian population providing a base of operations and the means to fade back into the local environment. The idea was to operate in relatively small units, launching surprise attacks followed by a rapid withdrawal from the field.[7]

There is one documented instance where Silas Deane, an American representative in Paris, commissioned sabotage work in England. The perpetrator was James Aitken, also known as "John the Painter." Aitken traveled to England on a French passport arranged by Foreign Minister Vergennes. It is difficult to ascertain whether the French understood Aitken's role, but they certainly knew that he was not traveling on a fake passport with plans to paint houses. On December 7, 1776, Aitken started a destructive fire at the Portsmouth dockyard. He then ignited another conflagration in Bristol. These fires created a furor in the British cabinet and had the newspapers reporting panic throughout the country. The heightened security brought on by the fires paid dividends when Aitken was caught. A speedy trial ensued, and he was hanged in Portsmouth on March 10, 1777.[8]

From Revolution to Civil War

George Washington left many legacies to the chief executives who followed him. One such was an answer to the question of which branch of the government—the executive or legislative—was to have primacy in dealing with the outside world. On July 1, 1790, the U.S. Congress—after some debate—approved Washington's request for a discretionary fund to be used for interactions beyond the boundaries of the new nation. The law establishing the Contingent Fund of Foreign Intercourse included an exception to the standard requirement for reporting expenses, whereby the president or secretary of state could certify that a certain amount had been expended, without having to provide specific details. Washington and his successors have used various forms of the Fund to conduct both open and hidden activities.

Most of Washington's successors have found it necessary to couple overt diplomacy with a less open backup plan. (See sidebar, *Taking Advantage*.) In fact, covert measures, particularly when the activity was in the hands of people who could not be linked to the president, saw frequent use in the republic's early years. In this way, the new and vulnerable nation could grow while reducing the need for the high-risk option of open warfare.[9]

Taking Advantage

Secretary of state and future president James Madison wrote: "Although it does not accord with the general sentiments or views of the United States to intermeddle with the domestic controversies of other countries, it cannot be unfair, in the prosecution of a just war, or the accomplishment of a reasonable peace, to take advantage of the hostile co-operation of others."

Source: James Madison to James Cathcart, August 22, 1802. *Annals of Congress*, 9th Congress, 2nd session, p. 709.

Thomas Jefferson, drafter of the Declaration of Independence, first secretary of state, second vice president, and third U.S. president (1801–1809), proved adept at conducting affairs on the dual overt and covert levels. During the negotiations that led to the Louisiana Purchase from France in 1803, Jefferson weighed actions other than diplomacy that might be necessary to bring the huge tracts of western land under U.S. control. He was prepared to clandestinely encourage uprisings by American settlers to create a pretense for American intervention. On the other hand, he cried treason when his former vice president, Aaron Burr, privately cultivated just such a scheme. It was, however, in Jefferson's dealings with the pirates of the Barbary Coast that his use of the dual-track approach comes most clearly into focus.

Some of the earliest expenditures out of the Contingent Fund paid off the Barbary States along the coast of North Africa—Algiers, Morocco, Tripoli, and Tunis—to release kidnapped American sailors and cease attacking American shipping in the Mediterranean. Prior to 1775, American vessels had been protected by British naval power and the blackmail Britain paid to the Barbary States. After the alliance with France, French naval ships and that nation's agreements with the pirates provided the same protection. With independence in 1783, the United States was on its own in dealing with the pirates. Initially, Congress appropriated the funds to bribe the Barbary leaders. In 1801, Pasha of Tripoli Yusuf Karamanli increased his demands.

Jefferson refused to pay, and the pasha declared war. The president responded by sending four U.S. ships to the Mediterranean. The grounding and capture of the *Philadelphia* and its crew in Tripoli harbor in 1803 produced a major embarrassment. Activity by the U.S. fleet brought the other Barbary leaders into treaties with the United States, but Tripoli continued the war alone.

Unable to negotiate with or defeat Tripoli, Jefferson decided on a covert operation, and positioned himself so he could deny any involvement. William Eaton, former U.S. consul in Tunis, returned to the Mediterranean in 1804 with the goal of raising a surrogate army, fomenting rebellion against Yusuf Karamanli, and replacing him with his more cooperative elder brother Hamet. With $20,000 supplied by Jefferson and a core of seven U.S. Marines and one midshipman, Eaton recruited a force in Egypt of about 600 Arabs more or less loyal to Hamet, Greek mercenaries, and Turkish and European soldiers of fortune. Eaton moved his force across 500 miles of Libyan Desert and, assisted by a bombardment from U.S. ships, captured the Tripolitan port of Derna in April 1805. As Eaton prepared to march on Tripoli, the pasha reopened negotiations with the U.S. consul general in Algiers for the release of the *Philadelphia*'s crew. A peace treaty was signed in June 1805; and U.S. ships hastily evacuated an unhappy Eaton, Hamet, the Marines, and the Europeans among the mercenaries. Hamet's Arab troops were left to their own devices.[10] Eaton's covert operation is memorialized in the first verse of the U.S. Marine Corps Hymn, "to the shores of Tripoli."

Jefferson's successor, James Madison (1809–1817), combined overt and covert efforts to extend American control over territory held by other countries. Spain controlled territory west of the Louisiana Purchase (from Texas to California) and areas in the south known as West and East Florida. The latter two areas became Madison's targets. West Florida reached along the 31st parallel from the Mississippi River to the Perdido River. Spain's control south of this line cut the territories of Mississippi and Alabama off from land access to the Gulf of Mexico. After the Revolutionary War, immigrants from the United States had moved into West Florida to take advantage of land grants offered by the Spanish government. With the connivance of the governors of the territories of Orleans and Mississippi, the president dispatched an executive agent, William Wykoff Jr., to West Florida. His role was to plant the idea that Washington would be open to a request for incorporation of West Florida into the United States. Wykoff incited the existing discontent among the Anglo-American settlers to a level where in September 1810 they "spontaneously" revolted against Spanish authority, declared the free and independent Republic of West Florida, and expressed the desire to be annexed by the United States. Madison could now intervene overtly "to protect the interests of the United States," and he sent in U.S. troops to maintain order. Ten weeks later, West Florida was incorporated into the Orleans Territory, essentially by the unilateral action of the president.[11]

Madison's covert foray into East Florida (essentially today's State of Florida) did not go as well. Madison's surrogate in the effort was George Mathews, a former governor of Georgia. The goal was to force the colonial authorities to surrender East Florida or, barring that, to encourage a rebellion to overthrow the Spanish regime and seek the protection of the United States. Mathews gathered a force from the Georgia-Florida borderlands and marched into East Florida in March 1812 under the guise of aiding a local rebellion. Backed by the offshore presence of American gunboats, Mathews captured the town of Fernandina and Spanish outposts north of St. Augustine. Following behind the insurrectionist force came regular U.S. troops to protect American lives and property. The looming war with Britain convinced Congress to oppose further involvement in the bid to take over East Florida. His covert plan to push the Spanish out of Florida having become too overt, Madison disavowed any connection with Mathews and cut off his covert support. Madison's abandonment of his surrogate force left behind a mess that dragged on as guerrilla warfare and reprisals until 1814 when the invading forces were finally pulled out.[12] It was not until 1821, in President James Monroe's administration, that Spain formally ceded Florida to the United States.

Madison showed great interest in the breakup of the Spanish Empire in the southern hemisphere. In 1810, he entrusted Joel Roberts Poinsett with a special mission to Argentina and Chile. The instructions given to Poinsett were broad and intentionally vague. He initially traveled under cover as a British businessman, and his first order of business was to determine whether the revolutionary governments in those countries were likely to become permanent. If so, he was to use his credentials as a chargé d'affaires to negotiate commercial treaties. After concluding a commercial agreement in Buenos Aires, Poinsett moved on to Chile, where a war with Peru (still under Spanish control) was underway. Poinsett served as a counselor to the revolutionaries, helped draft a provisional constitution, and even went so far as to accept a commission as a general in the revolutionary forces and lead troops into battle against the royalist army. His efforts, however, could not prevent the disintegration of the revolutionary junta through internal dissension, and he returned to the United States in 1814 without seeing Chile attain independence.

Poinsett was later asked by President James Monroe (1817–1825) to undertake a similar mission to Mexico in 1822–1823. Monroe wanted to know whether self-declared emperor Agustín de Iturbide had sufficient support to rule Mexico. Poinsett's conclusion that Iturbide was likely to be overthrown proved accurate. Then, in 1825, President John Quincy Adams (1825–1829) named Poinsett as the first U.S. ambassador to Mexico. In that position, he engaged in behind-the-scenes activities to create an opposition political party. His intervention in Mexico's internal affairs became so blatant that in 1829 the Mexican government requested his recall. For historian

Stephen F. Knott, "Joel Poinsett was the ideal covert operative for his time, an agent capable of broadly interpreting executive instructions in furtherance of objectives too sensitive to be acknowledged publicly."[13]

President Andrew Jackson (1829–1837) replaced Poinsett with Anthony Butler. Jackson wanted to expand U.S. boundaries by acquiring the Mexican territory of Texas, and he sent Butler off to Mexico with $5 million and instructions to purchase that border province. Finding the Mexican government uninterested in selling, Butler set out to bribe his way to his goal. Beyond filling the pocketbooks of some local officials, Butler's main "success" was to raise the apprehensions of successive Mexican governments about U.S. intentions toward Texas. The degree to which Jackson was involved in Butler's bribery schemes is a matter of dispute among historians. The fact that Jackson retained Butler as ambassador to Mexico until 1835 suggests the president may have achieved a degree of deniability that has withstood scrutiny all the way to the present.[14]

Despite Jackson's commitment to acquiring the Texas territory, it is generally accepted that he did not instigate the events leading to the Texas Revolution of 1835–1836. Neither Jackson nor his successor, Martin Van Buren (1837–1841), hurried to bring Texas into the Union. Issues included whether Texas would join as a slave-holding state, Mexico's refusal to recognize the Rio Grande River as the border, and reluctance on the part of some Texans to give up their independent status. It was not until the first year of President James K. Polk's (1845–1849) administration that Texas became a state.

John Tyler (1841–1845) may have been an "accidental president" (William Henry Harrison having died within a month of being inaugurated), but he did not shrink from using covert methods in pursuit of perceived American interests. In addition to the southern border issue between Texas and Mexico, Tyler inherited a long-standing dispute with Britain over the northern boundary between the United States and Canada. The Treaty of Paris of 1783 ended the Revolutionary War but left the boundary between Maine and the province of New Brunswick ill-defined, and the two sides had come close to war over the area in 1837–1839. Tyler and his secretary of state, Daniel Webster, were determined to end these tensions with Britain. The biggest impediment to a compromise was public opinion among Maine's citizens. Tyler and Webster set out to change this with a domestic covert operation paid for jointly from the Contingent Fund and by the British. The effort included the use of disinformation in the form of a probably forged map that supposedly had belonged to Benjamin Franklin and which seemed to support British claims, lobbying of state legislators, and well-directed propaganda in the form of planted articles supporting a compromise from Webster's paid "agent," Maine politician, former U.S. representative, and publisher Francis O. J. Smith. The effort succeeded, and the Webster-Ashburton Treaty was signed on August 9, 1842. Of the 12,000 square miles in dispute, Maine received 7,000 square miles and Canada 5,000.[15]

Four years later, the actions by Tyler and Webster were challenged in the House of Representatives. There was even discussion of whether Webster could be retroactively impeached for his "misuse" of the Contingent Fund. By then, James K. Polk was president, and he strongly supported maintaining executive secrecy in such matters. (See sidebar, *Polk on Contingent Fund.*) Polk's defense of executive secrecy came when he had already begun the series of actions—combining diplomacy, covert operations, and war—that would complete the annexation of Texas and acquire the Oregon, New Mexico, and California territories.

Polk on Contingent Fund

"The experience of every nation on earth has demonstrated that emergencies may arise in which it becomes absolutely necessary for the public safety or the public good to make expenditures the very object of which would be defeated by publicity. . . . In no nation is the application of such sums ever made public. . . . [I]t may often become necessary to incur an expenditure for an object highly useful to the country. . . . But this object might be altogether defeated by the intrigues of other powers if our purposes were to be made known by the exhibition of the original papers and vouchers to the accounting officers of the Treasury."

Source: President James K. Polk, Message to the House of Representatives, April 20, 1846, cited in Central Intelligence Agency, Center for the Study of Intelligence, "Our First Line of Defense: Presidential Reflections on US Intelligence: James K. Polk, 1845–49," at https://www.cia.gov/library/center-for-the-study-of-intelligence/csi-publications/books-and-monographs/our-first-line-of-defense-presidential-reflections-on-us-intelligence/polk.html.

In the dispute with Mexico over the boundary of Texas, Polk supported the Texans' position that the border was the Rio Grande River. Between his inauguration and Texas's vote to join the Union on October 13, 1845, Polk was prepared to provoke a war. Support in the Texas legislature for annexation short-circuited the war scenario. The annexation of Texas did not calm Polk's desire for the Rio Grande border and for the territory to the west of his Texas acquisition. In early 1846, Polk ordered U.S. troops into the disputed area north of the Rio Grande and precipitated the Mexican-American War, declared by the U.S. Congress on May 13, 1846.[16]

In preparing for war, Polk sent secret instructions to the U.S. consul in Monterey to stimulate separatist sentiment in California and support for annexation to the United States. Aware of the president's injunction, Captain John C. Frémont, with an armed force of about 60 men, crossed into California early in 1846. Frémont's presence was ostensibly part of his expedition of topographical exploration. However, he eventually led under the U.S. flag what began as the settlers' Bear Flag Revolt in June 1846. Whether he was acting in response to some vague presidential mandate remains in dispute, but his actions certainly matched what Polk wanted done in California. In addition, U.S. Navy ships, under the command of Commodore Robert F. Stockton, were available for support and provisions. The Treaty of Guadalupe Hidalgo, signed on February 2, 1848, ended the U.S.-Mexican War. While both his goals and his methods remain the subject of historical controversy, Polk—by the use of diplomacy, covert manipulations, and outright warfare— had, in a single term, pushed the borders of the United States all the way to the Pacific Ocean.

The American Civil War

Neither side in the American Civil War entered the conflict with a capability for covert operations. Nonetheless, both sides engaged in a range of covert activities, some militarily and others designed to garner international support or deny it to the opposing side. In fact, secret plans and actions played a prominent (but not decisive) part in the war. An early example is the clandestine slipping of President-elect Abraham Lincoln (1861–1865) into Washington, DC, before his inauguration, because of the threat of an assassination plot.[17]

One of the hopes of Confederate leaders was that they could obtain assistance from or even intervention by one or more European powers. The Confederate government not only engaged in diplomatic and covert efforts toward that end but also used the European nations to obtain war supplies and equipment. The Union's goal was to prevent external involvement and inhibit the movement of Confederate commerce across the Atlantic. Britain and France declared neutrality in the conflict, which in international law gave the Confederacy equal status with the United States as a recognized belligerent. U.S. representatives in Europe engaged in covert efforts to thwart the designs of those working for the Confederacy. The U.S. minister to Belgium, Henry Shelton Sanford, and the U.S. consul in Liverpool, Thomas Haines Dudley, were particularly active in this regard. Sanford's well-funded network of contacts reached throughout Europe and often allowed him to preempt planned Confederate purchases of supplies by buying them himself. He and the U.S. consul general in France, John Bigelow, former owner of the *New York Evening Post*, were skilled at placing pro-Union propaganda in major European newspapers.

Lacking a navy capable of breaking the Union's blockade of Southern ports, the Confederacy turned to Great Britain and France for procurement of ships to carry supplies through the blockade and for use as privateers. British and French neutrality necessitated that the activity be covert. British law forbade the arming of private vessels in its shipyards, and the cover for building the ships was that they were for private merchants. The Confederacy's primary shipbuilding agent was the Liverpool-based James Dunwoody Bulloch. The best known of the ships commissioned by Bulloch were the CSS *Florida* and CSS *Alabama*, both of which had success against Union shipping until 1864 when the *Florida* was captured in a covert boarding in a Brazilian port and the *Alabama* sunk in a battle with the USS *Kearsarge*. Bulloch moved to France in 1863 after the British seized two ironclad ships that were so obviously warships that it could no longer ignore the protests of U.S. consul Dudley. In France, Bulloch worked with Confederate commissioner John Slidell to initiate a covert warship procurement program, but was often frustrated by effective Union counterintelligence work and official protestations to the French government.[18]

One of the biggest obstacles for the Confederacy was the Europeans' strong aversion to slavery and, therefore, to the breakaway states. Southern representatives waged a substantial propaganda campaign to try to counter such sentiments. In addition to his quasiofficial activities as the Confederacy's representative in France, Slidell was active in paying European journalists to publish pro-Confederacy and/or anti-Union articles. Henry Hotze, a Swiss-born former U.S. diplomat in Belgium, managed a Confederate propaganda operation that reached from London into the major capitals of Western Europe. Hotze established his own outlet that appeared under the guise of being a British publication. His propaganda efforts made pro-Confederacy views available to a diverse readership that included government officials. However, there is no evidence that he was able to affect decisions made at the national levels in London, Paris, or other European capitals.[19]

Because the conflict was between regions connected by long and relatively porous borders and between deeply divergent views of what the world should look like, the Civil War gave birth to irregular and guerrilla forces beyond the specialized units created by the two militaries. The unconventional forces directly associated with the military structures of the two sides were identified by various terms, including *rangers*, *raiders*, and *scouts*. Named after Colonel John Singleton Mosby, Mosby's Rangers are one of the better known of such formal partisan commands. Although Mosby's Rangers practiced guerrilla-type tactics, frequently operating behind Union lines, attacking lines of communication, and collecting intelligence, the command was organized as the 43rd Battalion (later Regiment) of Virginia Cavalry—that is, its men were regularly enlisted soldiers who functioned under military discipline. Between operations, unit members were quartered with farm families over a wide area of northern Virginia. At a predetermined time or on special notification, the men would gather for missions. One of Mosby's more famous raids took place in March 1963, when he and 29 men infiltrated deep behind Union lines to the village of Fairfax Court House and captured Union general Edwin H. Stoughton and other personnel and escaped without a shot being fired. U.S. major general Philip H. Sheridan formed a counterpart unit to Mosby's Rangers in August 1864. Informally known as "Sheridan's Scouts" and dressed in Confederate uniforms or as civilians, they served as the general's eyes and ears in his campaign in the Shenandoah Valley and later in his James River expedition and the Appomattox Campaign in 1865. Operating as individuals and small units, the Scouts collected intelligence from within and behind Confederate lines, captured Southern couriers, hunted down enemy guerrillas, and occasionally engaged directly in combat.[20]

Some of the groups operating outside the military command structure were little more than criminal enterprises. Others may have begun as more organized irregular troops but degenerated into roving gangs that preyed as much on the local citizenry as on the opposing side. In Arkansas, Southern guerrilla groups, originally formed in response to a call from the commander of the Trans-Mississippi District, had by early 1863 begun to turn into little more than bandits. They began to consume the time and attention of regular Confederate forces trying to halt what was basically lawless pillaging. The violent conflict that began in 1854 in the Kansas-Missouri border region between armed pro- and antislavery forces continued to play out as banditry disguised as a guerrilla war during and beyond the Civil War. Confederate guerrillas, some with links to the central government but many without official sanction, were also a part of the war in northwestern Virginia, which broke off from the state and formed West Virginia; in eastern Tennessee and western North Carolina; and in Kentucky.[21]

There were substantial numbers in North and South who did not support their region's side of the conflict. Some engaged in what the target side termed *subversion*. In the South, dissidents might share one or a combination of antiwar, antisecession, and abolitionist views. These dissidents tended to band together in secret societies complete with their own constitutions, oaths, passwords, and signs. Their activities ranged across the spectrum of irregular operations. In addition to intelligence collection, they encouraged the avoidance of conscription, harbored individuals fleeing conscription, and initiated letter-writing campaigns to serving soldiers advocating desertion from the Confederate forces. Other groups carried out hit-and-run sabotage operations, striking railroads, bridges, and telegraph lines, or provided guides for Union cavalry raids behind Confederate lines. There is little evidence of organized efforts by Union authorities to coordinate these activities. On the other hand, the Confederates made several attempts to organize the Northern antiwar groups (collectively referred to under the label of *Copperheads*) for political and paramilitary operations.[22]

The existence of pro-Southern secret societies in the North, especially in Ohio, Michigan, Illinois, and Indiana, may have been of more value to the pro-Union governors of those states than to the Confederacy. Exaggerated fearmongering about these groups made excellent Union political propaganda. Raising the level of concern gave the authorities greater latitude to enact measures aimed at suppression of dissent under the label of fighting subversion. Nevertheless, Confederate agents appeared to put great store in the claims of the leaders of the secret societies, and projected a number of covert operations on the basis of promised support. Confederate general John Hunt Morgan's ill-fated foray into Indiana and Ohio in July 1863 was undertaken at least partially in expectation of local support—or even an uprising—from northern dissidents. By 1864, as the war increasingly turned against them, Confederate leaders believed that the way out of their situation was to energize their northern sympathizers. Technically neutral, Canada was exceptionally tolerant of Confederate covert activities. It became the locus for the South's plans to promote an uprising in what was then called the northwest but is today's Midwest. Thus, the Confederates' covert war became known as the Northwest Conspiracy.

After April 1864, Jacob Thompson, former interior secretary in the James Buchanan (1857–1861) administration, headed Confederate covert operations from Canada. Thompson arrived in Canada with $1 million approved for secret use by the Confederate Congress. He had available a diverse group of potential action officers, including Confederate soldiers who had escaped from northern prisoner of war camps, civilians who had fled to Canada, and assigned military personnel. Captain Thomas C. Hines, who has been captured with Morgan but had contrived his and the general's escape, usually led the latter. A succession of actions were undertaken, none successful in impacting the Confederacy's fortunes but sufficient to cause flurries of excitement in areas where activities were initiated. Hines and some of his forces were in Chicago in August 1864 prepared to attack Camp Douglas, a Union prisoner of war camp holding over 8,000 Confederate soldiers. However, the city's defenses had been reinforced because the Democratic National Convention was gathered there; and promised help from the Knights of the Golden Circle did not materialize. In September 1864, John Yates Beall, previously a privateer in the Chesapeake Bay area, and a small force of volunteers hijacked the ship *Philo Parsons* on Lake Eire. Their aim was to capture the main Union warship on the lake, the USS *Michigan*, and free the Confederate prisoners at Johnson's Island off Sandusky, Ohio. However, the agent who Beall had planted on the *Michigan* was discovered and the plan aborted.

In October 1864, about 20 Confederates raided the town of St. Albans, Vermont, 15 miles from the Canadian border. Before they fled back into

Canada on stolen horses, the group robbed the town's banks; but their effort to torch the town failed when their incendiary devices did not ignite. Hines made another attempt to free the prisoners in Camp Douglas in early November, but Union forces arrested the plotters before they could make their move. Hines managed another escape. Also in November, a team of Confederate agents, including Lieutenant John W. Headley, arrived in New York City with the goal of releasing Confederate prisoners of war being held at Fort Lafayette in New York harbor and igniting an uprising by Copperhead groups. Again, the promised support did not materialize. The eight members of the team managed to set fire to several hotels and other structures in New York City. The perpetrators got away, but the fires were easily contained and beyond causing alarmist newspaper headlines had little effect. John Yates Beall made several unsuccessful attempts to derail trains near Buffalo, New York, ostensibly to free Confederate prisoners being transported from Johnson's Island to Fort Lafayette. On his final attempt in December, he was captured, tried by a military commission, and hanged. Nevertheless, the Confederates in Canada were able to keep the authorities on the other side of the border on edge through a continuing stream of rumors and the planting of false stories of planned raids. A considerate number of U.S. troops were tied down throughout the war by the real and imagined threats generated from Canada.[23]

William A. Tidwell, a retired U.S. Army Reserve brigadier general and intelligence officer, produced two works that combined scholarship and inference to argue for the existence of one last, desperate Confederate covert action. Tidwell's careful marshaling of circumstantial evidence led him to the conclusion that President Lincoln's assassination was the end result of a plan—initiated at the highest levels of the Confederate government and supported by a clandestine Confederate network—to kidnap Lincoln. Tidwell argues that, faced with no other alternatives, John Wilkes Booth and the remaining members of his covert action team on April 14, 1965, killed Lincoln and wounded Secretary of State William H. Seward; the plotter assigned to murder Vice President Andrew Johnson decided to get drunk instead.[24]

From 1865 to World War II

Hawaii

As early as 1864, the United States was looking at the Hawaiian Islands as a site for a naval coaling station, but successive Hawaiian monarchs rejected a treaty granting base rights. Meanwhile, the struggle in Hawaii for political control between native Hawaiians and the descendants of New England whalers and missionaries (generally termed *haole*, the Hawaiian word for foreigner) intensified. By the 1870s, the haole business and plantation owners had wealth, land, and influence disproportionate to their 5–6 percent of the population. In 1876, a trade agreement removed the tariff previously levied on Hawaiian sugar. Putting the price of Hawaiian-produced sugar on a par with that from the mainland spurred growth in production at the islands' sugar plantations. This growth brought an influx of Chinese laborers—more than twice the number of haoles, followed by an even greater number of Japanese immigrants from the mid-1880s. Haoles' fears of losing their economic and political power provoked a constitutional crisis in 1887. King Kalakaua was forced to promulgate a new constitution that relegated the monarch to little more than a figurehead, established wealth and property ownership qualifications for running for the legislature, and gave American and European residents (but not Asian laborers) the right to vote.

The McKinley Tariff Act of 1890 nullified the trade treaty, and some of the planters and American businessmen in Hawaii began to talk about annexation to the United States. The turning point was the death of King Kalakaua in early 1891 and the succession of Queen Liliuokalani. The queen's accession was popular among Hawaiians, but petitions to her to change the 1887 constitution increased concerns among haoles. President Benjamin Harrison (1889–1893) let word be passed through Secretary of the Navy Benjamin Tracy to the leader of the annexationist group, Lorrin Thurston, that the United States would be open to considering annexation should such a request be forthcoming. When Liliuokalani announced in mid-January 1893 that she was going to promulgate a new constitution that would return actual rule to the monarch and give all citizens the right of franchise and candidacy, a haole-dominated "Committee of Safety" went into action. The committee maintained close contact with the U.S. representative in Hawaii, John L. Stevens. For his part, Stevens was acting on the basis of broad and vague instructions from Washington, which left him considerable latitude in handling matters. With encouragement from Stevens, the committee began planning a provisional government.

On January 16, 1893, Stevens brought sailors and Marines ashore from the USS *Boston*—to protect American lives and property—and housed them near the queen's palace. The next day, a provisional government was installed, government buildings were occupied, and martial law was proclaimed. Faced with the threat of U.S. military intervention, Liliuokalani surrendered. Stevens immediately recognized the new government as the de facto government of Hawaii. That timing can be everything was true for the coup plotters in Hawaii, as their effort to gain annexation encountered major obstacles. Although the Harrison administration sent an annexation treaty to the Senate in mid-February, a new president, Grover Cleveland (1893–1897), took office while the Senate was still debating the treaty. Cleveland repudiated the annexation given the circumstances surrounding the revolt. Annexation of Hawaii would come in 1898 after the outbreak of the Spanish-American War.[25]

Panama

Ten years after the Hawaiian revolt, President Theodore Roosevelt (1901–1909) made use of surrogates to achieve a long-sought-after goal of the United States. This time the surrogates were not fellow Americans but the people and leaders of what would become another country. Roosevelt's achievement was the agreements that made possible the building of the Panama Canal. Taking office after President William McKinley's assassination in 1901, Roosevelt was determined to move forward with building a U.S.-controlled water link between the oceans. The American experience in the Spanish-American War showed that such a connection was needed for U.S. national security. The question was whether the route would go through Nicaragua or the Panama part of Colombia. The French New Panama Canal Company offered to sell its Panama concession from Colombia for $109 million. When the U.S. House of Representatives voted overwhelmingly for the Nicaragua route, the French slashed their price to $40 million. Colombian chargé d'affaires Tomas Herrán on January 22, 1903, joined Secretary of State John Hay in signing a proposed treaty that granted the United States a 99-year lease on a 6-mile-wide strip across Panama at the cost of $10 million and a $250,000 annual payment. The agreement included a $40 million payment to the New Panama Canal Company. Ratified promptly by the U.S. Senate, the Hay-Herrán Treaty was rejected in Colombia.

Colombia's rejection of the treaty sent Panamanian business owners and politicians scurrying for support for splitting away from Colombia. Remote from the capital in Bogata, the Panamanians had generated sporadic revolts against Colombia's rule. Philippe Bunau-Varilla, one of the lead coupists, who also represented the French company wanting to sell the concession, left a visit to President Roosevelt clearly convinced he had the backing of the White House. On November 3, 1903, the insurrectionists seized control of Panama, and declared an independent Republic of Panama. An American cruiser, the USS *Nashville*, had arrived on the Caribbean side of Panama on November 2 with orders to prevent the landing of any armed forces. Since the Colombian government was the only party likely to attempt to land troops, this was an interventionist act. Two other U.S. warships converged on the Pacific side of the isthmus. In the immediate aftermath, the *Nashville* landed Marines in Colón, countering any thoughts those still loyal to Colombia might have had. The Roosevelt administration extended de facto recognition to the government of the Republic of Panama on November 6, 1903.

Fifteen days after the coup, the Hay–Bunau-Varilla Treaty provided the United States with use, occupancy, and control in perpetuity of a 10-mile-wide strip across the Isthmus of Panama. The new Republic of Panama received the offer that had originally been made to Colombia, Bunau-Varilla's New Panama Canal Company received the $40 million allocated for purchase of its concession, and Colombia was left with nothing.[26]

To World War II

In the years before World War I, the United States was less the initiator than the object of covert operations. Both sides of the conflict in Europe targeted neutral America. The German and Austrian governments initiated wide-ranging covert operations in the United States. Their agents engaged in propaganda, subversion in labor unions, and economic and physical sabotage. Political agitation, strikes, fires, and explosions all were part of the German covert campaign. British agents were also active, but their efforts focused on propaganda and activities designed to influence the Woodrow Wilson (1913–1921) administration and American public opinion over to their side.

When the Unites States entered the war in April 1917, it had little in the way of intelligence capabilities and no organized means for engaging in covert warfare. Much of the American covert activities during the war revolved around using existing assets (such as, attachés) in propaganda efforts targeted on reducing pro-German sentiment in neutral countries, particularly Spain and the Scandinavian countries. The naval attaché in Sweden organized an "Allied News Service" responsible for countering German propaganda. Within General John Pershing's Allied Expeditionary Force, the Propaganda Subsection of Army G2 (Intelligence) organized leaflet drops from balloons and airplanes. Leaflets targeting German soldiers were generally factual and projected such themes as the advantages of surrender and the inevitability of a German defeat. After the fall of the tsarist regime in Russia, covert propaganda efforts by the Americans and British to keep that country in the war on the side of the Allies were ultimately unsuccessful. Public opinion in Mexico was another active target for propaganda operations. There was also a propaganda campaign on the domestic front in support of the war and U.S. objectives. Created in April 1917 by executive order, the Committee on Public Information led this effort. Headed by George Creel, a former newspaperman, the activities of the Creel Committee encompassed all available forms of communication—newspapers, radio, posters, pamphlets, newsreels, and movies. Before it was abolished in August 1919, the committee had expanded its operations to nine overseas sites. This was America's first attempt at organized wartime propaganda.[27]

In the aftermath of World War I, U.S. intelligence capabilities were allowed to atrophy to only small pockets of activity in the army and navy. These organizations were engaged in monitoring radio and Teletype transmissions and breaking the codes and ciphers in which such broadcasts were made. It was not until the war clouds started to gather in Europe and the Far East in the late 1930s that the United States began the initial steps of organizing for the kinds of covert activity it would launch in World War II.

Notes

1. See John Bakeless, *Turncoats, Traitors and Heroes: Espionage in the American Revolution* (New York: Da Capo Press, 1998); and U.S. Central Intelligence Agency, *Intelligence in the War of Independence* (Washington, DC: U.S. Central Intelligence Agency, 1976), at: https://www.cia.gov/library/center-for-the-study-of-intelligence/csi-publications/books-and-monographs/intelligence/index.html.

2. John Frayler, "Privateers in the American Revolution," in *Stories from the Revolution* (U.S. Department of the Interior, National Park Service, n.d.), at: http://www.nps.gov/revwar/about_the_revolution/privateers.html.

3. Streeter Bass, "Beaumarchais and the American Revolution," *Studies in Intelligence* 14, no. 1 (Spring 1970): 1–18.

4. James Alton Jones, *Oliver Pollock: The Life and Times of an Unknown Patriot* (New York: Appleton-Century, 1937); and Barbara A. Mitchell, "Bankrolling the Battle of Yorktown," *MHQ* (Autumn 2010): 98–104.

5. See Edward J. Lovell, *The Hessians and the Other German Auxiliaries of Great Britain in the Revolutionary War* (New York: Harper and Brothers, 1884), at: http://www.americanrevolution.org/hessindex.html.

6. Bakeless, *Turncoats, Traitors and Heroes*, pp. 302–17. See also Sean Halverson, "Dangerous Patriots: Washington's Hidden Army during the American Revolution," *Intelligence and National Security* 25, no. 2 (April 2010): 139–41.

7. See Lance Q. Zedric and Michael F. Dilley, *Elite Warriors: 300 Years of America's Best Fighting Troops* (Ventura: Pathfinder Publishing of California, 1996), pp. 46–64.

8. See U.S. Central Intelligence Agency, *Intelligence in the War of Independence*; and Jessica Warner, *John the Painter: Terrorist of the American Revolution* (New York: Thunder's Mouth Press, 2004).

9. See Charles D. Ameringer, *U.S. Foreign Intelligence: The Secret Side of American History* (Lexington, MA: Lexington Books, 1990), pp. 29–48; Stephen F. Knott, *Secret and Sanctioned: Covert Operations and the American Presidency* (New York: Oxford University Press, 1996), pp. 87–136; and George J.A. O'Toole, *Honorable Treachery: A History of U.S. Intelligence, Espionage, and Covert Action from the American Revolution to the CIA* (New York: Atlantic Monthly Press, 1991), pp. 69–115.

10. See Richard Zacks, *The Pirate Coast: Thomas Jefferson, the First Marines, and the Secret Mission of 1805* (New York: Hyperion, 2005). See also Gerard W. Gawalt, "America and the Barbary Pirates: An International Battle against an Unconventional Foe," in *The Thomas Jefferson Papers* (Washington, DC: The Library of Congress, n.d.), at: http://memory.loc.gov/ammem/collections/jefferson_papers/mtjprece.

html; and Thomas Jewett, "Terrorism in Early America: The U.S. Wages War against the Barbary States to End International Blackmail and Terrorism," *Early American Review* (Winter-Spring 2002), at: http://www.earlyamerica.com/review/2002_winter_spring/terrorism.htm.

11. See Isaac Joslin Cox, *The West Florida Controversy, 1798–1818: A Study in American Diplomacy* (Baltimore: Johns Hopkins Press, 1918).

12. See James G. Cusick, *The Other War of 1812: The Patriot War and the American Invasion of Spanish East Florida* (Gainesville: University Press of Florida, 2003).

13. Knott, *Secret and Sanctioned*, p. 113. See also, Charles Janeway Stillé, *The Life and Services of Joel R. Poinsett: The Confidential Agent in South Carolina of President Jackson during the Nullification Troubles of 1832* (Philadelphia: 1888), at: https://archive.org/details/lifeandservices00stilgoog.

14. Quinton Curtis Lamar, "A Diplomatic Disaster: The Mexican Mission of Anthony Butler, 1829–1834," *The Americas* 45 (July 1988): 1–17.

15. See Gary May, *John Tyler* (New York: Henry Holt and Co., 2008), pp. 81–91; and Stephen F. Knott, "Covert Action Comes Home: Daniel Webster's Secret Operations against the Citizens of Maine," *International Journal of Intelligence and Counter-Intelligence* 5, no. 1 (Spring 1991): 77–87.

16. Ameringer, *U.S. Foreign Intelligence*, pp. 42–46. See John J. Carter, "Chapter 8: Covert Action and Westward Expansion in the Polk Administration, 1845–1849," in *Covert Operations as a Tool of Presidential Foreign Policy in American History from 1800 to 1920: Foreign Policy in the Shadows* (Lewiston, NY: The Edwin Mellen Press, 2000), pp. 79–89; and Anna K. Nelson, "Secret Agents and Security Leaks: President Polk and the Mexican War," *Journalism Quarterly* 52 (Spring 1975): 10–13.

17. Thomas Allen, *Intelligence in the Civil War* (Washington, DC: Central Intelligence Agency, 2007), at: https://www.cia.gov/library/publications/additional-publications/civil-war/index.html.

18. See James Dunwoody Bulloch, *The Secret Service of the Confederate States in Europe or, How the Confederate Cruisers Were Equipped*, 2 vols. (New York: G. P. Putnam's Sons, 1884); John D. Bennett, *The London Confederates: The Officials, Clergy, Businessmen and Journalists Who Backed the American South during the Civil War* (Jefferson, NC: McFarland & Co., 2008); and Walter E. Wilson and Gary L. McKay, *James D. Bulloch: Secret Agent and Mastermind of the Confederate Navy* (Jefferson, NC: McFarland & Co., 2012). On Union efforts to counter Confederate activities, see David Hepburn Milton, *Lincoln's Spymaster: Thomas Haines Dudley and the Liverpool Network* (Mechanicsburg, PA: Stackpole Books, 2003).

19. See Charles Painter Cullop, *Confederate Propaganda in Europe, 1861–1865* (Coral Gables, FL: University of Miami Press, 1969); Ella Lonn, *Foreigners in the Confederacy* (Chapel Hill: University of North Carolina Press, 1940), pp. 69–73; and Serge Noirsain, "Henry Hotze: Southern Propagandist," in *The Index*, Trans. Gerald Hawkins, at: http://www.chab-belgium.com/pdf/english/Index.pdf.

20. See John S. Mosby, *The Memoirs of Colonel John S. Mosby*, ed. Charles Wells Russell (New York: Little, Brown, & Co., 1917); Kevin H. Siepel, *Rebel: The Life and Times of John Singleton Mosby* (New York: Da Capo Press, 1997); and Allan L. Tischler, "Union General Phil Sheridan's Scouts," *America's Civil War* (November 2003), at: http://www.historynet.com/americas-civil-war-union-general-phil-sheridans-scouts.htm.

21. See Daniel E. Sutherland, *A Savage Conflict: The Decisive Role of Guerrillas in the American Civil War* (Chapel Hill: University of North Carolina Press, 2009). See also, Robert R. Mackey, *The Uncivil War: Irregular Warfare in the Upper South, 1861–1865* (Norman: University of Oklahoma Press, 2004), pp. 24–49.

22. See Georgia Lee Tatum, *Disloyalty in the Confederacy* (Lincoln: University of Nebraska Press, 2000); Frank L. Klement, *Dark Lanterns: Secret Political Societies, Conspiracies, and Treason in the Civil War* (Baton Rouge: Louisiana State University Press, 1984); and Jennifer L. Weber, *Copperheads: The Rise and Fall of Lincoln's Opponents in the North* (New York: Oxford University Press, 2006).

23. See John William Headley, *Confederate Operations in Canada and New York* (New York: Neale Publishing Co., 1906); James D. Horan, *Confederate Agent: A Discovery in History* (New York: Crown Publishers, Inc., 1954); and Oscar A. Kinchen, *Confederate Operations in Canada and the North: A Little-Known Phase of the American Civil War* (North Quincy, MA: Christopher Publishing House, 1970).

24. William A. Tidwell, with James O. Hall and David Winfield Gaddy, *Come Retribution: The Confederate Secret Service and the Assassination of Lincoln* (Jackson: University Press of Mississippi, 1988); and William A. Tidwell, *April '65: Confederate Covert Action in the American Civil War* (Kent, OH: Kent State University Press, 1995). See also, William Hanchett, *The Lincoln Murder Conspiracies* (Urbana: University of Illinois Press, 1986).

25. See William Adam Russ, *The Hawaiian Revolution (1893–94)* (Selinsgrove, PA: Susquehanna University Press, 1992); and Ruth M. Tabrah, *Hawaii: A History* (New York: W. W. Norton & Co., 1984). See also, Stephen Kinzer, *Overthrow: America's Century of Regime Change from Hawaii to Iraq* (New York: Times Books, 2006), pp. 9–30; and Knott, *Secret and Sanctioned*, pp. 150–52.

26. See David H. Burton, *Theodore Roosevelt: American Politician* (Cranbury, NJ: Associated University Presses, 1997), pp. 89–91; and Nathan Miller, *Theodore Roosevelt: A Life* (New York: William Morrow, 1992), pp. 398–409. See also, Philippe Bunau-Varilla, *Panama: The Creation, Destruction, and Resurrection* (New York: McBride, Nast & Company, 1914), pp. 159–431.

27. See Knott, *Secret and Sanctioned*, pp. 153–55; and Robert Jackall and Janice M. Hirota, *Image Makers: Advertising, Public Relations, and the Ethos of Advocacy* (Chicago, IL: University of Chicago Press, 2003), pp. 13–35. The "Records of the Committee on Public Information" are available on the National Archives site: http://www.archives.gov/research/guide-fed-records/groups/063.html#top.

CHAPTER 3

World War II

The Beginning of Organization

The U.S. Army and Navy established intelligence bureaucracies in the 1880s—the Navy in 1882 (the Office of Naval Intelligence or ONI) and the Army in 1885 (the Military Information Division or MID). The Department of State historically had expected its diplomats to report intelligence in the normal course of business. All of these activities focused on intelligence collection. Absent an organized covert operations capability, presidents from George Washington on used executive agents to conduct a wide range of covert activities. In wartime, the military tended to develop irregular war-related activities on an as-needed basis. Almost none of the wartime capabilities survived their wars.

The beginning of an institutionalized intelligence and covert operations capability came from the relationship of two Columbia Law School classmates, President Franklin D. Roosevelt (1933–1945) and Col. (later Maj. Gen.) William J. Donovan.[1] Nicknamed "Wild Bill," Donovan earned the Medal of Honor in World War I for leading an assault against German positions. In the interwar years, Donovan practiced law and dabbled in New York Republican politics. Beginning in the mid-1930s, Donovan made several ostensibly unofficial trips to Europe and North Africa to report on military matters for the War Department. In 1940, Roosevelt sent him to Europe to evaluate Britain's ability to withstand the German blitz. Another mission for the president in early 1941 sent Donovan to the Balkans and the Mediterranean to perform a strategic assessment.

Donovan's observations and his close contacts with British officials convinced him that the United States needed a centralized intelligence system outside the military services. The goal would be to centrally manage all aspects of intelligence activities—espionage, analysis, propaganda, psychological warfare, and paramilitary operations. Donovan proposed such an organization to the president in June 1941. An executive order of July 11, 1941, did not go that far, but authorized the coordinator of information (COI) to collect and analyze national security intelligence. Roosevelt gave the job to Donovan. Before December 7, 1941, Donovan worked on building COI's organizational structure, while planning an irregular warfare capability for his organization.[2]

The Office of Strategic Services

The onset of war created a new dynamic in Washington. On June 13, 1942, an executive order transferred Donovan's organization to the Joint Chiefs of Staff and renamed it the Office of Strategic Services (OSS). This move kept OSS outside a direct relationship with the army or navy, ensured a certain amount of operational autonomy, and provided greater access to military funding and personnel. OSS developed into America's first full-service human intelligence and covert operations agency. However, there were constraints on the scope and execution of the OSS's mission. The FBI under Director J. Edgar Hoover protected its mandate for collecting nonmilitary intelligence in Latin America. And as America's war effort developed, military commanders quickly established their own views about managing their theaters of operation.

Simultaneously with the creation of OSS, the use of propaganda was split between OSS and the newly established Office of War Information (OWI). The broadcasting responsibility for "white" (open or attributable) propaganda went to OWI, while OSS was responsible for "black" (covert or unattributed) propaganda. Under the leadership of CBS newsman Elmer Davis, OWI began as primarily a domestic information operation. It coordinated the release of war news and promoted the war effort. Congressional opposition to OWI's domestic activities—explaining the president's policies without appearing to advocate for them was the challenge—forced it more into overseas activities. In this work, it targeted both friendly and enemy peoples. By the end of the war, OWI was managing a substantial overseas propaganda campaign. However, the distribution of news and films and radio broadcasting to Latin America rested with Nelson Rockefeller's Office of the Coordinator of Inter-American Affairs. And OWI was never able to obtain operational jurisdiction over the propaganda activities of the OSS or the armed services. Executive Order 9608 abolished OWI on August 31, 1945; but the official government broadcasting service it established in 1942 lives on as the Voice of America.[3]

OSS had branches devoted to a wide range of covert operations. There was a branch for small-unit special operations, which worked directly with resistance groups. OSS also maintained larger commando-style operational groups (OGs) for attacks against specific targets. Its Morale Operations (MO) branch focused on waging psychological warfare through "black" propaganda and other means. A maritime unit's operations included delivering people and supplies to activities behind enemy lines and cooperating with the U.S. Navy in the preinvasion clearing of landing sites for U.S. forces. A "special projects" office engaged in such sensitive operations as searching for enemy atomic or chemical-biological weapons. Covert activities and irregular warfare units did not win World War II. Nevertheless, the covert war played a significant, if supporting, role in many of the steps that led to victory.

North Africa and Italy

An early test for OSS was supporting Operation TORCH, the British-American invasion of North Africa in November 1942. As early as October 1941, COI was coordinating the efforts of army and navy intelligence officers operating as vice consuls in North Africa. By January 1942, Donovan had his hand-picked action officer, Marine Lt. Col. William A. Eddy, in place in Tangier. In a memorandum to Roosevelt, dated December 22, 1941, Donovan laid out the role Eddy was called upon to play: "That the aid of native chiefs be obtained, the loyalty of the inhabitants be cultivated; fifth columnists organized and placed, demolition materials be cached; and guerrilla bands of bold and daring men organized and installed."[4]

The OSS contingent recruited agents from among local tribal leaders and sympathetic French military, police, and administrative personnel. Reporting from these agents helped identify the landing areas for the invasion. The OSS had guides waiting at the beaches to assist in directing the landing troops. One agent removed the fuses from demolition charges in a tunnel that connected the beach with the city of Oran. Later, a handful of the OSS members joined up with a Special Operations Executive (SOE) mission code-named BRANDON that was supporting the British First Army in Tunisia. The group's usual function was infiltrating German lines, sabotaging communications lines and transportation, and collecting tactical intelligence. However, at one point, Brandon was holding the northern flank of the Allied line.

Among the units landing in Operation TORCH was a precursor of the U.S. Army's special operations forces. The 1st Ranger Battalion, known as Darby's Rangers after their commander, Capt. William O. Darby, was organized in June 1942 and trained by British commandos. The battalion landed ahead of the main force, seized two Vichy-controlled forts guarding the entrance to the Algerian harbor of Arzew, and cleared the way for the landing of the

U.S. 1st Infantry Division. As an indicator of army attitudes toward unconventional forces, the Rangers often found themselves holding portions of the Allied frontline in the back-and-forth warfare in North Africa. However, the need for troops to spearhead future amphibious landings led to the formation of additional Ranger battalions. By the end of the war, six such units had served in Europe and the Pacific; but the lack of a doctrine for special operations haunted them. Despite their heroism on the beaches of Normandy, the 2nd and 5th Battalions rarely performed unconventional missions but rather functioned as line infantry in gap-filler situations and as reserve troops.

Lt. Gen. Mark Clark arranged to have an OSS contingent attached to his Fifth Army Intelligence (G-2) branch. During Clark's drive against the Italian mainland, the OSS Detachment landed on D-Day at Salerno in September 1943, and at Anzio in January 1944. The teams linked up with local resistance groups and established a capability for across-the-lines intelligence gathering and, later, subversion and sabotage. For their part, the Ranger battalions served as amphibious assault troops in the landings in Sicily and at Salerno and as line infantry in holding and expanding the Allied perimeters. The latter activities resulted in a high casualty rate for such lightly armed troops. A failed infiltration operation from the Anzio beachhead toward the town of Cisterna completed the destruction of the Ranger force, and it was deactivated. Some of the remaining soldiers were incorporated into the newly arrived 1st Special Service Force, a mixed U.S.-Canadian unit. Originally constituted to use a specialty vehicle (known as the weasel) for winter raids in Norway and Romania, the 1st Special Service Force was sent to Clark's Fifth Army in October 1943 as additional troops, not for its special capabilities. A commando-style raid by the unit in November 1943 helped open the German Winter Line and facilitated the later advance to Cassino. Nonetheless, the 1st Special Service Force found itself being deployed as line infantry. The army had neither the operational doctrine nor the inclination to use commando units for behind-the-enemy-lines operations in North Africa and Italy. Such activities were left largely to OSS and SOE.

The OSS also used its OGs to establish contact with resistance groups in occupied Italy. Agents, radio equipment and operators, and supplies were delivered deep into enemy territory via parachute, submarine, coastal landings, and direct penetration across battle lines. German lines of supply along roads and railways were targets of small-group attacks launched via nighttime landings on the coast. After the German retreat from Rome, coordination with resistance groups in northern Italy was such that guerrilla activities could be given tactical air support. In the final Allied offensive against the German Gothic Line in April 1945, OSS-supported partisans were able to occupy several towns ahead of the Allied advance. Not all operations went smoothly, as German military counterintelligence retained substantial resources, especially in terms of being able to triangulate and locate agent radio transmissions. Some operations came to the attention of the Germans through bad security practices by team members; in others, recruited individuals proved to be under German control and betrayed entire agent networks.

OSS's MO branch swung into action early in the Italian campaign. Prior to the landings in Sicily in July 1943, MO had a "black" radio ("Radio Italo Balbo") broadcasting from Tunisia and presenting itself as the voice of the Italian resistance. The programming sought to sow dissention between German and Italian Fascist troops and between Fascists and Italian civilians. Other MO operations included the production of "passes" through Allied lines for deserters or for surrendering to the resistance and the appearance behind the enemy lines of posters and leaflets in such profusion that perceptions of the strength of the Italian resistance were enhanced. Themes along the lines of "the war is lost" and "the Germans are using the Fascists to fight their war with your blood" were used in multiple variations. MO even produced and distributed an underground newspaper to German troops in Italy that purported to be the voice of a German peace party seeking to oust the Nazis and establish a democratically based state.[5]

OSS's Operation SUNRISE played a covert, hands-on role in ending the war in northern Italy days earlier than might have been the case. Between February and May 1945, Allen Dulles, head of the OSS mission in Bern, Switzerland, and a future director of central intelligence, engaged in a series of clandestine negotiations with SS general Karl Wolff for the surrender of the German and Fascist forces in northern Italy and southern Austria. Dulles met with Wolff in March, but the discussions were derailed when the Soviet Union demanded to be included and Washington told Dulles to break off negotiations. Renewed in April, the Dulles-Wolff dialogue resulted in the surrender of enemy forces on May 2, 1945.[6]

The War for Europe

OSS teams and their counterparts in Britain's SOE waged irregular warfare throughout German-occupied Europe. This war reached from Greece and the Balkans, to Denmark and Norway, to Czechoslovakia, and to France, and included Belgium, the Netherlands, and Poland for which SOE retained the primary responsibility. OSS and SOE teams organized and assisted local resistance groups in mounting opposition to occupying forces. Some guerrilla groups had been assisted by SOE before OSS arrived, and OSS found itself in a supporting role for operations being coordinated by SOE. Nonetheless, the resources available to OSS in terms of airlift capability and military supplies provided leverage in assuring the organization's leaders a role in the preparation for the Normandy invasion—Operation OVERLORD. The supreme

Allied commander in Europe, Gen. Dwight D. Eisenhower, recognized that the resistance groups in France (the Maquis) could help assure the success of the landings. In May 1944, the combination of SOE and OSS was designated Special Force Headquarters and placed directly under the command of Supreme Headquarters Allied Expeditionary Force.

Among the assets that the United States had to offer in the covert war was an Army Air Force special operations unit known as the "Carpetbaggers," after the codename for their activities—Operation CARPETBAGGER. Organized to meet OSS's needs, the Eighth Air Force's special bombardment groups in the United Kingdom, North Africa, and Italy flew clandestine missions deep into occupied Europe. They inserted and extracted agents behind enemy lines and made airdrops of equipment and supplies to resistance forces. From January 1944 to May 1945, the Carpetbaggers and their black-painted aircraft conducted 1,860 flights, delivering more than 1,000 parachutists and over 31,000 shipments of weapons, ammunition, and other supplies to resistance groups. The units also flew several thousand missions to drop propaganda leaflets and broadcast Allied radio messages.[7]

Well before D-Day on June 6, 1944, OSS OGs had begun augmenting the SOE's liaison with the French resistance. These teams provided the Maquis with training, arms, and other supplies; coordinated sabotage and guerrilla-style operations; and organized and led covert operations. Targets for sabotage included hydroelectric transmission lines, rail lines and trains, boat canals, and telephone lines. In the months before Operation OVERLORD, French partisans sabotaged over 100 factories producing materials for the German war machine. This was often the work of hit-and-run attacks by the Maquis, but occasionally the sabotage was accomplished with the complicity of the management of the factories. (See sidebar, *Internal Sabotage*.)

Internal Sabotage

"Agents pretending to be travelling salesmen, completely equipped with forged documents showing that they were legitimate representatives of existing French firms, called on the managers of a factory, requested that they permit the sabotage of certain machines, and threatened Allied bombing of the plant if they did not agree. Compliance was usual, since it saved the lives of countless French civilians, and prevented the destruction of the entire plant. For the Allies, successful operations of this kind meant that vital parts of important factories could be disabled with a large economy of men, aircraft and material, and with the greatest precision."

Source: Anthony Cave Brown, ed., *The Secret War Report of the OSS* (New York: Berkley Publishing Corp., 1976), p. 391.

Probably the best known of the teams supporting the invasion were the "Jedburghs." The three-man Jedburgh teams consisted of SOE, OSS, French, and/or other Allied military personnel in various combinations. Following the Normandy landings, some 90 such teams were parachuted behind German lines in France, Belgium, and the Netherlands to link up with local resistance forces. As a future Director of Central Intelligence but then a U.S. Army major, William E. Colby, described it years later, the mission of Jedburgh Team Bruce, comprised of himself and two members from General Charles de Gaulle's Free French organization, was

> "to contact . . . a *maquis* network operating in . . . central France, arrange for weapons and supplies to be parachuted to it, and coordinate its activities with that of Patton's Third Army, blowing bridges, ambushing patrols, attacking depots, sabotaging communications, blocking roads and rail lines, in a ceaseless series of hit-and-run harassing raids."[8]

Jedburgh teams were also put into place in advance of the Allied invasion of southern France on August 15, 1944. Following the breakout from the Riviera beachhead, the partisans launched harassing operations against the retreating Germans. The larger OSS OGs worked alone or in conjunction with Jedburghs and the Maquis in waging guerrilla warfare against German lines of communication and supply. However, not all the efforts of the Jedburgh and OG teams were successful. They, the resistance, and the Allied command had to learn that premature uprisings could be disastrous (as occurred in the Department of Vercours in July 1944) not only for the partisans but also for the civilian population when the lightly armed resistance forces were crushed and scattered by conventional German forces.[9]

While the Allies were waging war on the battlefield, MO Branch and its British counterpart—the Political Warfare Executive—were attacking the Axis forces with "black" propaganda. The British had begun efforts to undermine enemy military and civilian morale before America entered the war. "Black" or clandestine radios claiming to be of German origin carried news about how the war was turning against the Nazis. Claiming to be an official German armed forces radio station, *Soldatensender* used one of the most powerful transmitters of the day to beam broadcasts that reached from the front lines into Germany itself. The radio carried a combination of entertainment, real news, and rumor and gossip. The latter particularly targeted the German political and military leadership.[10]

Among MO's contributions to the psychological war against the Nazis was an effort to increase the audience for *Soldatensender* through the production of entertainment programming. Both standards and current popular songs were translated (and sometimes rewritten for a touch of propaganda), arranged, and recorded by a number of artists, including such well-known singers as

Marlene Dietrich. After the Allies freed Paris, MO went on the air with its own covert radio, *Volkssender Drei*, which purported to be the voice of the German Freedom Party. The station said it was located in the Alpine region and had been taken over by local partisans and station workers. *Volkssender Drei* sought to stimulate anti-Nazi activities among the German population. The capture of Radio Luxembourg in September 1944 gave the Allies access to one of the most powerful transmitters in Europe. OWI and Twelfth Army Group used the station in daylight hours for "white" propaganda broadcasts, typically relays of the Voice of America, the BBC, and the American Broadcasting Station in Europe, while OSS/MO operated Radio 1212 (Operation ANNIE) during the night. The broadcasts claimed they were coming from a Rhineland anti-Nazi organization. Radio 1212's subversive material included false evacuation and mobilization orders, real and exaggerated reports of the damage from Allied air raids, fabricated reports concerning the advance of Allied forces into Germany, and imaginary surrenders of German forces. Radio 1212 even played a role in inventing a resistance movement within Germany (the "New Germany" group), which people were encouraged to join. This campaign was reinforced by airdrops of the fictitious newspaper of the equally fictitious anti-Nazi peace group, *Das Neue Deutschland*.[11]

The Far East and Pacific

The war in the Far East and Pacific differed significantly from that in Europe or North Africa. The vast distances of the Far East and Pacific areas, the scattered landmasses, and the highly divergent terrains meant reversing Japan's early successes took multiple forms. The commanders in the combat theaters all had different views of the role of OSS and irregular warfare.

Pacific Ocean Areas

Commander of the Pacific Ocean Areas, Adm. Chester Nimitz, and his subordinate commanders tended to use Marines for the kinds of missions conducted by the Army Rangers in Europe. Nimitz saw no role for OSS covert operations in his theater. He did accept the assistance of a team of OSS operational swimmers ("frogmen") for prelanding inspections and obstacle demolition, and late in the war allowed the establishment on Saipan of a "black" radio station broadcasting to Japan.

OSS's "Voice of the People" went on the air in April 1945 broadcasting a 30-minute program daily. The station targeted the home front in Japan, claiming to represent the views of Japanese farmers, union members, and others who wanted the war to end before their country was destroyed. The broadcasts consisted of nostalgic music, news, and special features. One series of features was directed to Japanese women. It commiserated with the hardships war had brought to their lives; encouraged them to oppose continuation of the war; and in an effort to disrupt Japanese war production, recommended that they move to the countryside to get away from Allied bombings.[12]

South West Pacific Area

Gen. Douglas MacArthur, commanding the South West Pacific Area (SWPA), wanted nothing to do with OSS or its covert operatives, and he kept OSS out of the SWPA until the very end of the war.

The swiftness with which the Japanese attack on the Philippines breached MacArthur's defenses precluded leaving behind organized resistance. After MacArthur's dramatic escape in March 1942, command of U.S. forces passed to Lt. Gen. Jonathan Wainwright. Following Wainwright's decision in May to surrender all U.S. forces in the Philippines, small numbers of American and Filipino troops ignored the surrender order and retreated to the mountains to carry on guerrilla warfare. However, the geography of the Philippine islands and the animosities among some of the Filipino peoples worked against efforts to provide overall leadership of guerrilla operations. Early attempts to pull together the isolated guerrilla bands had an ad hoc nature that was only partially overcome when communications were established between some groups and MacArthur's headquarters in Australia.

To support SWPA headquarters and his drive back to the Philippines, MacArthur created his own intelligence agency—the Allied Intelligence Bureau (AIB)—as well as special operations units. The AIB was a joint venture with the Australians and coordinated Allied intelligence, covert operations, field propaganda, and irregular warfare for American, Australian, British, and Dutch units. The Australian Army's Director of Intelligence, Col. C.G. Roberts, headed the AIB; he reported to MacArthur's chief intelligence officer, Maj. Gen. Charles A. Willoughby. U.S. Capt. (later Col.) Allison Ind was Roberts's deputy and holder of the purse strings as finance officer. Although names and organizational structures changed over time, AIB began with four sections. Section A had been formed with assistance from the British SOE and was responsible for a range of covert operations, including disseminating propaganda, organizing local resistance groups and sabotage operations, and directing commando raids on enemy shipping and lines of communication. Section B was in charge of signals intelligence, encompassing both intercept and code-breaking functions. Section C included three different organizations that eventually became separate entities: The Coast Watch Organization, the Philippines Regional Section, and the Netherlands Forces Intelligence Section. Section D prepared propaganda for the operational sections.[13]

The Coast Watch Organization was built around the Australian navy's prewar system of volunteers. Coast watchers included Australians who had lived and worked in the islands before the war—missionaries, plantation owners, and schoolteachers—as well as island natives. They reported by radio on Japanese ship and aircraft movements. Their greatest challenge was the same as that faced by guerrillas—avoiding detection and capture. Observations by the coast watchers were a critical component in the intelligence available to Allied planners in the island-hopping campaign in the Pacific. Coast watchers also aided in the rescue of air and naval crews downed or sunk in hostile territory, such as the rescue of John F. Kennedy and his crew after the sinking of PT 109.[14]

In the Philippines, the guerrilla groups that developed on the archipelago's many far-flung islands confronted significant challenges of control, communication, supply, and leadership. Both Filipinos and Americans led the guerrilla bands. The most successful groups tended to be those that established continuing communication with SWPA and, therefore, received supplies from the theater command. By late 1942, SWPA was sending AIB teams into the Philippines to establish contact with the guerrillas. The head of AIB's Philippines section convinced the Seventh Fleet to loan "special mission" submarines to SWPA in return for establishing coast watch stations in the Philippines to provide the navy with intelligence on Japanese shipping. These submarines were used for covert supply runs from Australia with arms, ammunition, radios, medical supplies, and propaganda materials.

Lt. Col. Wendell W. Fertig led one of the largest guerrilla forces on the southern island of Mindanao. His group achieved early radio contact with SWPA and was among the first to be supplied by submarine. After some initial successes, Japanese reinforcements forced Fertig's guerrillas to retreat to the island's highlands. They remained isolated there, except for occasional small unit forays, until the Japanese began to move their forces back to the coast in anticipation of the U.S. invasion. By mid-1943, Col. Russell W. Volckmann had assumed command of the guerrilla movement in northern Luzon, the largest of the Philippine Islands and the one where Manila is located. Volckmann had escaped from Bataan with Capt. Donald D. Blackburn, who also earned renown as a leader of guerrilla forces, in his case for the band known as "Blackburn's Headhunters" in reference to the native tribesmen with whom he worked. Volckmann concentrated on organizational and training issues, avoiding large-scale attacks on the Japanese but using small ambushes and harassing tactics for training and supply replenishment purposes.

MacArthur's return to the Philippines began with the landing of the Sixth Army on the island of Leyte in October 1944 and was followed by the Sixth Army's assault on Luzon in early January 1945 and the attack by the Eighth Army on the central and southern islands. By that point, the better-prepared guerrilla groups could assist in liberating their homeland.

Prior to the assault on Luzon, guerrillas under Capt. Ramon Magsaysay (a future Philippine president) had driven the Japanese off the Zambales coast, which allowed the Americans to land unopposed. Overall, more than 300,000 Filipino guerrillas contributed to the war effort.[15]

The Sixth Army activated a special operations unit—the Alamo Scouts—in November 1943. Their roles included intelligence gathering, tactical reconnaissance, and organization and training of local guerrilla groups behind enemy lines and ahead of army landing operations. The Scouts operated in small teams, usually an officer and six or seven enlisted men, and often included Filipino and Dutch personnel. The Alamo Scouts conducted forward reconnaissance and provided tactical support in late January 1945 for another specialized unit—the 6th Ranger Battalion—in its covert operation to liberate the Cabanatuan Prisoner of War (POW) Camp on Luzon. A year earlier, the Sixth Army had created the battalion to meet its need for larger special operations units than the Alamo Scouts. Modeled on the Ranger units in Europe, the battalion was trained in commando-style tactics. As the Sixth Army advanced increasingly closer to the POW camp, concern grew about the safety of the prisoners. In an operation combining careful planning and skillful infiltration of enemy lines, over 500 Allied prisoners, many of them survivors of the Bataan Death March, were freed from Cabanatuan on January 30, 1945, and escorted and carried safely back to American lines, at a cost of two killed and seven wounded.[16]

SWPA complemented military operations with a psychological warfare campaign targeted on demoralizing Japanese forces. AIB's Section D (the Far Eastern Liaison Office or FELO) initially handled information and psychological warfare activities directed at both enemy troops and civilian populations in Australian, British, and Dutch territories. In preparation for the invasion of the Philippines, MacArthur established a Psychological Warfare Branch (PWB), incorporating some FELO personnel as well as a group of OWI staff members who had been cooperating with FELO. PWB's propagandists targeted the enemy with truthful reporting in order to establish and maintain the credibility of their information. Particular emphasis was given to the greater material and industrial resources available to the Allies. The propagandists avoided criticizing the Japanese emperor, portraying him as a victim of militarists. Leaflets distributed from aircraft were the primary means for delivering the propaganda message, with some 400 million disseminated during the war.

China-Burma-India Theater

Gen. Joseph "Vinegar Joe" Stilwell wore multiple hats—commander of U.S. forces in the China-Burma-India (CBI) Theater, chief of staff to CBI commander Generalissimo Chiang Kai-Shek, and until October 1944, deputy supreme Allied commander for the South East Asia Command (SEAC) under Adm. Lord Louis Mountbatten. Stillwell accepted OSS participation in his theater as the only help available.

By the time the Philippines fell in early May 1942, the Japanese had over-run Burma, French Indochina, Malaya, and Thailand. These conquests, cou-pled with Japan's victories in Hong Kong and Singapore, closed off Allied access by land to China, which Japan had invaded in 1937. The Allied strategy was to assist China in tying down as large a portion of the Japanese army as possible. This strategy did not include the commitment of large num-bers of American troops to CBI, focusing instead on supplying the Chinese with munitions, money, and military advisers. Although Stilwell was not an enthusiast of unconventional warfare, his desire to reverse the loss of Burma and reopen a land route to China represented a strong incentive to wage the best war he could with the resources available. He reluctantly accepted Don-ovan's offer of OSS assistance, and the nucleus of Detachment 101 headed for India under Capt. (later Col.) Carl F. Eifler.[17]

Detachment 101 was built around a small number of Americans working with Anglo-Burmese military personnel who had escaped to India. After extensive training focused on waging guerrilla warfare in the mountains and jungles of Burma, Detachment 101 parachuted its first group of covert operatives into central Burma in early February 1943. Expanded contacts with the indigenous Kachin natives led to guerrilla warfare deep behind the Japanese lines. Within a year, Detachment 101's Kachins were col-lecting intelligence, harassing Japanese units in their areas, relaying target information for the Tenth Air Force, evaluating air strike results, and pro-viding safe havens and escape routes for downed Allied pilots and crews. The Kachins proved adept at jungle ambushes and hit-and-run attacks. When American engineers began work on a road from Ledo, India, to the north Burmese city of Shingbwiyang, it was Detachment 101 and the guer-rillas that screened that effort from Japanese attacks. In December 1943, Donovan visited Detachment 101 in the field and flew to an operating base behind enemy lines. At that time he replaced Eifler, who had been injured in a raid, with Lt. Col. (later Lt. Gen.) William R. "Ray" Peers. Thus, it was Peers who led Detachment 101 and its Kachin guerrilla forces when Stillwell launched an offensive in December 1943 to recover north-ern Burma. Detachment 101 and the Kachins provided intelligence on enemy positions, served as guides for Stilwell's forces through the jungles and mountains, slowed the Japanese withdrawal by blowing up bridges and troop-carrying trains, and mopped up isolated Japanese troops left behind in the retreat of the main force.[18]

In February 1944, another specialized unit arrived—the 5307th Composite Unit (Provisional). Codenamed GALAHAD, the unit's three battalions (about

3,000 troops) were at the time the only American ground combat troops in the CBI Theater. Soon to be called Merrill's Marauders after their commanding officer, Brig. Gen. (later Maj. Gen.) Frank D. Merrill, the 5307th was trained and equipped to replicate the British long-range-penetration units. It undertook covert missions against objectives deep behind the enemy lines and facilitated the taking of key points by Stilwell's main forces. When operating in the field, the unit traveled by foot and pack mule (in some instances, by cargo-bearing elephants), and received airdrops of food, ammunition, equipment, medical supplies, and other material. Although two actions in March and April 1944 had produced significant losses, the Marauders, a Chinese regiment, and some of Detachment 101's Kachin guerrillas were sent on a long march over mountainous terrain to seize the airfield at Myitkyina. In the ensuing siege, the lightly armed 5307th was used as line infantry. When Myitkyina fell to the Allies in August 1944, the Marauders were so depleted by being pressed into a role for which they were not equipped (only some 200 men of the original unit remained) that they were linked with other units in a new long-range penetration group, the Mars Task Force.[19]

At the end of October 1944, Stilwell was pulled out of CBI at Chiang Kai-Shek's insistence. His replacement for the India-Burma Theater was Lt. Gen. Daniel I. Sultan, previously Stilwell's deputy, while Maj. Gen. Albert C. Wedemeyer became Chiang's new chief of staff and chief of the China Theater. The Allied offensive continued with Detachment 101 guarding the flanks of advancing Allied armies, while Kachin partisans used ambushes and even substantially sized raids to cut the lines of communication of the Japanese forces. By mid-January 1945, patrols from Detachment 101 and the Mars Task Force were in contact with the Burma Road. When the Japanese evacuated Lashio on March 7, 1945, Stilwell's road from Ledo in India was linked to the Burma Road and a land route to China reestablished. Detachment 101 and its Kachin guerrillas, joined by Shan, Karen, Gurkha, and Chinese volunteers, then helped open the Burma Road all the way to Rangoon. Its reason for being behind it, Detachment 101 was deactivated on July 12, 1945; the Kachins returned to their homes, and the small group of OSS personnel moved on to other wartime endeavors prior to Japan's surrender on August 14, 1945.

In China, dozens of Allied intelligence organizations expended most of their time and energy struggling among themselves and with Chiang Kai-Shek and his intelligence chief, Tai Li. It was early 1945 before OSS was allowed to put together and train Chinese commando units and July before they were deployed in the field. The same kinds of frustrations impaired OSS's efforts to initiate black propaganda broadcasts to the Japanese occupation forces. It was not until late April 1945 that OSS made its first clandestine radio broadcast from Chinese territory.[20]

With the Japanese surrender, Wedemeyer made locating and rescuing Allied POWs and civilians being held by the Japanese his top priority. OSS organized a series of rescue missions, parachuting teams behind Japanese lines to establish control of prison camps and the POWs being held there. Maj. (later Maj. Gen.) John "Jack" Singlaub, whose long career in covert operations was just starting, led the rescue operation on Hainan Island. At Sian, 100 miles north of Mukden, in late August, an OSS team rescued Wainwright, who had been in Japanese hands since he surrendered the Philippines in 1942, and British Lt. Gen. Sir Arthur E. Percival, captured when Singapore fell. Capt. Roger F. Hilsman, a veteran of both Merrill's Marauders and Detachment 101, volunteered for the rescue mission to Manchuria in hopes of locating his father, Col. Roger Hilsman, Sr. The younger Hilsman had the pleasure of finding and evacuating his emaciated but alive father from Hoten prison camp.[21]

Indochina and Thailand

Covert operations against the Japanese in Thailand and Indochina achieved mixed results. U.S. efforts in each ran up against divergent attitudes on the part of allies—Britain in the case of Thailand and France in Indochina.

After its leader allied himself with the Japanese, Thailand declared war on the United States and Britain on January 25, 1942. The United States chose to ignore that action, but the British responded with their own declaration of war. Thus, U.S. and British policies were moving in different directions from the beginning. The Americans were convinced that creation of an internal Thai opposition was possible, while the British were planning to invade Thailand and defeat it militarily. In August 1942, OSS was tasked with recruiting, training, and infiltrating Thai agents into their homeland, using officials and students (the "Free Thai") who had refused repatriation when war was declared. There were also indications of the existence of an anti-Japanese underground within Thailand, led by one of the young king's regents—Pridi Phanomyong (codenamed RUTH by the OSS). The initial effort by OSS to infiltrate agents into Thailand was not a success. In June 1944, when its agents crossed the border from China, the Thai police killed two and captured and incarcerated six others in Bangkok. A governmental change in July brought a moderate opposition group led by Pridi to power. In September, OSS airdropped two Thai agents into their homeland. The Thai police arrested one agent, but the other was able to contact Pridi. This led to the earlier agents being given access to their radio equipment, and they began to send low-level intelligence. In January 1945, Donovan dispatched two OSS officers to Bangkok, where Pridi's men sheltered them in the midst of the Japanese occupation force. An offer by Pridi to foment a revolt against the Japanese came with the proviso that his forces needed arms and training. After much foot-dragging in SEAC, a plan for raising a Free Thai force was approved by the U.S. military command. Supplies and trainers for guerrilla warfare were parachuted into Thailand beginning in May. However, the war ended before fighting was initiated. After that, the OSS primarily monitored the peace talks between the British and the Thais and advocated for a settlement that would insure the independence of Thailand.[22]

French Indochina—today's Cambodia, Laos, and Vietnam—was another region where the American covert role ended up being more political than military. The French desire to reestablish control of Indochina made working relations with the U.S. military and civilian authorities, focused on fighting the Japanese, difficult. OSS efforts to support guerrilla warfare by the Vietnamese also clashed with a refusal to cooperate with anything in which the French were involved. By 1944, there was an active resistance to the Japanese from the anticolonialist Viet Minh movement, led by longtime communist Ho Chi Minh. The OSS was not averse to cooperating with communist-led partisan organizations to take the fight to the Axis nations. Such cooperation also occurred in Italy, France, and Yugoslavia. Nonetheless, the OSS decision to work with Ho remains controversial. In a meeting with OSS officer Marine Lt. Charles Fenn in March 1945, Ho agreed to allow OSS agents and radio operators into Vietnam if the United States would supply arms and medicine to the Viet Minh. Another meeting followed in April between Ho and the head of OSS operations in Indochina, Army Capt. Archimedes Patti. In July, two OSS teams were parachuted into areas of Vietnam controlled by the Viet Minh. The war ended before the several hundred OSS-trained Vietnamese could be committed to combat. Within months the French and the Viet Minh were at war.[23]

Notes

1. See Thomas F. Troy, *Donovan and the CIA: A History of the Establishment of the Central Intelligence Agency* (Frederick, MD: University Publications of America, 1981); Thomas F. Troy, *Wild Bill and Intrepid: Bill Donovan, Bill Stephenson, and the Origin of CIA* (New Haven, CT: Yale University Press, 1996); and Douglas Waller, *Wild Bill Donovan: The Spymaster Who Created the OSS and Modern American Espionage* (New York: Free Press, 2011).

2. For the organization and activities of the COI, see U.S. War Department, Strategic Services Unit, *War Report of the OSS (Office of Strategic Services)*, vol. 1 (New York: Walker & Co., 1976), pp. 9–95. See also Michael Warner, "The COI Came First," in *The Office of Strategic Services: America's First Intelligence Agency* (Washington, DC: Central Intelligence Agency, 2000), at: https://www.cia.gov/library/center-for-the-study-of-intelligence/csi-publications/books-and-monographs/oss/art02.htm.

3. See Allan Winkler, *The Politics of Propaganda: The Office of War Information, 1942–1945* (New Haven: Yale University Press, 1978).

4. U.S. War Department, Strategic Services Unit, *War Report*, p. 94. On Eddy's role in North Africa, see Robert E. Mattingly, "One of a Kind, Unique," in *Herringbone Cloak—GI Dagger: Marines of the OSS* (Quantico, VA: Marine Corps Command and Staff College, 1979), pp. 22–39, at: http://www.ibiblio.org/hyperwar/USMC/USMC-OSS/index.html#index. For a full-scale biography of Eddy, see Thomas W. Lippman, *Arabian Knight: Colonel Bill Eddy USMC and the Rise of American Power in the Middle East* (Vista, CA: Selwa Press, 2008).

5. On OSS operations in North Africa and Italy, see Anthony Cave Brown, ed., *The Secret War Report of the OSS* (New York: Berkley Publishing Corp., 1976), pp. 134–54 and 185–249. On Darby's Rangers and 1st Special Service Force, see David W. Hogan Jr., "Special Operations in the Mediterranean," in *U.S. Army Special Operations in World War II*, pp. 11–28 (Washington, DC: Department of the Army, 1992), at: http://www.history.army.mil/books/wwii/70-42/70-42c.htm. Erasmus H. Kloman, *Assignment Algiers: With the OSS in the Mediterranean Theater* (Annapolis, MD: Naval Institute Press, 2005), provides a first-hand account. For clandestine broadcasting to Italy, see Lawrence C. Soley, *Radio Warfare: OSS and CIA Subversive Propaganda* (New York: Praeger Publishing, 1989), pp. 102–14.

6. See Allen Dulles, *The Secret Surrender* (New York: Harper & Row, 1966); and Bradley F. Smith and Elena Agarossi, *Operation Sunrise: The Secret Surrender* (New York: Basic Books, Inc., 1979).

7. Statistics from the National Museum of the U.S. Air Force, "Operation Carpet-bagger: Night Flights over Occupied Europe," at: http://www.nationalmuseum.af.mil/factsheets/factsheet.asp?id=1502. See also Air Force Special Operations Command, "Heritage of the Special Operations Professionals: World War II in North Africa and Europe," at: http://www.afsoc.af.mil/Portals/1/documents/history/heritage_special_ops_prof.pdf; and Jerry L. Thigpen, *The Praetorian STARShip: The Untold Story of Combat Talon* (Maxwell Air Force Base, AL: Air University Press, 2001), pp. 1–4.

8. William E. Colby, with Peter Forbath, *Honorable Men: My Life in the CIA* (New York: Simon & Schuster, 1978), pp. 25–26.

9. See Will Irwin, *The Jedburghs: The Secret History of the Allied Special Forces, France 1944* (New York: Public Affairs, 2005); Robert R. Kehoe, "1944: An Allied Team with the French Resistance," *Studies in Intelligence* (Winter 1998–1999): 15–50; and S. J. Lewis, *Jedburgh Team Operations in Support of the 12th Army Group, August 1944* (Ft. Leavenworth, KS: U.S. Army Command and General Staff College, Combat Studies Institute, 1991), at: http://usacac.army.mil/cac2/cgsc/carl/download/csipubs/lewis.pdf. On OSS's OGs, see "Office of Strategic Services Operational Groups," at: http://www.ossog.org/index.html.

10. See David Garnett, *The Secret History of PWE: The Political Warfare Executive, 1939–1945* (London: St. Ermin's Press, 2002); and Denis Sefton Delmer, *Black Boomerang* (London: Secker & Warburg, 1962).

11. On MO branch generally, see Brown, *Secret War Report*, pp. 525–40; and Clayton D. Laurie, "The OSS Morale Operations Branch in Action, 1943–1945," in *The Propaganda Warriors: America's Crusade against Nazi Germany* (Lawrence: University

Press of Kansas, 1996), pp. 192–209. On MO's radio operations targeting Germany, see Soley, *Radio Warfare*, pp. 123–55. For some examples of MO black propaganda, see Herbert A. Friedman, "Poison Cornflakes for Breakfast," at: http://www.psywarrior. com/Cornflakes2.html.

12. See Allison B. Gilmore, *You Can't Fight Tanks with Bayonets: Psychological Warfare against the Japanese Army in the Southwest Pacific* (Lincoln: University of Nebraska Press, 1998). On the tribulations of OSS in getting black broadcasts underway in the Pacific area, see Soley, *Radio Warfare*, pp. 183–88.

13. See William B. Breuer, *MacArthur's Undercover War: Spies, Saboteurs, Guerrillas and Secret Missions* (Edison, NJ: Castle Books, 1995); and Allison Ind, *Allied Intelligence Bureau: Our Secret Weapon in the War against Japan* (New York: David McKay, 1958).

14. See Eric Feldt, *The Coast Watchers* (Melbourne: Oxford University Press, 1946); and Alan Powell, *War by Stealth: Australians and the Allied Intelligence Bureau, 1942–1945* (Melbourne: Melbourne University Press, 1996).

15. See Hogan, *U.S. Army Special Operations in World War II*, pp. 64–95. On Fertig's guerrillas on Mindanao, see John Keats, *They Fought Alone* (Philadelphia: J.B. Lippincott & Co., 1963). Volckmann tells his story in Russell W. Volckmann, *We Remained: Three Years behind the Enemy Line in the Philippines* (New York: W.W. Norton & Co., 1954). Blackburn's exploits are told in Philip Harkins, *Blackburn's Headhunters* (New York: W.W. Norton & Co., 1955).

16. On the rescue mission at Cabanatuan POW Camp, see Hampton Sides, *Ghost Soldiers: The Forgotten Epic Story of World War II's Most Dramatic Mission* (New York: Random House, 2002). On the Alamo Scouts generally, see Lance Q. Zedric, *Silent Warriors of World War II: The Alamo Scouts behind Japanese Lines* (Ventura, CA: Pathfinder Publishing, 1994). See also, the website of the Alamo Scouts Association at: http://www.alamoscouts.org. On the 6th Ranger battalion see Hogan, *U.S. Army Special Operations in World War II*, pp. 83–89.

17. See Barbara W. Tuchman, *Stilwell and the American Experience in China, 1911–45* (New York: Macmillan Co., 1970), pp. 229–504.

18. See Richard Dunlop, *Behind Japanese Lines: With the OSS in Burma* (New York: Rand McNally, 1979); Roger Hilsman, *American Guerrilla: My Life Behind Japanese Lines* (New York: Brassey's, 1990); Thomas M. Moon and Carl F. Eifler, *The Deadliest Colonel* (New York: Vantage, 1975); and William R. Peers and Dean Brelis, *Behind the Burma Road: The Story of America's Most Successful Guerrilla Force* (Boston: Little, Brown, 1963).

19. See the account of the unit's second in command: Charles N. Hunter, *Galahad* (San Antonio, TX: Naylor Co., 1963). See also Gary J. Bjorge, *Merrill's Marauders: Combined Operations in Northern Burma in 1944* (Fort Leavenworth, KS: Combat Studies Institute, U.S. Army Command and General Staff College, 1996), at: http:// usacac.army.mil/cac2/cgsc/carl/download/csipubs/bjorge.pdf; Historical Section of the India-Burma Theater, *Merrill's Marauders: February–May 1944* (CMH Pub. 100–4) (Washington, DC: Military History Division, U.S. War Department, 1945), at: http:// www.history.army.mil/books/wwii/marauders/marauders-fw.htm; and Hogan, *U.S. Army Special Operations in World War II*, pp. 113–20.

20. On the OSS's tribulations in China, see Maochun Yu, *OSS in China: Prelude to Cold War* (New Haven, CT: Yale University Press, 1996). See Soley, *Radio Warfare*, pp. 172–83, for a discussion of MO Branch's efforts to conduct black propaganda in China.

21. Hilsman, *American Guerrilla*, pp. 233–44. See also, John Whiteclay Chambers II, *OSS Training in the National Parks and Service Abroad in World War II* (Washington, DC: U.S. National Park Service, 2008), pp. 465–70, at: https://www.cia.gov/library/center-for-the-study-of-intelligence/csi-publications/csi-studies/studies/vol53no4/oss-training-in-the-national-parks-and-service.html.

22. See Stewart Alsop and Thomas Braden, *Sub Rosa: The O.S.S. and American Espionage* (New York: Reynal & Hitchcock Publishers, 1948), pp. 98–115; Chambers, *OSS Training in the National Parks*, pp. 401–6; E. Bruce Reynolds, "The Opening Wedge: The OSS in Thailand," in *The Secrets War: The Office of Strategic Services in World War II*, ed. George C. Chalou (Washington, DC: National Archives and Records Administration, 1992), pp. 328–50; and R. Harris Smith, *OSS: The Secret History of America's First Central Intelligence Agency* (New York: Dell Publishing Co., Inc., 1972), pp. 286–317.

23. See Dixee R. Bartholomew-Feis, *The OSS and Ho Chi Minh: Unexpected Allies in the War against Japan* (Lawrence: University Press of Kansas, 2006); Chambers, pp. 407–14; Charles Fenn, *At the Dragon's Gate: With the OSS in the Far East* (Annapolis, MD: Naval Institute Press, 2004); Archimedes L. A. Patti, *Why Viet Nam? Prelude to America's Albatross* (Berkeley: University of California Press, 1980); and Smith, *OSS: The Secret History*, pp. 320–38.

CHAPTER 4

Beginning the Cold War

Out with the Old

The United States has historically concluded its wars by demobilizing its citizen forces. Specialized or elite forces rarely survived the end of the conflict, and the few that did were usually mere skeletons. The end of World War II was no different. The army continued some greatly diminished units incorporating psychological warfare capability. A limited capacity for unconventional warfare existed within a handful of Ranger battalions, but there was no cohesive military doctrine for the use of special warfare forces.

America's first attempt to institutionalize intelligence functions and covert warfare capabilities in a single entity was dismembered. That was not the result that Maj. Gen. William J. Donovan had envisaged for the Office of Strategic Services (OSS). In late 1944, Donovan proposed to President Roosevelt that OSS form the basis for centralizing intelligence activities in an independent organization. The plan was not warmly received at the State Department; the Federal Bureau of Investigation (FBI) wanted to extend its wartime operations in Latin America to cover the world; and the armed services were adamantly opposed. In early February 1945, the *Chicago Tribune* ran a series of articles denouncing the concept of a "central intelligence service" as un-American, a New Deal plot to "snoop" on American citizens, and the equivalent of the hated Nazi Gestapo. The damage was too great to be reversed by more accurate reporting elsewhere.

On September 20, 1945, the new president, Harry S. Truman (1945–1953), ordered that OSS be disbanded effective October 1. The research and analysis function was passed to the State Department along with the remnants of the two "white" propaganda organizations, the Office of War Information and Office of Inter-American Affairs. OSS's espionage units were parked in the War Department as the Strategic Services Unit (SSU). Operational units in the field were eliminated. Personnel demobilized, joined the SSU or the U.S. Army's Counterintelligence Corps, or returned to regular army units. The capability to conduct paramilitary operations disappeared. Some of the officers previously detailed to OSS resurfaced in the early 1950s as driving forces in the creation of the U.S. Army's Special Operations Forces (SOF). Others, civilian and military, played significant roles when covert operations were later resurrected.[1]

Searching for Coordination

Truman's actions did not mean he was unaware of the need for improvements in American intelligence. The president tasked Secretary of State James F. Byrnes with developing a comprehensive and coordinated foreign intelligence program. The focus was on intelligence collection, analysis, and counterespionage. No attention was given to covert operations.

Absent agreement on whether intelligence should be housed in a single unit or decentralized to geographical divisions, the State Department was ill prepared to address the president's mandate. A growing unease about the intentions of the Soviet Union and concerns about the lack of coordination in prewar intelligence gave a sense of urgency to the effort to rationalize American intelligence functions. Truman grew impatient with the lack of progress, and on January 22, 1946, announced his decision in a presidential directive addressed to the secretaries of state, war, and navy. The directive created the National Intelligence Authority (NIA), comprised of a presidential representative and the three secretaries. The NIA was to supervise the work of a new organization, the Central Intelligence Group (CIG), headed by a director of central intelligence (DCI).[2] The CIG was staffed with personnel on loan from other departments and its funding came proportionally from the three departments. The result was a bureaucratic morass that only partly provided the president with the coordination of intelligence activities he was seeking.

The National Security Act of 1947

Days before leaving the DCI position in June 1946, Rear Adm. Sidney Souers recommended that the NIA and CIG be given a statutory foundation and an independent budget. His successor as DCI, Lt. Gen. Hoyt S. Vandenberg, set out to establish CIG as a comprehensive and independent national intelligence service with a legislatively recognized mandate.

On July 26, 1947, President Truman signed the National Security Act of 1947 (P.L. 80–235, 61 Stat 496). This legislation was the basic charter of the U.S. national security establishment for 57 years and, with the changes introduced by the Intelligence Reform and Terrorism Prevention Act of December 2004, remains in effect. The 1947 Act merged the war and navy departments and the newly independent air force into what became the Department of Defense, under a secretary of defense. It created the National Security Council (NSC) and made it responsible for advising the president on policies relating to national security. The Act replaced the CIG with an independent agency within the executive branch—the Central Intelligence Agency (CIA). The CIA was headed by a presidentially appointed DCI, responsible to the president through the NSC. Thus was created America's first peacetime civilian intelligence service. In addition to coordinating governmental intelligence activities, the Act tasked the CIA with performing "such other functions and duties related to intelligence affecting the national security as the [NSC] may from time to time direct."[3] It was on the basis of this vague phrasing that the task of conducting covert operations fell to the newly created CIA.

The Early Cold War

The Cold War stretched from the immediate post–World War II years to 1989 (the fall of the Berlin Wall) or 1991 (the demise of the Soviet Union). Whether the Cold War was "won," absorbed into a changing world, or expired when one of the competing ideologies reached a logical dead end is a question that historians will debate. The conflict reached every corner of the globe. It had such hot spots as Korea and Vietnam; but the principal opponents mostly avoided direct military confrontation. Much of the early tension related to Europe, but antagonism soon spread to Asia and, as colonial empires disintegrated, to the Middle East and Africa.

Europe

When World War II ended, the physical, economic, and social structures of West European countries—victorious and defeated alike—lay substantially in ruin. With Joseph Stalin's armies occupying northeastern Germany and communist regimes being established in Eastern Europe, the military threat to Western Europe loomed large in the minds of U.S. policy makers. In addition, communist parties in West European countries—notably Greece, France, and Italy—had gained credibility from their contributions to the resistance movements. By 1946–1947, there was deep concern that the countries of

Western Europe were so vulnerable that democratic processes could bring antidemocratic communist parties to power.

America's initial foray into stopping a communist takeover of a national government was overt and came in Greece. On March 12, 1947, the president announced the Truman Doctrine, whereby the United States would provide political, economic, and military assistance to democratic governments being threatened by totalitarian forces. American financial and military assistance helped stabilize the Greek government and allow it to reduce and isolate the communist guerrilla forces. Truman's next step was equally open. On June 5, 1947, Secretary of State George C. Marshall proposed that the European nations address their physical destruction and economic dislocation by establishing a reconstruction program—with U.S. assistance. One of the centerpieces of American national security policy in the postwar years—the Economic Recovery Program or Marshall Plan—was formalized in the Economic Assistance Act of 1948. The Soviet Union and the East European countries refused to participate. This economic partnership between the United States and Western Europe was accompanied in 1949 by the creation of the North Atlantic Treaty Organization, a military alliance.[4]

Initiating Covert Operations

While the overt mechanisms for rebuilding and defending Europe were being created, the administration supplemented those efforts with less open actions to counter political turmoil being caused by the Soviet Union. In mid-December 1947, Truman approved NSC 4-A, officially launching the United States into the business of "covert psychological operations." DCI Rear Adm. Roscoe H. Hillenkoetter was given the responsibility for conducting such activities. (See sidebar, NSC 4-A.) The threat of a communist victory in the April 1948 national elections in Italy became the first target.

NSC 4-A

"The National Security Council, taking cognizance of the vicious psychological efforts of the USSR, its satellite countries and Communist groups to discredit and defeat the aims and activities of the United States and other Western powers, has determined that, in the interests of world peace and U.S. national security, the foreign information activities of the U.S. Government must be supplemented by covert psychological operations. . . . [T]he National Security Council directs the Director of Central Intelligence to initiate and conduct . . . covert psychological operations designed to counteract Soviet and Soviet-inspired activities."

Source: *FRUS, 1945–1950—Truman Series: Emergence of the Intelligence Establishment,* Document 257 (Washington, DC: GPO, 1996).

Much of the effort to convince the Italian people to reject the communists was overt. Grain and foodstuffs marked as coming from the United States flowed into Italy; Italian Americans engaged in a letter-writing campaign focused on the perils of communism; statements by prominent Italian Americans were broadcast to and in Italy; and Truman threatened to withhold aid to any government that included communists. The covert effort relied heavily on the use of American dollars and "black" propaganda. The efforts were aided greatly in February 1948 when a communist coup replaced the democratic government in Czechoslovakia. Millions of dollars were funneled covertly to the centrist Christian Democrat party. Other dollars were spread among the Italian media to fund negative propaganda about communist candidates. When the Christian Democrats obtained a workable parliamentary majority, the United States had an early victory in the political Cold War.[5]

As tensions mounted with the Soviet Union, sentiment grew in Washington that the United States needed to conduct covert operations beyond propaganda and political action. Pressure in this direction came from the State Department's Policy Planning Staff, headed by George F. Kennan. Six months after promulgating NSC 4-A, the NSC took the next step in institutionalizing peacetime covert operations. On June 17, 1948, the NSC approved NSC 10/2, establishing the Office of Special Projects (soon renamed the Office of Policy Coordination or OPC) to plan and conduct covert operations. Organizationally, the OPC was technically under the DCI and part of the CIA; but the Secretary of State selected the head, and OPC was to operate independently of other CIA components. And it received its direction and approval for actions through a process involving a panel of State and Defense department officials. This awkward arrangement persisted until 1952, when DCI Walter Bedell Smith merged the OPC with the CIA's intelligence gathering unit, the Office of Special Operations, to form the Directorate of Plans (later the Directorate of Operations and, most recently, the National Clandestine Service). NSC 10/2 also codified the concept of plausible denial, and provided a wide-ranging definition of covert operations. (See sidebar, *NSC 10/2.*) The Secretary of State selected Frank G. Wisner, an OSS veteran and deputy assistant secretary of State for occupied countries, to head OPC.

NSC 10/2

"As used in this directive, 'covert operations' are understood to be all activities . . . which are conducted or sponsored by this Government against hostile foreign states or groups or in support of friendly foreign states or groups but which are so planned and executed that any US Government responsibility for them is not evident to unauthorized persons and that if uncovered the US Government can plausibly disclaim any responsibility for them. Specifically, such operations shall include any covert activities related to: propaganda, economic warfare; preventive direct action, including sabotage, anti-sabotage, demolition and evacuation measures; subversion against hostile states, including assistance to underground resistance movements, guerrillas and refugee liberation groups, and support of indigenous anti-communist elements in threatened countries of the free world."

Source: *FRUS, 1945–1950—Emergence of the Intelligence Establishment*, Document 292.

By the end of October 1948, Wisner was circulating a plan of action that envisaged covert activity in four functional areas: psychological warfare, political warfare, economic warfare, and preventive direct action, including support of guerrillas.[6]

Wisner chose the tiny communist, Adriatic coast country of Albania for OPC's initial foray into organizing paramilitary resistance groups. As early as 1947, the British Secret Intelligence Service (SIS or MI6) sent émigré agents into Albania hoping to foment a civil war. Funding issues sent the British to the United States for assistance in the spring of 1949. For its paramilitary force, OPC used the groups from which the British had drawn their Albanian agents—émigrés and refugees. Western Europe after World War II was awash with refugees from Eastern Europe and Russia, many living in "displaced persons" camps. Motivations for these individuals to participate in infiltration programs ranged from the noble to the sinister. Some were ardent nationalists who had fought both communists and Nazis. Others were opportunists or common criminals who worked for anyone who paid them. It was from such raw material that OPC's operators, such as William Sloan Coffin, tried to train and activate resistance forces to be launched covertly against the USSR and the occupied countries from the Baltic to the Adriatic.

From October 1949 to the early 1950s, OPC persisted in inserting small paramilitary partisan units into Albania, Poland, Ukraine, and the Soviet Union (Britain was doing the same in the Baltic countries). Infiltration routes into Albania included the Adriatic coast, parachute drops, and overland from Greece. Almost always the authorities killed or captured the members of the groups soon after arrival. No foothold in Albania was ever established. The Albanian operation was likely compromised by MI6's liaison officer in Washington, H.A.R. "Kim" Philby, a Soviet agent who participated in the planning sessions for the joint U.S.-British infiltrations. However, blaming Philby for reverses in the covert war is limited to early efforts in Albania; beyond that, it is necessary to look for other reasons. Chief among the culprits was Soviet and East European counterintelligence services. The émigré groups in the West and their in-country counterparts were thoroughly penetrated by communist services. Most, like the Polish Freedom and Independence movement (*Wolnose I Niepodleglose* or WIN), were revealed to have been fabrications of Soviet and satellite intelligence.[7]

Another cause of the lack of success in infiltration activities was the basic assumption on which they rested—that is, the belief that the peoples of Eastern Europe were ready to rise up and overthrow their oppressive regimes and all that was needed was to give them a little help. However, liberation only came to Western Europe through massive military force, not through direct actions by resistance forces. The question remains as to why OPC continued such operations for as long as it did. Here, there may be support for the argument that covert operations tend to have their own momentum. Once you begin training groups in the techniques of covert warfare, it is difficult to figure out what to do with them when they have no further use. However, paramilitary operations were not the sole aspect to the covert struggle in Europe. Other activities garnered a higher success rate.

Propaganda and Culture

When NSC 10/2 enumerated the activities included in covert operations, propaganda was first on the list. Both radio and print media became the means for waging the "propaganda war." The earliest entries in the effort to communicate information via the radio belonged to the "white" propaganda category. The Voice of America (VOA) began Russian language broadcasts in February 1947 and by 1951 was broadcasting in minority languages across the USSR. VOA focused on contrasting the evils of communism with the positive features of America.

The U.S. military also participated in the propaganda war. Early in the occupation of Germany, the military established two radio stations: Armed Forces Network allowed the military command to communicate informally with American troops and Radio in the American Sector (RIAS) provided German civilians accurate information about occupation policies and efforts to restore a semblance of normalcy. Over time, RIAS expanded its offerings to news, current affairs, music, and light entertainment. It broadcast until 1992, and remained an important (if illegal) source of information for East

Germans to the end of a divided Germany. On the "black" propaganda side (actually more "gray" than "black," there being little doubt from where the activities originated but only as to their source of funding), two enduring symbols emerged—Radio Free Europe (RFE) and Radio Liberty (RL).

During the discussions that culminated in NSC 10/2, the State Department's Policy Planning Staff had proposed forming a public organization to sponsor selected political refugee committees. The proposal envisaged that the organization would be overt but would "receive covert guidance and possibly assistance from the Government."[8] The National Committee for a Free Europe (later the Free Europe Committee) was incorporated in mid-1949, with such luminaries as Dwight D. Eisenhower and Allen Dulles on its Board. The committee was ostensibly an open, publically supported entity, and engaged in large-scale fund-raising campaigns. The "Crusade for Freedom" began in 1950 and included parades, public gatherings, and the signing of "Freedom Scrolls." None of these efforts raised enough money to fund the committee's activities. Consequently, RFE and its publishing arm (Free Europe Press) were funded by and received policy guidance from the U.S. government via OPC/CIA. RFE began broadcasting in mid-1950 with a workforce drawn from among East European émigrés and refugees. Its first broadcasts targeted Czechoslovakia; and over the following months, it added broadcasts to Romania, Poland, Hungary, Bulgaria, and Albania. The American Committee for the Liberation of the Peoples of the USSR (later the American Committee for Liberation or AMCOMLIB) was incorporated as a public corporation in January 1951. In 1953, Radio Liberation (the name changed to Radio Liberty in 1964) began broadcasting to the Soviet Union in Russian; broadcasts in minority languages of peoples living within the USSR were later added.

RFE and RL broadcasts sought to become a surrogate free press for the nations behind the Iron Curtain. They provided audiences with news and commentary about events in their countries and the world beyond what was in their government-controlled media. Programming included Western music banned in the USSR and its satellites. Reportage and commentary were hard-hitting in their opposition to the communist regimes and their leaders. However, the object was not to disseminate "black" or false propaganda but rather, free from the limitations associated with official media, to give a voice to those who had been dispossessed by the communist takeovers of their countries and to provide a rallying point—internally and externally—for those who desired to oppose those regimes.[9]

Many believe that the real impact of the radios was to extend hope to the captive peoples of Eastern Europe and the Soviet Union; others counter, given the events in Hungary in 1956, that the effort raised false hopes of something other than verbal support for their internal struggle. A CIA assessment in 1969 characterized RFE and RL as "the oldest, largest, most costly, and probably most successful covert action projects aimed at the Soviet Union and Eastern Europe."[10] Individuals coming fresh to the subject are often surprised at how little control the CIA exercised over the day-to-day and editorial operations of the radios.

OPC/CIA used multiple other means of delivering propaganda to the Eastern Bloc. From late 1951 until 1956, the Free Europe Committee released balloons in the West to transport hundreds of millions of pieces of printed propaganda into the Eastern Bloc. The earliest efforts used surplus World War II meteorological balloons. These balloons were hydrogen-filled and carried about three pounds of leaflets (approximately 3,000) each. They burst at 30,000 feet, thereby distributing the materials indiscriminately over a wide area. (For text of one such leaflet, see sidebar, *Winds of Freedom*.) Later releases used large, clear plastic, hydrogen-filled balloons with an ingenious timing device—dry ice. The payload—leaflets, books, posters—was suspended below the balloon in a loosely covered cardboard carton; below the carton, carefully balanced envelopes carried dry ice. When the dry ice evaporated, the cartons would tip and release the contents. By calibrating the weight of the dry ice, the amount of hydrogen, the weight of the payload, and the direction and velocity of the wind, launches could be targeted for specific populations. That the program went beyond being just an annoyance to the communist regimes may be indicated by occasional attempts to shoot the balloons down and reports that police in the cities ordered people to turn in the materials they found.[11]

Winds of Freedom

The following is text of one of the propaganda leaflets directed at the people of Czechoslovakia in a balloon release in August 1951: "A new wind is blowing. New hope is stirring. Friends of freedom in other lands have found a new way to reach you. They know that you also want freedom. Millions of free men and women have joined together and are sending you this message of friendship over the winds of freedom which in the upper air always blow from West to East. There is no dungeon deep enough to hide truth, no wall high enough to keep out the message of freedom. Tyranny cannot control the winds, cannot enslave your hearts. Freedom will rise again."

Source: Herbert A. Friedman, "Free Europe Press Cold War Leaflets," at: http://www.psywarrior.com/RadioFreeEurope.html.

Western Europe was the stage for a cultural Cold War. The Soviet Union and the communist parties of the West European countries made a well-coordinated drive to control national and international labor, youth, women's, and other mass opinion organizations. In October 1947, the Soviets launched their "peace offensive" with a writer's conference in Berlin, and followed this with a broader gathering in 1948 in Wroclaw. Soviet planners then convened their next conference in New York City in March 1949. New York anti-Stalinist intellectuals, led by Sidney Hook, staged a counter conference, and infiltrated the communists' carefully orchestrated discussion panels, asking tough questions of the party-line presenters. Sensing they were on to something, Wisner and the OPC tried to disrupt the next Soviet-organized conference in Paris in April 1949 by funding the presence of a number of anti-Stalinist intellectuals. However, OPC found the assembled group difficult to manage, as anti-American and/or anti-capitalist diatribes often accompanied the anticommunist rhetoric of participants.

In the aftermath of the Paris conference, OPC picked up on a proposal from Michael Josselson, working with the American occupation government, for a cultural and intellectual conference in Berlin. With support from OPC and U.S. military authorities, the Congress for Cultural Freedom (CCF) in June 1950 was a propaganda success—an outcome aided by its coinciding with the communist invasion of South Korea. OPC then turned the CCF into a continuing campaign under Josselson's management. For the next 16 years, the CCF was a major OPC/CIA conduit for covert U.S. government funding to noncommunist social and intellectual endeavors. Money passed to the recipients through such middleman "cutouts" as cooperating legitimate foundations and specially created "private" entities. The CCF's dollars mounted art exhibitions, arranged concerts, sustained publication of literary and political affairs magazines, subsidized publication of books, and funded anticommunist international conferences as a counterweight to conferences sponsored by the Soviet Union through its front organizations. Subsidies to the U.S. National Student Association, for example, provided the organization with the means to sustain democratically based international student groups in the competition with their communist-controlled counterparts. Similarly, covert financial assistance to the New York-based women's group, the Committee of Correspondence, provided the opportunity for the injection of a gendered voice in the West-East debate over what constituted the elements of "peace" and its corollaries of freedom and democracy. OPC/CIA directed other financial assistance to noncommunist political parties, newspapers, and labor unions (often with the assistance of the AFL-CIO). The providing of subsidies to political parties and labor unions reinforced the effects of the Marshall Plan in stabilizing the economies and rebuilding the West European industrial base. The covert funding of voluntary and educational organizations continued into the 1960s.[12]

Asia

Korean War

The Far East also presented problems for the makers of U.S. national security policy after World War II. The fall of China to Mao's communists in 1949 was a seminal event. The reconstruction effort in Japan drew its share of attention. And there was significant concern about communist insurgents in the Philippines. Nevertheless, it was the invasion by the Democratic Republic of Korea (DPRK—North Korea) of the Republic of Korea (ROK—South Korea) on June 25, 1950, that put the spotlight on the Far East. U.S. combat troops had been withdrawn from Korea a year prior to the attack, leaving only the small U.S. Korean Military Advisory Group (KMAG) in South Korea. President Truman immediately authorized U.S. naval and air support to the ROK. Then, on the basis of a UN resolution (passed in the absence of the Soviet delegation), Truman committed U.S. troops to the battle. However, by the end of August 1950, the South Korean and U.S. forces had been pushed into a constricted area around the southeastern city of Pusan.

The U.S. services had virtually no troops, infrastructure, or doctrine for irregular operations, yet the army, navy, and air force all initiated covert activities in Korea. The CIA also organized guerrilla and other covert operations into North Korea. A scramble ensued to rebuild unconventional warfare capabilities discarded at the end of World War II. As the war wore on, there was a proliferation of organizations conducting covert and special operations.

Even in the absence of experienced and trained personnel, the Tokyo-based Far East Command (FEC), the U.S. Eighth Army, and individual service components moved to initiate special operations. The FEC began organizing Korean nationals for tactical ("line-crossers") and strategic (long-range penetrations via parachute) missions behind enemy lines. FEC's small Psychological Warfare Branch quickly had propaganda leaflets printed and airdropped. And psychological warfare broadcasts began from prewar Radio Japan studios in Tokyo. The U.S. Navy's maritime muscle forced North Korea to withdraw its naval offensive capability from coastal waters. Despite a lack of proper training and equipment, the Navy's Task Force 90 began in early August 1950 using Underwater Demolition Team (UDT) personnel, often referred to as *frogmen*, to conduct onshore raids. Several such interdiction missions by Navy frogmen and a Marine reconnaissance unit were directed against the North Korean railway system up to 200 miles behind enemy lines. Seaborne UDT attacks targeted other types of North Korean infrastructure, including harbor facilities and shore installations. The UDT teams, originally organized to conduct beach reconnaissance, had begun a transition to becoming the Navy's commandos.

The war brought growth in the size and capability of OPC's paramilitary operations. In July 1950, OPC chief Wisner sent Hans Tofte to the theater to organize covert paramilitary operations. By September, the OPC/CIA was using Korean agents to run intelligence collection missions into areas along North Korea's northern borders with China and the USSR and working with the air force to establish escape and evasion routes for U.S. pilots shot down over enemy territory. CIA operational planning and training of the Korean agents was done under the cover name of the Joint Advisory Commission, Korea.

By late November 1950, General MacArthur's advance toward the Yalu River boundary between North Korea and the People's Republic of China (PRC) had been reversed by the intervention of several hundred thousand Chinese troops. The UN retreat was so precipitous that large numbers of anticommunist North Koreans were left behind the battle lines. These individuals, some already part of quasi-organized partisan groups, became the basic material—some suggest "fodder"—for the development by the Eighth Army and OPC/CIA of guerrilla warfare and covert operations. Korea's east and west coasts are dotted with small islands, some quite close to the North Korean mainland. Because UN naval forces controlled Korean coastal waters, these islands became the training and staging areas for covert operations by the military and the CIA.

Cease-fire negotiations began in July 1951, but it was another two years before an armistice was concluded. Conventional and unconventional warfare continued. Raids into North Korea by partisan teams from the offshore islands were accelerated, as were air force-supported deep penetration, parachute drops of military and CIA agents for intelligence collection and sabotage. The communication and supply lines from China were particularly targets for guerrilla activities. Air force support to the unconventional war was reinforced in mid-1952 with the deployment of the newly formed 581st Air Resupply and Communications Wing. The 581st and its mixed complement of aircraft and helicopters performed covert support services analogous to the Carpetbaggers of World War II. As the negotiations went forward and the frontlines became relatively fixed, the always dangerous missions into enemy-held territory became even more so, since the communists could redirect line units into internal security. The dangers extended to the air force crews who flew agent insertion/extraction and psychological warfare missions. The 11 men of the crew of a B-29 shot down while making leaflet drops over North Korea were held and brutally interrogated by the Chinese from February 1953 until their release in August 1955. In May 1953, as part of the armistice negotiations, the UN began disarming and withdrawing partisan forces from islands north of the 38th parallel. The withdrawal of the partisans from their island bases created the problem of what to do with them. The South Koreans were not pleased with having to integrate these unhappy "northerners" and their families into their society.[13]

One of the more positive outcomes of the unpreparedness for the Korean War was the U.S. Army's belated recognition of the need for special operations capability. The small number of regular Ranger companies encountered the same problems as their World War II counterparts. There was a tendency among army commanders to throw the lightly armed Rangers at the most dangerous aspects of conventional warfare, such as patrolling forward of friendly lines and spearheading attacks on fixed positions. The high casualty rate among Ranger companies led to the units in Korea being disbanded in August 1951. Back in Washington, veterans Col. Aaron Bank and Col. Russell Volckmann teamed with Brig. Gen. Robert A. McClure, head of the Office of Psychological Warfare, to convince the army to initiate a new era in unconventional warfare units. Known as the "father of Special Forces," Bank was named the first commander of the 10th Special Forces Group (Airborne), established in June 1952 at Fort Bragg, North Carolina. Drawing on his Jedburgh experience in World War II, Bank helped establish the basic unit organization—the 12-man A-Detachment—of the SOF. At the end of 1953, a second group, the 77th Special Forces Group (Airborne), was activated. However, the aftermath of the Korean War saw a continuation of the cycle where such forces were built up during times of a crisis and then reduced after the conflict had passed.[14]

Operations against Mainland China

Beyond the battlefields of Korea, U.S. geopolitical goals in Asia, as articulated in NSC 48/5, signed by President Truman on May 17, 1951, were to separate China from its alliance with the Soviet Union and remove or change the character of the communist regime. A commitment to supporting anticommunist groups inside and outside of the Chinese mainland was included in these broader goals.[15] A range of covert operations were undertaken despite intelligence estimates that assessed the potential of guerrilla forces in China in less than glowing terms. (See sidebar, *Estimating Chinese Guerrilla Potential.*)

Estimating Chinese Guerrilla Potential

"The maximum total number of effective guerrillas throughout China . . . is approximately 175,000. . . . Active guerrilla forces are located for the most part in inaccessible areas—mountainous regions and on Nationalist-held offshore islands. . . . Guerrilla forces suffer from a lack of central direction and coordination, . . . from serious deficiencies in arms and ammunition, and . . . from an almost total lack of communication facilities. . . . Chinese Communist countermeasures against dissident elements have been most successful; and . . . guerrilla strength and activity under present circumstances will probably continue to decline. . . . Anti-Communist guerrillas . . . do not have the capability to: (a) Delay or disrupt the movement from one front to another of the Chinese Communist armies; (b) Seriously interdict Chinese Communist lines of communications or logistic support; (c) Attract to their ranks substantial numbers of defectors from the Communists; (d) Significantly aid military operations should a Nationalist invasion be launched in the near future. . . . Guerrilla capabilities are unlikely to increase without sizable outside support."

Source: Central Intelligence Agency, "Tab D: Estimate of the Present Strength and Capabilities of Anti-Communist Guerrillas in China," in *Special Estimate: The Probable Consequences of Certain Possible US Courses of Action with Respect to Communist China and Korea*, SE-20, December 22, 1951, at: http://www.foia.cia.gov/sites/default/files/document_conversions/89801/DOC_0000205489.pdf.

OPC/CIA sought to work with what was believed to be a "Third Force" existing inside and outside China, that is, a force neither communist nor Nationalist in its political orientation. Keeping the Third Force separate from the Nationalists was necessary because Chiang Kai-shek's regime was seen as largely discredited on the mainland. The Third Force concept called for linking small teams of CIA-trained Chinese anticommunist agents with local, noncommunist guerrilla groups believed to be operating on the mainland. The goal was to support and promote internal anticommunist guerrilla operations and, after China intervened in the Korean War, to divert Chinese resources away from that war. Third Force agent teams were parachuted or inserted from the sea into China. The target area was largely Manchuria along the Yalu River border with North Korea. Their orders included contacting dissident forces, recruiting local agents, collecting intelligence, setting up networks to assist downed U.S. aircrews, and reporting back to their CIA handlers via radio transmissions. Modeled after the OSS experience in Europe during World War II, a crucial element was lacking in the situation in China—that is, a population desirous and willing to cooperate in actions against the communist government.[16]

Insertion and retrieval of covert agents and resupplying Third Force and other clandestine groups often involved flights deep inside China by Civil Air Transport (CAT) pilots and planes. Lt. Gen. Claire Chennault, of World War II "Flying Tigers" fame, founded CAT to fly relief supplies to war-torn areas of China but developed it into a commercial carrier. By the 1950s, it had been purchased by the CIA and become a covert proprietary company. It operated regular passenger and cargo flights, but the reason for CAT's continued existence was to support CIA operations. Flying covert missions into communist China was hazardous work. A November 1952 mission went badly wrong for all involved. A five-man Third Force team deployed into Manchuria in July had established radio contact soon after insertion, was twice resupplied, and was then augmented by an agent with courier responsibilities. In November, the team requested exfiltration by "air snatch" of the agent to carry out documents that had been obtained. Such aerial pickups involved a line strung between two poles, a harness into which the agent was strapped, and a low-flying aircraft trailing a hook to catch the line between the poles. After catching the line, the agent was carried into the aircraft by a winch. In this instance, individuals in the team had been captured and were cooperating with the authorities. When CAT's C-47 aircraft came in low and slow for the snatch, antiaircraft fire shot it down. The CAT pilots, Americans Norman Schwartz and Robert Snoddy, were killed in the crash; and CIA paramilitary officers, John Downey and Richard Fecteau, were captured. It was two years before the two men resurfaced to the outside world, after being presumed dead. A show trial was held in November 1954 that included the officers and crew of the U.S. Air Force B-29 psychological operations flight shot down in February 1953. Downey was sentenced to life imprisonment and Fecteau to 20 years. Fecteau was released in 1971, but it was 1973 before the Chinese freed Downey.[17]

Another OPC/CIA venture supported Nationalist remnants isolated in northern Burma. Gen. Li Mi and several thousand troops had retreated to the area, rather than heading east for Taiwan. Truman tasked the CIA with initiating a covert paramilitary operation against China using Li Mi's forces. Beginning in March 1951, the CIA airlifted equipment, Nationalist soldiers from Taiwan, and U.S. advisors to Li Mi. Incursions of Li Mi's troops into Yunnan Province in 1951 and 1952 were turned back by PRC forces. By late 1952, it was clear Li Mi was not going to be able to gain a foothold in Yunnan. After the CIA ended its support for Li Mi, Nationalist contacts continued; and a long-term problem of how to dispose of these forces emerged. In early 1953, the Eisenhower administration convinced Chiang Kai-shek's government to evacuate its troops back to Taiwan. Not all left, however, and they continued to receive support from Taiwan well into the mid-1960s. In the end, these remnants turned to banditry and opium smuggling, with only occasional forays into Yunnan Province.[18]

In March 1951, OPC/CIA launched an operation with the Nationalist Chinese to use the thousands of irregular Chinese troops who had taken up residence on the islands in the straits between Taiwan and the southeastern coast of the mainland. The best known of the islands are Quemoy/Jinmen and Matsu/Mazu. Some of the groups on the islands had maintained a semblance of military discipline. Others had fallen into smuggling and piracy. On the U.S. side, the effort was organized under an ostensibly civilian import-export firm, Western Enterprises Incorporated (WEI), in reality a CIA proprietary. Lt. Col. (later Lt. Gen.) William R. "Ray" Peers, commander of OSS's Detachment 101 in Burma in World War II, was the initial head of WEI's operations. Peers was typical of many individuals who served with OPC in its early days. He had been "sheep-dipped," that is, he was regular military on loan to OPC/CIA after having gone through a mock resignation from active duty and being hired by WEI. When such tours with CIA were completed, the process was reversed and individuals returned to their military careers. Included among the sheep-dipped military personnel was a future Marine Corps Commandant, Maj. (later Gen.) Robert H. Barrow, who headed a WEI unit from late 1952.

WEI trained and equipped paramilitary forces for incursions into Mainland China. The operation also had a psychological warfare element that prepared and distributed anticommunist propaganda by drops from aircraft and by leaving materials behind in coastal raids. The original plan called for "blind" (without on-ground reception committees) air insertions by CAT of individuals or small groups into remote regions of China, where ethnic minority guerrillas were known to be holding out. There were also coastal landings of several hundred guerrillas, who moved inland seeking to establish "safe havens" where they could link up with anticommunist stay-behind forces, collect intelligence, and be resupplied by airdrops. Neither of these approaches produced the desired results. Those involved in blind-drop operations disappeared almost as soon as they hit the ground. They might be heard from again if a show trial was desirable for perusal of the world media. Tellingly, there was no indication of local support for these groups, although the guerrillas were often from the areas where they landed.

After those experiences, WEI and the Nationalists moved to hit-and-run attacks on isolated islands and coastal areas. These raids enjoyed more success. They usually used motorized junks, towing sampans, or rubber boats. Nationalist navy vessels provided security for such operations; at times, there was limited air cover from the Nationalist air force. In addition, taking a page from the Australians' World War II playbook, CIA-sponsored coast-watching networks were established throughout the islands to track communist and international shipping. As the war in Korea began to stabilize, the PRC responded to the island-based operations by rotating seasoned units from Korea to the southeastern coastal area. After mid-1953, the PRC increasingly took more direct action against the most exposed of the island bases. By this time, CIA involvement in covert offensive operations from the islands was being scaled back, and essentially ceased after the shooting ended in Korea. However, CIA personnel provided guerrilla warfare training to Nationalist teams for several years after ending the active management of operations from the islands.[19]

Counterinsurgency in the Philippines

When the United States granted the Philippines independence in 1946, the new government faced an armed insurrection from a guerrilla group seen in Washington as an extension of the worldwide communist threat. By 1950 the Hukbo ng Bayan Laban Sa Hapon or People's Anti-Japanese Army—the Huks—had changed their name to Hukbalahap or People's Liberation Army and, rather than their original vaguely agrarian socialism, were espousing a Marxist ideology. Using classic guerrilla tactics, the Huks had gained control over a significant portion of central Luzon, the main island, and were potentially capable of threatening Manila, the capital. Much of the U.S. assistance to the Philippine government took the form of military aid, managed by the Joint U.S. Military Assistance Group. At the initiative of both the State Department and the Joint Chiefs of Staff, OPC head Wisner selected an OSS veteran with previous experience in the Philippines, Air Force Lt. Col. (later Maj. Gen.) Edward G. Lansdale, to provide covert advice and assistance to the Philippine government.

Lansdale arrived in Manila in September 1950 at the same time Ramón Magsaysay was appointed the country's secretary of National Defense. The teaming of Lansdale, whose prewar experience had been in advertising, and Magsaysay, a hero of the wartime guerrilla resistance, was a potent combination. The counterinsurgency campaign they launched had both military and psychological warfare aspects. The military goal of U.S. aid was to enlarge, train, rearm, and reorganize the Philippine military to effectively fight the Huk guerrillas. This involved a switch in military tactics to greater reliance on small-unit operations. Magsaysay sought to maintain pressure on the guerrillas and reduce their sense of security in areas they previously controlled. On the psychological warfare side, Lansdale's advice was targeted on gaining the support of the populace and denying that support to the guerrillas. Magsaysay and Lansdale launched a psychological and political action campaign that included establishing community centers where modern agricultural methods and health care were taught. A propaganda campaign seeking to reduce pro-Huk feelings among villagers encompassed funding pro-government community organizations and disseminating anticommunist materials. Taken together, these actions and Magsaysay's reforms in the military gradually reduced the insurgency as a serious threat. In 1953, with U.S. backing in the form of both money and political advice, Magsaysay was overwhelmingly elected president of the Philippines. Lansdale returned to the United States that same year. His reputation as a psychological warfare guru led in 1954 to his assignment to another unconventional warfare challenge in Vietnam.[20]

Notes

1. See Thomas F. Troy, *Donovan and the CIA: A History of the Establishment of the Central Intelligence Agency* (Frederick, MD: University Publications of America, 1981), pp. 217–304. See also, Arthur B. Darling, *The Central Intelligence Agency: An Instrument of Government, to 1950* (University Park: Penn State Press, 1990), pp. 22–41.

2. *FRUS, 1945–1950—Truman Series: Emergence of the Intelligence Establishment*, Document 71. See also Ludwell Lee Montague, *General Walter Bedell Smith as Director of Central Intelligence, October 1950–February 1953* (University Park: Penn State Press, 1992), pp. 15–34; and Michael Warner, "The Creation of the Central Intelligence Group," *Studies in Intelligence* 39, no. 5 (1996): 111–20.

3. *National Security Act of 1947* (July 26, 1947), Sec. 103(d)(1)-(5), at: http://research.archives.gov/description/299856. The legislative debate that preceded passage is detailed in Troy, *Donovan and the CIA*, pp. 365–402.

4. See "The Truman Doctrine, 1947," at: http://history.state.gov/milestones/1945-1952/truman-doctrine. On the Marshall Plan, see "For European Recovery: The Fiftieth Anniversary of the Marshall Plan," at: http://www.loc.gov/exhibits/marshall/.

5. See G.J.A. O'Toole, *Honorable Treachery: A History of U.S. Intelligence, Espionage, and Covert Action from the American Revolution to the CIA* (New York: Atlantic Monthly Press, 1991), pp. 434–37; Sallie Pisani, *The CIA and the Marshall Plan* (Lawrence: University Press of Kansas, 1991), 81–105; and Thomas Powers, *The Man Who Kept the Secrets: Richard Helms and the CIA* (New York: Knopf, 1979), 28–31. ·

6. *FRUS, 1945–1950—Emergence of the Intelligence Establishment*, "Memorandum from the Assistant Director for Policy Coordination (Wisner) to Director of Central Intelligence Hillenkoetter," dated October 29, 1948, Document 306.

7. See Peter Grose, *Operation Rollback: America's Secret War behind the Iron Curtain* (New York: Houghton Mifflin Co., 2000). On Albania, see John Prados, *Safe for Democracy: The Secret Wars of the CIA* (Chicago: Ivan R. Dee, Publisher, 2006), pp. 58–64.

8. *FRUS,1945–1950—Emergence of the Intelligence Establishment*, Document 269.

9. On RFE and RL generally, see Richard H. Cummings, *Cold War Radio: The Dangerous History of American Broadcasting in Europe, 1950–1989* (Jefferson, NC: McFarland, 2009); A. Ross Johnson, *Radio Free Europe and Radio Liberty: The CIA Years and Beyond* (Palo Alto, CA: Stanford University Press, 2010); Arch Puddington, *Broadcasting Freedom: The Cold War Triumph of Radio Free Europe and Radio Liberty* (Lexington: University Press of Kentucky, 2000); and George R. Urban,

Radio Free Europe and the Pursuit of Democracy: My War within the Cold War (New Haven, CT: Yale University Press, 1997). On the Crusade for Freedom, see Richard H. Cummings, *Radio Free Europe's "Crusade for Freedom": Rallying Americans behind Cold War Broadcasting, 1950–1960* (Jefferson, NC: McFarland, 2010).

10. *FRUS, 1969–1976, Vol. XXIX, Eastern Europe; Eastern Mediterranean, 1969–1972,* "Memorandum for the 303 Committee," dated January 27, 1969, Document 28.

11. See Richard H. Cummings, "Balloons over East Europe: The Cold War Leaflet Campaign of Radio Free Europe," *Falling Leaf: The Quarterly Journal of the PsyWar Society* 166 (Autumn 1999), at: http://www.psywarsoc.org/FallingLeaf/balloons.php. For examples of the materials, see Herbert A. Friedman, "Free Europe Press Cold War Leaflets," at: http://www.psywarrior.com/RadioFreeEurope.html.

12. See Helen Laville, "The Committee of Correspondence: CIA Funding of Women's Groups, 1952–1967," *Intelligence and National Security* 12, no. 1 (January 1997): 104–21; Pisani, *CIA and the Marshall Plan*; Frances Stonor Saunders, *The Cultural Cold War: The CIA and the World of Arts and Letters* (New York: New Press, 2000); Michael Warner, "Origins of the Congress for Cultural Freedom, 1949–50," *Studies in Intelligence* 38, no. 5 (1995), pp. 89–98; and Hugh Wilford, *The Mighty Wurlitzer: How the CIA Played America* (Cambridge, MA: Harvard University Press, 2008).

13. See Ed Evanhoe, *Darkmoon: Eighth Army Special Operations in the Korean War* (Annapolis, MD: Naval Institute Press, 1995); Michael E. Haas, *In the Devil's Shadow: U.N. Special Operations during the Korean War* (Annapolis, MD: Naval Institute Press, 2000); Ben S. Malcom, with Ron Martz, *White Tigers: My Secret War in North Korea* (Washington, DC: Brassey's, 1995); and Curtis Peebles, *Twilight Warriors: Covert Air Operations against the USSR* (Annapolis, MD: Naval Institute Press, 2005), pp. 65–84.

14. See Thomas K. Adams, *U.S. Special Forces in Action: The Challenge of Unconventional Warfare* (London: Frank Cass Publishers, 1998), pp. 51–52, 54–55; Aaron Bank, *From OSS to Green Berets: The Birth of Special Forces* (Novato, CA: Presidio Press, 1986); and Susan L. Marquis, *Unconventional Warfare: Rebuilding U.S. Special Operations Forces* (Washington, DC: Brookings Institution, 1997), pp. 11–13.

15. NSC 48/5, "United States Objectives, Policies and Courses of Action in Asia," May 17, 1951, in *FRUS, 1951, Vol. VI, Asia and the Pacific,* pp. 33–63.

16. Nicholas Dujmovic, "Extraordinary Fidelity: Two CIA Prisoners in China, 1952–73," *Studies in Intelligence* 50, no. 4 (2006): 22. On the Third Force generally, see James Lilley, *China Hands: Nine Decades of Adventure, Espionage, and Diplomacy in Asia* (New York: PublicAffairs, 2004), pp. 78–83.

17. See William M. Leary, *Perilous Missions: Civil Air Transport and CIA Covert Operations in Asia* (Tuscaloosa: University of Alabama Press, 1984). On Downey and Fecteau, see Dujmovic, "Extraordinary Fidelity," pp. 21–36. On Schwartz and Snoddy, see CIA, 2007 Featured Story Archive, "Remembering CIA's Heroes: Norman Schwartz & Robert Snoddy," November 29, 2007, at: https://www.cia.gov/news-information/featured-story-archive/2007-featured-story-archive/schwartz-and-snoddy.html. On the CIA's "air snatch" device, see "A Look Back . . . The CIA

and the All American System," at: https://www.cia.gov/news-information/featured-story-archive/2010-featured-story-archive/the-cia-and-the-all-american-system.html.

18. See John W. Garver, *The Sino-American Alliance: Nationalist China and American Cold War Strategy in Asia* (Armonk, NY: M.E. Sharpe, Inc., 1997), pp. 148–64; Lilley, *China Hands*, pp. 78–83; and Peebles, *Twilight Warriors*, pp. 85–105.

19. On WEI, see Frank Holober, *Raiders of the China Coast: CIA Covert Operations during the Korean War* (Annapolis, MD: Naval Institute Press, 1999).

20. See Edward Geary Lansdale, *In the Midst of Wars: An American's Mission to Southeast Asia* (New York: Fordham University Press, 1991).

CHAPTER 5

The Heyday: 1953–1961

New Leadership Arrives

When Dwight D. Eisenhower (1953–1961) succeeded Harry Truman as U.S. President, the Cold War was firmly established as the guiding principle of American national security policy. There is irony in the situation where the Republicans' mantra in 1952—denouncing the "passive" policy of containment in favor of "liberating the captive nations"—had been tried by the outgoing administration and was winding down because it was not working. The Republicans' rhetoric was blunted by the death of Stalin in March 1953. The possibility of achieving a less threatening existence with the post-Stalin leadership opened the door to viewing the Soviet Union as a dangerous adversary with whom it was necessary to contend vigorously, rather than an enemy whose defeat was essential to the well-being of the Western world.

Spearheaded by an activist State Department, under John Foster Dulles, and with a Central Intelligence Agency (CIA) led by younger brother Allen Dulles as its chosen implement, the Eisenhower administration endorsed covert operations as an integral part of the struggle with the Soviet Union. The use of covert operations became the preferred option in seeking to prevent or reverse the spread of communism.

Organizing for Covert Operations

President Eisenhower established his own methodology for managing covert operations. In March 1954, he approved National Security Council 5412 (NSC 5412). The directive reaffirmed the CIA's responsibility for conducting covert operations, under the direction of the NSC. The director of Central

Intelligence (DCI) was to coordinate with the State and Defense departments to ensure that covert operations were planned and conducted consistent with U.S. policies.

NSC 5412 and subsequent iterations laid out an ambitious anticommunist
agenda that called for covert operations to:

> "a. Create and exploit troublesome problems for International Commu-
> nism, impair relations between the USSR and Communist China and
> between them and their satellites, complicate control within the USSR,
> Communist China and between them and their satellites, and retard the
> growth of the military and economic potential of the Soviet bloc.
>
> "b. Discredit the prestige and ideology of International Communism,
> and reduce the strength of its parties and other elements.
>
> "c. Counter any threat of a party or individuals directly or indirectly
> responsive to Communist control to achieve dominant power in a free
> world country.
>
> "d. Reduce International Communist control over any areas of the
> world.
>
> "e. Strengthen the orientation toward the United States of the peo-
> ples and nations of the free world, accentuate, wherever possible, the
> identity of interest between such peoples and nations and the United
> States as well as favoring, where appropriate, those groups genuinely
> advocating or believing in the advancement of such mutual interests,
> and increase the capacity and will of such peoples and nations to resist
> International Communism.
>
> "f. In accordance with established policies and to the extent practi-
> cable in areas dominated or threatened by International Communism,
> develop underground resistance and facilitate covert and guerrilla oper-
> ations and ensure availability of those forces in the event of war, includ-
> ing wherever practicable provisions of a base upon which the military
> may expand these forces in time of war within acting theaters of opera-
> tions as well as provision for stay-behind assets and escape and evasion
> facilities."[1]

Old Problems

New leadership does not mean the disappearance of old problems. As promised, Eisenhower brought the stalemated war in Korea to a conclusion with the
armistice agreement in July 1953. The UN-U.S. forces had already begun to
decommission the Korean partisan units that had been the core of the special
warfare tactics used against the North. CIA covert paramilitary operations in
Korea and those directed against Mainland China from the Nationalist-held
offshore islands also wound down with the armistice. In Western Europe,
covert financial support of labor, student, women's, and cultural groups, as

well as Radio Free Europe and Radio Liberty, continued. With the end of the shooting war in Korea, military special operations regressed into primarily providing physical support to CIA-directed paramilitary actions.

Iran and TPAJAX

Iran had been on and off the national security agenda since the end of World War II. Britain and the Soviet Union had jointly occupied Iran, to assure a transportation route for wartime lend-lease supplies to the Soviets. A January 1942 treaty committed the two nations to withdraw their forces within six months of the end of the war. The United States also had strategically placed troops in Iran. The Americans and British withdrew their troops on schedule, but the Soviets pushed their occupied territory further south and set up two puppet governments. Although the Soviets finally pulled out in the spring of 1946, concerns remained about Moscow's designs on the Iranian oil fields and its perceived desire to develop a pro-Soviet Iran as a land link and extension of Soviet power to the Gulf of Oman.[2]

The early 1950s crisis in Iran[3] began when the Majlis, the Iranian legislature, voted in March 1951 to nationalize the Anglo-Iranian Oil Company (AIOC), which had held a monopoly on the production and sale of Iranian oil since early in the century. The Majlis pressured the shah, Mohammed Reza Pahlavi, into appointing as prime minister the strongly nationalistic, anti-British, and personally erratic Mohammed Mossadegh. The British government, half-owner of AIOC, found it impossible to negotiate with Mossadegh, and initiated an economic embargo. In October 1952, Mossadegh ordered the closure of the British Embassy, thus depriving the British of direct access to those inside Iran who would support a coup against Mossadegh. The British approached the United States for assistance in removing Mossadegh, but President Truman was more in tune with the nationalistic sentiments of the day than with British desires to maintain their grip on Iranian oil.

By early 1953, Iran was nearing chaos. Mossadegh's National Front was falling apart from internal strife, and he looked for support from the well-organized and well-financed Iranian communist party, the Tudeh. Fear of Soviet efforts to take advantage of the situation led Eisenhower to agree to a British proposal for a covert operation to remove Mossadegh. Given that diplomacy had failed and military action was not feasible, a covert operation offered the kind of "third option" that this and future administrations found attractive. It also offered the president "deniability" should something go wrong. By mid-July, the British prime minister and the U.S. president had approved a joint CIA and British Secret Intelligence Service (SIS or MI6) plan. (See sidebar, *TPAJAX Operational Plan.*) CIA Tehran station began passing its agents an initial batch of anti-Mossadegh propaganda materials. Kermit Roosevelt, grandson of Theodore Roosevelt and chief of the CIA's Near East Africa Division, arrived in Iran on July 19, 1953, to coordinate the effort on the ground. He had at his disposal a stable of agents, some paid by the CIA and others left in place by SIS when Mossadegh closed the British embassy.[4]

TPAJAX Operational Plan

"The policy of both the US and UK government requires replacement of Mossadegh as the alternative to certain economic collapse in Iran and the eventual loss of the area to the Soviet orbit. Only through a planned and controlled replacement can the integrity and independence of the country be ensured. . . . The total estimated expenditure required to implement this plan will be the equivalent of $285,000 of which $147,500 will be provided by the US Service and $137,500 by the UK Service. . . . This plan is based on the assumption that the cooperation of the Shah will be obtained. Such cooperation will give a military coup the best chance of success. However, it also envisages the same type of operation through the involuntary involvement of the Shah in this plan."

Source: The " 'London' Draft of the TPAJAX Operational Plan," is available at: http://www.nytimes.com/library/world/mideast/iran-cia-appendix-b.pdf.

Mossadegh strengthened the hands of the coupists in early August 1953 by staging a rigged referendum on dissolution of the Majlis, an act that constitutionally rested with the shah. This act alienated both liberal and conservative Iranians, and provided fodder for the CIA/SIS-subsidized opposition press.[5] Among other themes, the propaganda linked Mossadegh and the Iranian communists to the threat of a Soviet takeover. Attacks on Mossadegh in the Iranian press were supplemented by "black" propaganda, such as threats against religious leaders in the name of the Tudeh Party. A bombing of the home of a religious leader was carried out in such a way as to assign blame on the Tudeh.[6] On August 13, 1953, the shah dismissed Mossadegh and named Gen. Fazlollah Zahedi prime minister. The first effort at a military coup on August 15 failed, because of a leak from within the Iranian military plotters. The approach then became one of convincing the Iranian public—and the army—that Zahedi was the legal head of government and Mossadegh the usurper. The shah fled the country for Baghdad and later Rome.

Mossadegh and his supporters then made a mistake by launching a strong propaganda attack on the shah, increasing public resentment against the prime minister. By the evening of August 18, small-group violence had begun in the streets of Tehran, primarily between Tudeh Party activists and a grow-ing pro-shah element. Gangs claiming to act in the name of the Tudeh Party engaged in looting and vandalism, acts that generated additional resentment. By August 19, the shah's royal decree (firman) was being widely circulated; and the street crowds, with some outside encouragement but also from cleri-cal opponents of Mossadegh, were ransacking pro-Tudeh and anti-shah news-papers.[7] As the crowds grew, military and police officers began to provide leadership and fighting broke out as pro-royalist crowds occupied the main government buildings. The taking of Radio Tehran allowed the royalists to broadcast news of their success to the provincial cities, and provided Zehedi a platform to call for the people to rally around his government. By the end of the day, it was mostly over. Roosevelt left Tehran a few days later—clandestinely, just as he had entered.

It is easy to regard TPAJAX as a success for the concept of covert politi-cal action in that it achieved its stated purpose. A short-term problem was solved. The role of the shah was strengthened, and he kept his country in the Western orbit (more or less) for the next 25 years. Internally, he developed into a despot, and laid the groundwork for his eventual overthrow. None-theless, it seems a stretch to blame the events in Iran of 1979 on TPAJAX. Given the chaotic situation of Tehran (admittedly helped by CIA agents) and the steadily weakening hold of Mossadegh on the people, it is difficult to imagine Iran being on the road to democracy.

Guatemala and PBSUCCESS

The Eisenhower administration's next concern about communist encroac-hment beyond the borders of the Bloc came in America's "backyard." There are multiple interpretations as to why the administration decided to oust Guatemalan president Jacobo Arbenz Guzmán.[8] The prevailing scholarship suggests that while Arbenz was probably more a nationalist than a commu-nist, he was influenced by and willing to make common cause with the com-munists. The plan for his overthrow was developed with the participation of the CIA, State Department, Pentagon, and White House.

Washington was uneasy about communist influence in the government and labor unions in Guatemala before Arbenz was elected president in 1950. As Arbenz's new regime edged toward radical personnel and positions, the Truman administration overtly signaled its displeasure. Aid and construction projects were delayed and loans discouraged. In 1952, Arbenz launched a new land reform, with the involvement of the leaders of the Guatemalan Commu-nist Party. The land reform was not particularly radical, but it increased tension between the government and the landowners and American-owned compa-nies, such as the United Fruit Company. When the Guatemalan Supreme

Court declared the reform decree unconstitutional, Arbenz dismissed the justices. By this time, the countryside was experiencing substantial disorder; landowners, the Catholic Church, and the army all perceived a threat to the established order, but leadership was lacking. By early 1952, Washington had identified a potential leader of military action against Arbenz. Carlos Castillo Armas had fled to Honduras after leading an abortive uprising against the government in late 1950. An initial plan to provide Castillo Armas with arms was scuttled when its cover was blown, but the CIA paid him enough to keep his small force in place.

Just over two months after its covert success in Iran, the Eisenhower administration issued the guidelines for its "Basic National Security Policy." Dated October 30, 1953, NSC Paper No. 162/2 (NSC 162/2) endorsed in plain language the use of covert measures to challenge Soviet encroachments into the free world. (See sidebar, *NSC 162/2*.) Reporting from Guatemala by government sources and American journalists about the "radical" agenda being pursued by Arbenz and the growth of communist influence convinced Eisenhower to approve a covert operation. The plan provided for a full range of overt and covert tactics from all elements of the U.S. national security establishment—military and economic aid to neighboring countries, propaganda and psychological warfare, economic and diplomatic pressure, and paramilitary action.[9] The operation established a training base in the Canal Zone, recruited pilots to fly unmarked ("black") aircraft, set up a clandestine radio station, and assisted Castillo Armas in creating a revolutionary committee as the public face of the operation.

NSC 162/2

"As a means of reducing Soviet capabilities for extending control and influence in the free world, the United States should:

"a. Take overt and covert measures to discredit Soviet prestige and ideology as effective instruments of Soviet power, and to reduce the strength of communist parties and other pro-Soviet elements.
"b. Take all feasible diplomatic, political, economic and covert measures to counter any threat of a party or individuals directly or indirectly responsible to Soviet control to achieve dominant power in a free world country.
"c. Undertake selective, positive actions to eliminate Soviet-Communist control over any areas of the free world."

Source: National Security Council Paper No. 162/2 (NSC 162/2), "Note by the Executive Secretary to the National Security Council on Basic National Security Policy," dated October 30, 1953, *FRUS, 1952–1954, Volume II, Part 1, National Security Affairs*, Document 100.

Much of PBSUCCESS depended on propaganda and psychological warfare. The early propaganda effort focused on intimidating the Arbenz government and convincing Guatemalans of the existence of a strong underground resistance. Student groups were active in producing antigovernment graffiti, while a women's group proved adept at spreading rumors and distributing anticommunist leaflets at the markets. These efforts brought on increasingly harsh reactions, as newspapers and radio stations were shut down or intimidated into silence. Psychological warfare was waged against the Guatemalan army to undermine its neutral stance in the country's political turmoil. The message was that the army had to act to prevent something worse from happening, such as, an American invasion. After May 1, 1954, these themes were reinforced by the CIA's clandestine radio, the Voice of Liberation (Operation SHERWOOD). The radio claimed to be transmitting from the jungle inside Guatemala, but the programming was prepared in Florida and sent to Honduras for broadcast. Meanwhile, training for Castillo Armas's forces proceeded at bases in Honduras, Nicaragua, and the Canal Zone.

In the middle of May, Arbenz gave the U.S. government a pretext for action—a ship carrying several tons of Czech weapons arrived in Guatemala. The Czech arms became the centerpiece in the argument that the Soviet Union was preparing Guatemala as a beachhead in the Americas. The United States launched a naval blockade, stopping and searching ships, including those of Britain and France. This was accompanied by using Castillo Armas's air force of CIA-supplied aircraft and pilots to buzz the capital city and drop anticommunist, anti-Arbenz leaflets. The result was a building sense of panic in the government.

On June 18, 1954, Castillo Armas led about 500 troops across the Honduras border into Guatemala. The "invasion" was more bluff than real, and minimal resistance from government forces tended to bring it to a halt. Nonetheless, the Voice of Liberation announced that Castillo Armas was marching on Guatemala City at the head of several thousand troops and scoring great victories along the way. Planes flown by CIA contract pilots bombed a fuel depot and other visible points, and dropped propaganda leaflets. Convinced they were seeing the beginning of a much larger U.S.-supported invasion, the Guatemalan army abandoned Arbenz. The government collapsed, and was replaced by a military junta that eventually, with some arm-twisting from the Americans, accepted Castillo Armas as president.

PBSUCCESS achieved its stated policy goal of removing a national leader and replacing him with a handpicked successor. However, the initial feeling that the operation had lived up to its name did not last long. The history of PBSUCCESS, written 40 years later by a member of the CIA's history staff, sums up the aftermath:

The Agency's initial jubilation gave way to misgivings as it became clear that victory in Guatemala had been neither as clear nor as unambiguous as originally thought. . . . Castillo Armas's new regime proved embarrassingly inept. Its repressive and corrupt policies soon polarized Guatemala and provoked a renewed civil conflict.[10]

New Challenges

Revolt in Indonesia

By the mid-1950s, there was growing apprehension among U.S. national security policy makers about the political direction of Indonesia.[11] Consisting of three major islands and thousands of smaller islands, the country gained its independence from the Netherlands in 1949, and had been showing an increasing tendency toward political chaos. The center of power rested in Djakarta on the main island of Java, but control over the outlying islands and their mixture of ethnic, religious, and language groups weakened in proportion to their distance away from the center. Washington's concerns were reinforced by the efforts of Sukarno, the country's first president, to increase economic and military aid from both the People's Republic of China and the Soviet Union. The level of Washington's anxiety is expressed in NSC 5518, dated May 3, 1955: "The loss of Indonesia to Communist control would have serious consequences for the U.S. and the rest of the free world."[12] In Indonesia's first national elections in September 1955, a CIA political action operation reportedly distributed $1 million to the Moslem Masjumi Party, which finished second in the overall voting.[13] At the same time, the Indonesian Communist Party (PKI) received 16 percent of the popular vote. Follow-on elections in 1957 saw a further growth in the PKI vote.

By early 1957, separate civilian and army groups on the western island of Sumatra and the eastern island of Sulawesi (Celebes) were in virtually open revolt against the central government. Both the Indonesian government and the dissidents would eventually lobby for assistance in the struggle. In September 1957, a Special Report by the Ad Hoc Interdepartmental Committee on Indonesia for the NSC recommended that the United States "employ all feasible covert means to strengthen the anti-Communist forces in the outer islands." Eisenhower accepted the reasoning in the Special Report and approved a two-track approach to Indonesia: First, to continue economic aid to the government and support to noncommunist elements within the military; and, second, to initiate a covert operation focused on strengthening the anticommunist forces on the islands beyond Java.[14]

Meetings between CIA officers and dissident representatives in the summer and fall of 1957 began a flow of money to the Sumatran rebels. In early 1958, the first of several CIA officers landed in Sumatra and the Agency began direct shipments of arms, first, from the sea and, later, by airdrops. On February 15, 1958, the rebels in Sumatra broke formally with Djakarta and established the Revolutionary Government of the Republic of Indonesia (PRRI). The dissidents on Sulawesi followed suit, and the Indonesian government reacted on February 21 and 22 by staging airstrikes on dissident strongholds. Urged on by Secretary of State Dulles, Washington decided to supply the rebels with airplanes and heavy weapons. Although doing so raised the profile and increased the risk of exposure of U.S. involvement, it was too late to save the PRRI. In mid-March, Djakarta launched an air and sea offensive on Sumatra, and a month later was in control of the rebel "capital" in Padang. The five-man CIA team that had been in Padang fled into the hills, but eventually made it to the seashore where they arranged to be picked up by submarine.[15]

On Sulawesi, the CIA created an air force for the rebels. Planes were bought from the Philippine air force and the CIA proprietary Civil Air Transport (CAT) and flown by Filipino and Polish civilian mercenaries. CIA officers and Filipino military personnel provided ground support for the airplanes, and fuel and ammunition were ferried in from a U.S. base in the Philippines by CAT aircraft and pilots. When two of the Polish pilots were killed in a crash, the other two quit; CAT pilots, ostensibly operating on their own as "soldiers of fortune," replaced them. Aided by their air force—which included U.S. Air Force advisors, Nationalist Chinese pilots, and Filipino mechanics—the Sulawesi rebels made gains against government forces. The whole covert operation collapsed when on May 18, 1958, a CIA/CAT pilot named Allen Pope, against all orders carrying his identity papers, was shot down on a bombing run and captured by government forces. U.S. "deniability" was already thin, and this was too much exposure. Secretary of State Dulles terminated covert support for the Indonesian rebels,[16] leaving the operation well short of achieving any of the administration's goals.

Tibet

Tibet's long history records both expansions and contractions in status. The latest contraction occurred in 1950 when Mao Tse-tung sent the People's Liberation Army to take control of Tibet. The feudal and localized tribal forces were overwhelmed. Chinese policies, including forced collectivization and desecrations of monasteries, convinced the often-feuding Tibetan elite that their Buddhist religion, historical freedom, and unique way of life were doomed. They turned first to India for assistance in sustaining an existing but poorly armed and uncoordinated resistance movement and, rejected there, approached the West.[17]

As the Chinese sought to change the ways of Tibetans in the country's out-lying regions, tensions mounted. In the spring and summer of 1956, uprisings in eastern Tibet brought on brutal retaliations that included air and ground operations and the destruction of the ancient monastery of Litang. These actions helped grow a local rebellion into a national resistance movement. The existence of an active resistance together with requests from the Dalai Lama's brothers for assistance convinced Secretary of State Dulles that Tibet offered an opportunity to, at a minimum, harass the Chinese communists. The decision by the NSC in the summer of 1956 to aid the Tibetans set in motion a small-scale but complex covert operation that ended only in 1972. The CIA initially sent six Tibetans to Saipan for training in radio commu-nications and guerrilla warfare tactics. By late May 1958, training had been moved to higher altitudes at the deactivated U.S. Army Camp Hale near Leadville, Colorado. The first two-man team was infiltrated by parachute in September 1957. A second three-man team followed soon after, and arms drops began in July 1958. Over the next three years, there would be over 30 airdrops of personnel, arms, and supplies. The flights transited out of a U.S. base in Thailand. Crews for these physically demanding and dangerous flights came from the CIA's proprietary airline, CAT.[18] By 1958, the Tibetan parti-sans numbered upward of 100,000 and caused the PRC to divert significant manpower and supplies to the area.

In March 1959, affairs took a fateful turn for the Tibetans when the Dalai Lama concluded that he had to flee Lhasa or risk bloodshed among his sup-porters. The revolt in Lhasa turned violent, with the Chinese shelling the palace the Dalai Lama had just vacated. The Chinese dissolved the Tibetan government, and the Dalai Lama responded by declaring his own free Tibetan government and seeking asylum in India. The Chinese moved quickly and massively to put down the revolt. On April 23, 1959, DCI Allen Dulles reported to the NSC that the Chinese had "severely beaten" the resistance fighters and pushed them into "a relatively small area." The Chinese military had proved to be a very effective force, utilizing Korean War veterans and "making very efficient use of aircraft." The rebel forces in the Kham region "had been pretty well knocked to pieces," and it was likely that the same out-come was true in the area around Lhasa.[19] Covert airdrops had to be put on hold until secure locations could be found. Airdrops of teams, arms, supplies, propaganda materials, and mimeograph machines where pockets of resistance remained resumed in September 1959. However, the resistance fighters never adopted the mentality necessary for guerrilla warfare. They tended to travel with their families and herds, and to establish encampments that became fixed targets for the Chinese. Group after group was attacked and its members killed, captured, or dispersed. Then, after a U.S. U-2 was shot down over the Soviet Union on May 1, 1960, President Eisenhower put a hold on covert overflights that might be provocative in nature. Efforts to sustain a large-scale resistance movement inside Tibet by airdrops were over. As a new administration took over in January 1961, covert support for the Tibetan resistance was becoming focused in Nepal, across the border from Tibet.

The Congo

Until Belgium granted independence to the Belgian Congo on June 30, 1960, Washington had paid little attention to the region. As the newly minted Republic of the Congo descended into an internal struggle perceived as having implications for the Cold War, that attitude changed. In a countrywide parliamentary election held a month prior to independence, no party secured a plurality. The head of the party with the largest single bloc of votes in the Chamber of Representatives, Patrice Lumumba, became prime minister and the leader of a rival party, Joseph Kasavubu, became president. Within days of independence, the Belgian-officered Congolese army, the *Force Publique*, mutinied, bringing chaos to an already unstable situation. Less than a week later, the country's richest region, Katanga, seceded under the leadership of the provincial governor, Moise Tshombe. A month later, southeastern Kasai province declared its independence as well. In mid-July 1960, U.S. military aircraft began transporting UN peacekeeping forces drawn from several African countries to the Congo in an effort to restore law and order.

By the summer of 1960, concern in Washington about Lumumba and his influence on the course of events in the Congo had grown to such an extent that it has been averred that, at a NSC meeting on August 18, 1960, Eisenhower raised the possibility of assassinating Lumumba. Director of the NSC Secretariat Robert H. Johnson told the Senate Select Committee on Intelligence on June 18, 1975, that it was his recollection that

> at an NSC meeting during the summer of 1960, "President Eisenhower said something—I can no longer remember his words—that came across to me as an order for the assassination of Lumumba." Johnson stated that this was his impression at the time but that, in retrospect, he was uncertain whether it was an accurate reading of the President's meaning.[20]

A week later, the NSC subcommittee responsible for planning covert operations discussed plans for an anti-Lumumba campaign. The next day, DCI Allen Dulles informed the CIA chief of station in the Congo that Lumumba's "removal must be an urgent and prime objective and that under existing conditions this should be a high priority of our covert action."[21]

Acting in close collaboration with the American ambassador, the CIA initiated a range of political action operations targeting Lumumba and supporting Congolese leaders who seemed favorable to U.S. and Western interests. These included using recruited agents and the outlay of small sums of money to foment and organize anti-Lumumba demonstrations, having agents plant anti-Lumumba articles and editorials in the local newspapers, providing advice and even guidance to the anti-Lumumba president Kasavubu and other government officials, and countering the financial support being provided by the Soviets to pro-Lumumba parliamentarians. On September 14, 1960, Army chief of staff Joseph Mobutu led a bloodless coup in the name of the army.

Even a Lumumba out of power remained a rallying point for discontent and a focus for potential Soviet intervention in Congolese affairs. In the main, there was nothing unusual about the combination of diplomatic and covert efforts directed toward maintaining a government in the Congo friendly to the United States. However, there was a deeply troublesome aspect to the covert anti-Lumumba actions. In September 1960, CIA station chief Larry Devlin was hand-delivered poisons and told to plan and implement the assassination of Lumumba. He was given to understand that the order came from President Eisenhower. Devlin's response was to go into delaying mode in the hope that the Congolese would take care of Lumumba themselves. Eventually, that is what happened when the central government authorities handed Lumumba and two of his associates over to the Katanga secessionists. Lumumba was probably killed on January 17, 1961. But the fact of such plotting combined with its being made public in 1975 in the Church Committee report left a stain on U.S. policies toward Africa and provided Soviet propagandists with ready-made anti-U.S. material for many years.[22] Even with Lumumba gone, problems in the Congo and covert operations designed to support the central government continued into the next two administrations.

Beginning the Long War

Vietnam

As World War II drew to a close, the French moved to reassert colonial control over Vietnam, Cambodia, and Laos. Although neither the Truman nor the Eisenhower administrations held pro-colonialist sympathies, both were drawn into supporting the French. Cooperation with Ho Chi Minh's Viet Minh in wartime, established by the Office of Strategic Services (OSS), gave way to concerns about the Viet Minh's communist foundation. Assistance to the French in their war with the Viet Minh became the precursors of America's involvement in Indochina. In 1950, Truman approved a military aid package that went predominantly to the French forces in Indochina.

Eisenhower resisted directly assisting the French with U.S. troops or bombers; but in the spring of 1953, he approved the loan of C-119 "Boxcars," appropriately repainted to look like French aircraft, to be flown by CAT pilots and maintained by civilian-clothed U.S. Air Force mechanics. By the spring of 1954, the French were losing their war. They had made the strategic and tactical mistake of choosing to confront the Viet Minh from a stronghold at Dien Bien Phu, located in a valley surrounded by higher ground covered in vegetation and laced with caves. Because of its location, Dien Bien Phu had to be resupplied by aircraft; and the French did not have the available airlift to support Dien Bien Phu. The administration loaned the French 22 B-26 attack-bombers, to be flown by French crews, as well as 200 U.S. Air Force personnel to maintain them. And CAT pilots would fly resupply flights in U.S. C-119s loaned and maintained by the U.S. Air Force.[23] None of this saved the French garrison. Its fall in May 1954 and the Geneva Accords of July 1954 ended French colonial rule in Indochina and left a Vietnam divided along a truce line at the 17th parallel. On one side was the well-organized communist north and on the other a disorganized noncommunist south.

Washington's goals in Indochina in 1954 were to prevent a communist takeover in the south and to create a viable anticommunist government. To this end, the administration turned to the covert hand of Col. Edward Lansdale, on loan to the CIA from the U.S. Air Force. The hope was that he could duplicate the successful counterinsurgency and nation building he helped generate in the Philippines. Working with the CIA's Saigon Military Mission, Lansdale's efforts to disrupt the Viet Minh's takeover from the French in Hanoi and to organize "stay-behind" networks in the north garnered scant results. His "black" propaganda efforts to encourage Catholics to emigrate south during the 300 days allowed by the Accords for the exchange of population may have been more successful. In the south, Lansdale sought to turn the administration's handpicked head of government, Ngo Dinh Diem, into a popular democratic leader in the model of Ramón Magsaysay in the Philippines. This neither he nor his CIA successors was able to do. However, their covert advice and assistance to Diem and his brother, Ngo Dinh Nhu, helped Diem consolidate and maintain his position as the head of the South Vietnamese government. He managed to hold power until a new administration abandoned him, and he was overthrown in a coup and killed in November 1963.

For the first four years of the existence of the two Vietnams, Diem in the South and Ho in the North focused on suppressing possible opposition within and consolidating their respective regimes. As part of the military assistance promised Diem by the Eisenhower administration, U.S. Army Special Forces' teams were sent to South Vietnam in 1957 and 1960 to train Vietnamese forces in counterinsurgency tactics. In early 1959, the North Vietnamese removed the restraints on their compatriots in the South, and the National Liberation Front for South Vietnam (or Viet Cong) launched a full-fledged insurgency. As an integral part of that decision, the North Vietnamese army established the 559th Transportation Group to move men and equipment from north to south along what became known as the Ho Chi Minh Trail. From the summer of 1959 into early 1960, the attacks by the insurgents grew sufficiently strong to frighten the Diem administration into accepting the need for cooperative covert operations against the North. However, it was the end of 1960 before the first cross-border foray into the North was undertaken, and by then a new administration was coming to Washington.[24]

Laos

When the Geneva Conference ended France's aspirations for continuing its empire in Indochina, the Kingdom of Laos, a landlocked country that borders on Cambodia, China, Thailand, Vietnam, and Burma (Myanmar), was left with a weak central government, multiple contenders for power, and its two northern provinces in the hands of the Pathet Lao, the Laotian communist front controlled by the North Vietnamese Viet Minh. The United States did not sign the armistice agreement but said it would not use force to effect change in it. Concerned about the inadequacies of the Royal Lao Army (*Forces Armées Royales*, FAR) but unwilling to overtly violate the agreement, the Eisenhower administration established a covert military mission in Vientiane, the Programs Evaluation Office (PEO), at the end of 1955. U.S. military personnel in civilian clothes who had been removed from active-duty rosters staffed the PEO. American military aid over the next several years essentially paid for the salaries and general upkeep of the Lao armed forces.

In mid-1959, fighting broke out between the widely dispersed Lao forces and North Vietnamese regular army units along the border with North Vietnam. The Vietnamese would lead the attack on a defended position, then fall back after taking the site, leaving the Pathet Lao as the occupying force. It was through much of this territory that North Vietnam began building the Ho Chi Minh Trail. In 1959, the United States initiated a new effort to shore up the Laotian military forces. In Operation WHITE STAR, U.S. Army Special Forces personnel began operating in coordination with the CIA and under the control of the U.S. Ambassador as mobile training teams. The objective was to train the FAR in counterinsurgency and unconventional warfare tactics. The WHITE STAR teams served six-month rotations in Laos. Lt. Col. Arthur D. "Bull" Simons, already a legendary figure in U.S. special operations, headed the first and sixth rotations. In 1960, the U.S. role in Laos was extended when the CIA reached an agreement with Maj. Vang Pao, deputy commander of the Laotian army in Xieng Khouang district. A member of the Hmong minority, Vang Pao was one of the few ethnic minorities among Laotian army officers and, consequently, an influential figure among the loosely affiliated Hmong clans. This agreement led to the development of a Hmong-based and CIA-funded parallel military force. Thus, the initial elements of what became a complex, multifaceted covert operation in Laos were in place when John Kennedy took office in January 1961.[25]

Political Action in Japan

The Eisenhower administration also began a series of covert political action operations in Japan. The Allied occupation of Japan lasted from 1945 to 1952. By 1947, the concerns that characterized the Cold War elsewhere were surfacing in Japan. In particular, the specter of a strong Japanese Communist Party (JCP) led the occupation authorities to lend quiet advice and assistance to the more moderate parties. Even after the occupation ended, political groups that represented neither the extreme nationalists nor the extreme left received advice and assistance from U.S. sources.

Concern about the JCP's potential in the elections for the Japanese lower house in May 1958 led Eisenhower to direct the CIA "to provide a few key pro-American and conservative politicians with covert limited financial support and electoral advice."[26] Prime Minister Nobusuke Kishi and the Liberal Democratic Party were returned to power and the Treaty of Mutual Cooperation and Security was signed in January 1960. Low-level covert financial subsidies continued to be provided to specific Japanese politicians into the 1960s.

Another covert effort in Japan, beginning in 1959, sought to create a more pro-American opposition party through a CIA program to divide the left-wing Japan Socialist Party and use the moderate group as the basis for a new party. The program's cost for 1960 was $75,000, and it continued basically at that level through the early 1960s. The covert subsidizing of Japanese politicians was phased out in 1964 as no longer needed and as an operation where the risks of exposure outweighed the benefits. One further covert operation involving propaganda and social action activities, targeted on encouraging "key elements in Japanese society to reject the influence of the extreme left, continued to be funded at moderate levels—$450,000 for 1964, for example—throughout the Johnson administration."[27]

The Castro Problem

Relations between Cuba and the United States deteriorated quickly after the rebel forces of Fidel Castro Ruz overthrew Cuban dictator Fulgencio Batista in January 1959.[28] Even before the success of his revolutionary movement, the question of whether Castro was a communist was being discussed in cables from the U.S. Embassy in Havana. Intelligence gathering on Castro, his associates, and the forces allied with him were well underway by early 1958. After Castro took power, Washington was alarmed by the arrest, imprisonment, and even execution of former Batista supporters. Then, the regime began expropriating foreign-owned properties and companies. The thought that a communist regime was being established just off the shores of the United States was more than Washington policy makers could countenance. There was also growing concern that the Cubans would seek to "export" their revolution to other countries in Latin America. The administration's NSC Special Group approved a range of low-level covert operations, including psychological, political, and economic warfare as well as agent-insertion and other paramilitary operations.

On March 17, 1960, Eisenhower formally approved a plan, developed by CIA's Western Hemisphere Division and vetted by the NSC, for a covert operation to overthrow Castro.[29] The original plan was modeled to some extent on the operation in Guatemala. It called for forming an exile political opposition to serve as the focal point for all of the anti-Castro elements, launching a propaganda offensive, developing a robust intelligence network within Cuba, and creating a Cuban exile paramilitary force. The latter force would be provided the logistical support for conducting covert military operations on the island. All aspects of the operation were to be predicated on "plausible deniability," that is, the hand of the United States should not be evident. The paramilitary concept envisaged recruiting and training outside the United States a core group of Cubans who could deploy into their country to recruit, organize, train, and lead guerrilla forces in establishing centers of resistance to the Castro government.

Although the CIA was the lead element in organizing and implementing propaganda and paramilitary activities, the White House saw the endeavor as a total U.S. effort involving both overt and covert means. Substantial coordination with other government agencies, especially the departments of State and Defense, was a necessary element. The U.S. Navy moved and installed the transmitters for the "black" radio broadcasts, which began from Swan Island in the Caribbean in May 1960. The U.S. Army was involved in the refurbishment of Fort Randolph in the Canal Zone for use as a covert training site. Major air and ground training sites were ultimately established in Guatemala and Nicaragua with the blessings of their presidents. U.S. Army Special Forces personnel were used as part of the training contingent. In addition, officers on loan from the services were in charge of the overall paramilitary effort and the paramilitary training—Marine Col. Jack Hawkins and Army Lt. Col. Frank Egan, respectively.

By the autumn of 1960, the proposed operation had expanded in concept from infiltrating and supporting small-unit guerrilla forces that would seek haven in and operate out of the Cuban mountains, to a conventional amphibious assault by a sizable invasion force to seize and hold a section of Cuban real estate. Although a new president was to be inaugurated on January 20, 1961, anti-Castro planning continued. Then, on January 10, the *New York Times* published a story describing the training of anti-Castro forces in Guatemala. The fabric of plausible denial was wearing thin.[30]

While the paramilitary aspect was changing in scope and objectives, the propaganda and psychological warfare side of the Cuban operation went forward at full speed. The centerpiece of the propaganda effort took shape after approval of the large-scale operation. U.S. Navy Seabees constructed the necessary infrastructure and installed two transmitters—one 50 kilowatt and one 7.5 kilowatt—for a clandestine radio facility on Swan Island. At that time, this small island in the Caribbean was claimed by both the United States and Honduras (it went back to Honduras in 1972) but housed a small U.S. Weather Bureau station and a Federal Aviation Agency radio beacon for a navigational aid to pilots. The first transmissions from Radio Swan came in mid-May 1960. Broadcasts focused around a theme developed by the State Department of "The Revolution Betrayed." CIA propaganda specialists and opposition groups developed the station's materials. Taped programs by Cuban exiles were air expressed to stations in other countries around the Caribbean. The CIA also supported the production in Miami of several Spanish-language newspapers, including *Avance in Exile*, and a magazine, *Bohemia Libre*. Radio Swan broadcast selected articles from these publications; and copies along with other printed material were carried into Cuba by agents inserted by airdrops or maritime landings for dissemination by underground groups. Teams of trained agents also established mobile clandestine radio transmitters inside Cuba, and published a clandestine newspaper in Havana.[31]

Notes

1. *FRUS, 1950–1955, The Intelligence Community, 1950–1955*, "Note From the Executive Secretary of the National Security Council (Lay) to the National Security Council," March 15, 1954, Document 171.

2. "New Evidence on the Iran Crisis 1945–46," *Cold War International History Project Bulletin* 12/13 (July 7, 2011): 309–14, at: http://www.wilsoncenter.org/sites/default/files/New_Ev_IranCrisis.pdf.

3. See the heavily redacted Scott A. Koch, *"Zendebad, Shah!": The Central Intelligence Agency and the Fall of Iranian Prime Minister Mohammed Mossadeq, August 1953* (Washington, DC: History Staff, Central Intelligence Agency, June 1998), at: http://www2.gwu.edu/~nsarchiv/NSAEBB/NSAEBB126/iran980600.pdf; Kermit Roosevelt, *Countercoup: The Struggle for the Control of Iran* (New York: McGraw-Hill,

1979); and Donald Wilber, *Clandestine Service History: Overthrow of Premier Mossadeq of Iran, November 1952–August 1953* (Washington, DC: Central Intelligence Agency, March 1954), at: http://www.nytimes.com/library/world/mideast/041600iran-cia-index.html. See also, Stephen Kinzer, *All the Shah's Men: An American Coup and the Roots of Middle East Terror* (New York: Wiley, 2008).

    4. Wilber, *Overthrow of Premier Mossadeq*, pp. 7, 9, 23–24.

    5. Ibid., p. 32.

    6. Ibid., p. 37.

    7. Ibid., pp. 63, 65–66.

    8. See Nicholas Cullather, *Operation PBSUCCESS: The United States and Guatemala, 1952–1954* (Washington, DC: History Staff, Center for the Study of Intelligence, Central Intelligence Agency, 1994), at: http://www2.gwu.edu/~nsarchiv/NSAEBB/NSAEBB4/cia-guatemala5_b.html; and *FRUS, Eisenhower Administration, 1952–1954, Guatemala*. See also, Piero Gleijeses, *Shattered Hope: The Guatemalan Revolution and the United States, 1944–1954* (Princeton, NJ: Princeton University Press, 1991); and Stephen Schlesinger and Stephen Kinzer, *Bitter Fruit: The Untold Story of the American Coup in Guatemala* (Garden City, NY: Doubleday Publishing, 1982).

    9. *FRUS, Eisenhower Administration, 1952–1954, Guatemala*, "Memorandum for the Record," September 11, 1953, Document 51.

    10. Cullather, *Operation PBSUCCESS*, pp. 81, 84.

    11. See *FRUS, 1955–1957, Vol. XXII, Southeast Asia*, Documents 79–341. For a relatively brief, well-written overview, see David Brichoux and Deborah J. Gerner, *The United States and the 1958 Rebellion in Indonesia* (Washington, DC: Institute for the Study of Diplomacy, School of Foreign Service, Georgetown University, 2002).

    12. *FRUS, 1955–1957, Vol. XXII, Southeast Asia*, "U.S. Policy on Indonesia," May 3, 1955, Document 95.

    13. Joseph Burkholder Smith, *Portrait of a Cold Warrior* (G. P. Putnam's Sons, New York, 1976), p. 211–13.

    14. *FRUS, 1955–1957, Vol. XXII, Southeast Asia*, "Report Prepared by the Ad Hoc Interdepartmental Committee on Indonesia for the National Security Council," September 3, 1957, Document 262; and *FRUS, 1958–1960, Vol. XVII, Indonesia*, "Memorandum from the Assistant Secretary of State for Far Eastern Affairs (Robertson) to Secretary of State Dulles," January 2, 1958, Document 1. See Kenneth Conboy and James Morrison, *Feet to the Fire: Covert Operations in Indonesia, 1957–1958* (Annapolis, MD: Naval Institute Press, 1999), pp. 16–17.

    15. Conboy and Morrison, *Feet to the Fire*, pp. 23, 25, 32–33, 38–39, 52–59, 63–66, 72, 95–97, 108–11; Brichoux and Gerner, *1958 Rebellion*, p. 5. See also, *FRUS, 1958–1960, Vol. XVII, Indonesia*, "Editorial Note," Document 18, and "Memorandum from the Under Secretary of State (Herter) to Secretary of State Dulles," February 21, 1958, Document 23.

    16. Conboy and Morrison, *Feet to the Fire*, pp. 71–72, 88–91, 112–14, 121–22, 132–33, 139, 142–43. *FRUS, 1958–1960, Vol. XVII, Indonesia*, "Memorandum of Conversation," May 18, 1958, Document 103.

17. John Kenneth Knaus, *Orphans of the Cold War: America and the Tibetan Struggle for Survival* (New York: Public Affairs, 1999); and John Prados, *Safe for Democracy: The Secret Wars of the CIA* (Chicago: Ivan R. Dee, 2006), pp. 184–203. See also Kenneth Conboy and James Morrison, *The CIA's Secret War in Tibet* (Lawrence: University Press of Kansas, 2002); and Roger E. McCarthy, *Tears of the Lotus: Accounts of Tibetan Resistance to the Chinese Invasion, 1950–1962* (Jefferson, NC: McFarland, 1997).

18. Knaus, *Orphans of the Cold War*, pp. 153–55.

19. *FRUS, 1958–1960, Vol. XIX, China*, "Editorial Note," Document 371.

20. *FRUS, 1958–1960, Vol. XIV, Africa*, "Memorandum of Discussion at the 456th Meeting of the National Security Council," August 18, 1960, Document 180, footnote 1.

21. See Larry Devlin, *Chief of Station, Congo: A Memoir of 1960–67* (New York: Public Affairs, 2007), pp. 62–63; and *FRUS, Vol. XIV, 1958–1960, Africa*, "Editorial Note," Document 189.

22. Devlin, *Chief of Station, Congo*, pp. 94–97, 113–14, 130–31, 260–63. See also, U.S. Congress, Senate, Select Committee to Study Governmental Operations with Respect to Intelligence Activities, *Interim Report: Alleged Assassination Plots Involving Foreign Leaders*, 94th Congress, 1st Session, S. Report No. 94–465, pp. 13–70 (Washington, DC: GPO, 1975), at: http://www.intelligence.senate.gov/pdfs94th/94465.pdf.

23. William M. Leary, *Perilous Missions: Civil Air Transport and CIA Covert Operations in Asia* (Washington, DC: Smithsonian Institute Press, 2003), pp. 157–67, 180–94.

24. See Thomas L. Ahern Jr., *CIA and the House of Ngo: Covert Action in South Vietnam, 1954–63* (Washington, DC: Center for the Study of Intelligence, Central Intelligence Agency, 2000), pp. 119–33, at: http://today.ttu.edu/wp-content/uploads/2009/03/02-cia-and-the-house-of-ngo.pdf; and Thomas L. Ahern Jr., *The Way We Do Things: Black Entry Operations into North Vietnam* (Washington, DC: Center for the Study of Intelligence, Central Intelligence Agency, 2005), pp. 7–10, at: http://today.ttu.edu/wp-content/uploads/2009/03/05-the-way-we-do-things.pdf.

25. See *FRUS, 1955–1957, Volume XXI, East Asian Security; Cambodia; Laos*, "Telegram From the Legation in Laos to the Department of State," January 15, 1955, Document 262, and successive documents. The military aid figure for 1955 is given in Document 302. See also, Kenn Finlayson, "Operation White Star: Prelude to Vietnam," June 2002, at: http://www.militaryphotos.net/forums/showthread.php?27936-Operation-White-Star-prelude-to-Vietnam.

26. *FRUS, 1964–1968, Vol. XXIX, Part 2, Japan*, "Editorial Note," Document 1.

27. Ibid.

28. See Don Bohning, *The Castro Obsession: U.S. Covert Operations against Cuba, 1959–1965* (Washington, DC: Potomac Books, Inc., 2005). See also, *FRUS, 1958–1960, Vol. VI, Cuba*; and *FRUS, 1961–1963, Vol. X, Cuba, January 1961– September 1962*.

29. See *FRUS, 1958–1960, Vol. VI, Cuba*, "A Program of Covert Action against the Castro Regime," March 16, 1960, Document 481; and Kornbluh, ed., *Bay of Pigs Declassified*, pp. 103–9.

30. Paul Kennedy, "U.S. Helps Train an Anti-Castro Force at Secret Guatemalan Air-Ground Base," *New York Times*, December 10, 1961, p. 1.

31. On the CIA's propaganda program, see Pfeiffer, *Official History*, pp. 204–33; undated interview with David Atlee Phillips, at: http://www2.gwu.edu/~nsarchiv/ NSAEBB/NSAEBB29/docs/doc08.pdf; and "Propaganda Action Plan in Support of Military Forces," n.d., at: http://www2.gwu.edu/~nsarchiv/NSAEBB/NSAEBB29/ docs/doc01.pdf.

CHAPTER 6

Challenging Times: 1961–1973

When John F. Kennedy (1961–1963) became President, he already supported using unconventional warfare to confront communist aggression. Thus, it is not surprising he continued a wide range of ongoing covert and special operations initiated under his predecessors.

Attacking Castro

The covert operation against Castro[1] envisaged an armed invasion by exile forces to seize a foothold on Cuban soil. The final training of the Cubans began in mid-January 1961 when U.S. Special Forces arrived at the training camp in Guatemala. A month before the planned attack, Kennedy decided a daytime landing at the original site was too visible and ordered that alternatives be identified. The choice was a nighttime landing at the Bay of Pigs (Playa Girón). To further reduce visibility, strikes by the exiles' B-26 bombers on Castro's air force were halved to eight. Carried out two days before the landing, the strikes destroyed only half of Cuba's combat aircraft. The president also delayed follow-up air strikes planned for D-Day until an airfield inside Cuba could be captured.

When the exile brigade went ashore after midnight on April 17, 1961, constrained geography, lack of air support, and availability of Cuban combat aircraft made the beachhead a trap. By day three, the *brigadistas* were scattering into the swamps, to be rounded up by Castro's forces.[2] The official count was 114 killed and over 1,200 captured. A Military Tribunal sentenced those captured to 30 years hard labor, and set a ransom of $62 million. In December 1962, surviving members were released and transported to the United States, together with family members, in exchange for over $50 million in medicines and food.

Kennedy asked former Army chief of staff Gen. Maxwell D. Taylor to chair a committee—comprised of Taylor, Attorney General Robert Kennedy, Chief of Naval Operations Admiral Arleigh Burke, and Director of Central Intelligence (DCI) Allen Dulles—to investigate the causes of the failure. The group found mistakes in the assumption that deniability could be maintained in such a large operation, a lack of coordination among U.S. agencies, operational control remaining in Washington, and limitations on an already marginal operation. The failure of the joint chiefs of staff (JCS) to offer strong objections sent the message they approved the revised plan.[3]

In November 1961, the President authorized a new program to undermine Castro. Operation MONGOOSE was placed under Air Force Brig. Gen. Edward G. Lansdale, known for his counterinsurgency work in the Philippines. However, Robert Kennedy was the driving force behind the project. MONGOOSE involved overt and covert efforts to disrupt the Cuban government. Most of the covert operations involved inserting small "resistance teams" along Cuba's coastline. Their responsibilities included sending back localized intelligence and organizing resistance cells. The latter goal became increasingly difficult as Castro tightened his hold on all aspects of Cuban life. There was a particularly unsavory aspect to MONGOOSE that the players kept out of written notes. This involved efforts to use Mafia personnel to assassinate Fidel Castro. It remains difficult to conceive that the potential for disaster for such an alliance was not apparent to all involved.[4]

The Vietnam War

The failure in Cuba did not blunt Kennedy's enthusiasm for covert operations. The covert war in Vietnam had two different lead agencies. From 1961 to 1963, it was the CIA. After 1963, the U.S. military took charge of the covert war against North Vietnam.[5] Kennedy expected actions similar to those conducted by the Office of Strategic Services in occupied Europe during World War II. That inserting guerrillas behind enemy lines to link up with indigenous resistance forces had proved ineffective against the Soviet bloc, North Korea, and Communist China did not diminish the commitment to this mode of warfare.

CIA Operations

The CIA chief of station in Saigon, William Colby, responded to Washington's demands by reenergizing insertions in the North of ethnic Vietnamese agents. CIA officers and "on-loan" army and navy special operators provided the training. Insertions began with coastal landings; then, airborne teams of Vietnamese originally from the North were dropped close to their former villages. The first airborne insertion was in May 1961. That team and others that followed were quickly captured and brought under the control of Democratic Republic of Vietnam (DRV) security forces.

The CIA also expanded psychological warfare and "black" propaganda operations; initiated coastal harassment; and used paramilitary forces drawn from local tribes for cross-border, hit-and-run sabotage raids. None of these actions yielded much to report in response to the president's expectation of guerrilla operations inside North Vietnam. When the CIA's efforts failed to produce results, Kennedy gave the covert war to the Pentagon. Military Assistance Command, Vietnam (MACV) drafted Operational Plan 34A (OPLAN 34A), which reflected Defense Secretary Robert McNamara's view that more military muscle was needed. Implementing OPLAN 34A was the task of MACV's covert operations unit, the Studies and Observation Group (SOG).

SOG Operations

The tortuous approval process for SOG operations illustrates the controversy surrounding military covert operations. SOG's monthly schedule of proposed actions passed through the MACV commander and Pacific Command before going to Washington. At the Pentagon, the offices of the defense secretary and the JCS chairman had to approve. From the Pentagon, the proposals went to the State Department, the CIA, and the White House, where some were passed to the president. Approvals, disapprovals, and changes went back through the same channels. Then, individual operations had to be approved before they could be conducted.

The attitude of the military's top leadership exacerbated SOG's challenges. While accepting that President Kennedy expected (see sidebar, *Kennedy to McNamara*) the services to undertake counterinsurgency and anti-guerrilla activities, the senior leadership at the JCS and regional commands did not believe in unconventional warfare, and their actions reflected that viewpoint.

Kennedy to McNamara

"I am not satisfied that the Department of Defense, and in particular the Army, is according the necessary degree of attention and effort to the threat of Communist-directed subversive insurgency and guerrilla warfare. . . . The effort devoted to this challenge should be comparable in importance to preparations for conventional warfare. . . . [A]t this time I do not see that this degree of effort is being made."

Source: "Memorandum from President Kennedy to Secretary of Defense McNamara," dated January 11, 1962, *FRUS, 1961–1963. Vol. VIII, National Security Policy*, Document 67.

Waging Covert War

SOG's covert war revolved around four core missions: (1) insertion of individual agents and agent teams, (2) maritime operations, (3) psychological warfare, and (4) reconnaissance against the Ho Chi Minh Trail.

Agent Insertions

Few special operations personnel had experience in creating and handling agents meant to function in hostile environments, so SOG adopted the CIA's techniques. Recruits came via their South Vietnamese counterpart, the Strategic Technical Directorate. Insertion into northern territory was primarily through "blind drops"—parachuting individuals or teams into areas where it was hoped their landing would go unnoticed. The results were the same as the CIA experienced: eventual discovery that all the teams were under the DRV's control. Hanoi's counterintelligence and internal security were too much to overcome. In late 1968, Washington ordered all operations that involved physically crossing the DRV's borders to cease.

Maritime Operations

The same order ended the maritime operations of SOG's Naval Advisory Detachment. Navy SEAL and Marine reconnaissance personnel trained South Vietnamese commandos for cross-beach raids (U.S. personnel could not participate in operations in DRV territory). As with land and air operations, Washington and the military command structure tightly managed maritime raids. The operations caused the North Vietnamese to move additional resources to the coastal areas, but doing so did not seem to hamper their ability to wage the war against South Vietnam.

Psychological Warfare

SOG's psychological warfare included creating a fictitious North Vietnamese resistance movement. The basic concept for the Sacred Sword of the Patriot League (SSPL) originated with the CIA, but SOG developed the idea. The SSPL claimed to represent communists disillusioned with the takeover of the North Vietnamese party by politicos allied with the People's Republic of China (PRC). SOG created a fictitious slice of North Vietnam on an island off the coast of South Vietnam. Maritime operations teams would "snatch" unsuspecting peasants in cross-beach raids or fishermen from vessel searches and take them to the enclave. They were told they were in a part of North Vietnam under SSPL control. Trained South Vietnamese personnel would treat and feed them well while indoctrinating them with the SSPL message. After a couple of weeks, the detainees would be returned to the North, where they would be picked up and interrogated.

The SSPL message was reinforced by broadcasts over SOG's "black" radio, *The Voice of SSPL*, and by leaflet drops from overflights and materials left behind in cross-beach intrusions. Another SOG "black" radio, *Radio Red Flag*, claimed it, too, was located in the North and represented the views of dissident communist military officers. SOG also ran a "snuggling" operation, essentially creating a fake Radio Hanoi. Snuggling involves transmitting directly adjacent to the signal that is being mimicked, and broadcasting the same material with carefully prepared insertions. Other "black" radio operations involved "ghosting," putting a fake signal on top of another. This technique was used to distribute fake orders to North Vietnamese units fighting in the South.[6]

Cross-Border Operations

Although the CIA and Special Forces trained ethnic minorities and South Vietnamese for intelligence collection missions against the Ho Chi Minh Trail, U.S. personnel could not participate in the actual operations. It was a year after SOG assumed responsibility before U.S.-led insertions were approved. SOG also struggled with limitations dictated by U.S. ambassadors to Laos, who controlled the parameters of cross-border operations. U.S.-led incursions into Laos, except for rescue missions, ended in early 1971.

By 1967, the DRV was clearly transshipping military supplies through the Cambodian port of Sihanoukville. These supplies moved across Cambodia to base camps in eastern Cambodia and Laos, and moved into South Vietnam over the Ho Chi Minh Trail. In May, SOG began conducting covert cross-border operations into Cambodia. In April 1970, the president announced that a U.S.–South Vietnamese force had invaded Cambodia. The invasion sparked a wave of protests, and U.S. troops had pulled out by the end of June.[7]

Son Tay Rescue Mission

Personnel known or assumed to be prisoners of war (POWs) were an enduring problem in the Vietnam War. After discovery of a relatively isolated compound potentially holding U.S. prisoners, Special Assistant for Counterinsurgency and Special Operations Brig. Gen. Donald D. Blackburn convened a rescue feasibility study group in June 1970. The JCS endorsed the group's plan in July.

Training for the mission began at Eglin Air Force Base, Florida, in August. There were hours of rehearsals on a replica of the Son Tay compound and precision planning on a CIA-supplied scale model of the camp. The attack force launched on November 20 from Udorn Air Base in Thailand. Under cover of darkness, the force flew in helicopters to the site less than 25 miles west of Hanoi. Well planned and executed, the raid nevertheless came up empty.

The prisoners had been moved, an outcome that gave the mission a feeling of failure. However, the North Vietnamese apparently reacted by consolidating their POW camps, ending years of isolation for some POWs. Morale among the POWs reportedly rose when news of the raid reached them.[8]

The Phoenix Program

The terms *pacification* and *counterinsurgency* symbolized a two-pronged effort in South Vietnam: "to win the hearts and minds" of the rural population and to root out from that population the Viet Cong "shadow government." The goal was to provide the authorities in Saigon a stable base for governing.

As early as 1954, the CIA began working with the South Vietnamese on creating village defense and civilian civic action programs. After 1961, additional overt and covert pacification programs funded and advised by civilian agencies proliferated. The military also had thousands of advisers working in the outlying areas and reporting through their own chain of command. In May 1967, the Johnson administration centralized management of pacification and anti-Viet Cong activities. The Civil Operations and Revolutionary Development Support (CORDS) program was a component of MACV but under the overall authority of the U.S. Ambassador. One of the elements within CORDS, the Phoenix Program, has received the most attention. The program represented the American advisory role to the South Vietnamese Phung Hoang program targeting the Viet Cong Infrastructure (VCI). One action element of Phung Hoang was the paramilitary Provincial Reconnaissance Units (PRUs). These units were trained, paid, and advised by CIA or on-loan military personnel. Comprised of South Vietnamese generally native to the province in which they served, the PRUs' primary mission was to capture communist cadres and use them for intelligence purposes. There were abuses, but whether they were so endemic as to justify making them the defining image of the program is arguable. With the withdrawal of U.S. forces after Vietnamization began in 1969–1970, most of the pacification programs withered away from lack of engagement by the Saigon government.[9]

The War in Laos

Before President Kennedy took office in January 1961, the confusing political situation in Laos had been further scrambled by a coup, the beginning of a Soviet airlift of military supplies to the communist Pathet Lao, and the commitment of North Vietnamese troops to the fighting. The outgoing administration passed on a sense of urgency about Laos, even more so than Vietnam, to the new president.[10]

Over the next year, the DRV–Pathet Lao pushed back the pro-Western forces and their U.S. military advisers. In July 1962, the United States, USSR, PRC, DRV, Thailand, and nine other countries signed the Declaration on the Neutrality of Laos and its accompanying Protocol (the Geneva Accords). The Accords created a tripartite government for Laos, with neutralists holding the balance of power, and mandated the withdrawal of foreign troops.[11] Laos was essentially partitioned between the DRV and the Laotian government, leaving Hanoi in control of the vital Ho Chi Minh Trail. The U.S. military advisers (the White Star teams) pulled out, while the North Vietnamese increased the number of their troops in Laos and intensified work on the Ho Chi Minh Trail. The administration countered the growing threat by expanding covert support to the noncommunist forces of the government, including Vang Pao's Hmong. After late 1962, the war grew beyond its original size, scope, and covert nature, becoming a multifaceted and complex, if not totally covert, operation.[12] (See sidebar, *Answering Questions*.)

Answering Questions

"Arming and training a guerrilla army . . . could not be entirely concealed. As early as March 1961 American journalists were digging for the facts of US support for the Hmong. . . . The solution was threefold: first, to acknowledge some US Mission support of Col. Vang Pao, in his capacity as a [Laotian Army] commander; secondly, to play down the importance of the Hmong militia . . . and finally, to avoid confirming an Agency role. It was an uneasy compromise, leading eventually to allegations . . . of a rogue CIA running its own 'secret war' in Laos. But it sufficed . . . to minimize publicity about the origin and extent of support to the Hmong."

Source: Thomas L. Ahern Jr., *Undercover Armies: CIA and Surrogate Warfare in Laos, 1961–1973* (Washington, DC: Center for the Study of Intelligence, Central Intelligence Agency, 2006), p. 57.

Strategic and even operational guidance for Laos operations came from Washington, primarily from an often-contentious collaboration among State, Defense, and CIA but also involving close attention from the White House. Operational and at times tactical oversight rested with a succession of strong-willed U.S. ambassadors in Vientiane. Training, arming, provisioning, and paying of troops, logistical and intelligence support, and varying levels of tactical direction were the responsibility of CIA paramilitary officers, CIA contract employees, and military personnel "on detached duty." The fighting on the ground was split initially between Vang Pao's Hmong-based forces and regular Royal Lao Army units in northeastern Laos and a mix of Laotian army and irregular units organized by the CIA from among indigenous tribes in the central and southern portions of the elongated country. Efforts after 1964 to interrupt the flow of troops and supplies along the Ho Chi Minh Trail included covert air interdiction attacks by U.S. Air Force and Navy aircraft. As the war progressed, small teams of troops drawn from an elite Thai Police group called the Police Air Reconnaissance Unit were brought in to train and fight alongside the Hmong. Later, Thai irregular troops recruited, trained, and paid by the United States supplemented and in the later stages of the war replaced the depleted in-country forces.

Air America

By 1961, it was clear that the use of surrogate forces would require air sup-port for the delivery of supplies and equipment, rapid movement of fighting forces, and evacuation of wounded and troops about to be overrun by superior North Vietnamese forces. The CIA-owned proprietary airline Air America (renamed from Civil Aviation Transport in 1959) and several smaller propri-etaries formed the backbone of that support.[13]

Air Commandos

The need for another layer of U.S. commitment—close-air support—came into focus in 1964. In the spring, the North Vietnamese and Pathet Lao launched a full-scale attack across the strategically located Plain of Jars. Named for the megalithic iron-age stone jars found in the plateau region of north central Laos, control of the 500-square-mile plateau was viewed as a gateway to the Laotian capital of Vientiane. Washington responded by cre-ating an air strike capability for the forces supporting the Lao government. A Special Air Warfare detachment was deployed to the Royal Thai Air Force (RTAF) Base at Udorn, Thailand.

Members of the Air Commando detachment served six-month tours and were "sheep-dipped" for this assignment, that is, they were removed from active-duty rosters, carried nonmilitary identification, and wore civilian clothes. The detachment's original mission was to train Royal Lao Air Force pilots, aircrews, and mechanics on Korean-era, AT-28 Trojan ground-attack aircraft declared excess by the U.S. Air Force and transferred off the books. Lacking enough Lao candidates, the Air Commandos trained Air America pilots and sheep-dipped RTAF "volunteers" for combat missions. Use of Thai pilots continued until 1970, when sufficient Lao pilots were available. The Air Commandos also trained a small contingent of Hmong to fly combat missions. The U.S. ambassador tightly controlled in-country air operations. In late 1966, the U.S. Air Force's commitment to the war in Laos was increased with the activation of the 56th Air Commando Wing at Nakhon Phanom RTAF Base, under the command of Col. (later, Brig. Gen.) Harry C. "Heinie" Aderholt. Having worked alongside the CIA in Korea and the Tibetan covert operation, Aderholt developed much of the doctrine and practice in the use of Air Force assets in covert operations.[14]

Butterflies and Ravens

The introduction of combat aircraft necessitated another layer of covert activity—airborne Forward Air Controllers (FACs) to provide targeting for attack aircraft in the rugged, jungle-covered terrain. Some Air Commando sergeants working with the CIA began using smoke rockets fired from small, slow-moving Air America aircraft to mark ground targets for attack. This group became known as "Butterflies." In 1966, the commander of the Seventh Air Force ordered that FACs must be officers and pilots. Replacing the Butterflies were volunteer U.S. Air Force officers and jet-qualified pilots who had flown as FACs in South Vietnam. This small group, wearing civilian clothes and carrying no military identification, become known as "Ravens," their radio call sign. The Ravens operated in hazardous conditions in often-hostile areas, and suffered a casualty rate estimated to be as high as 30 percent.[15]

Tactical Air Navigation

The U.S. Air Force responded to the mountainous terrain and rapidly changing weather patterns in Laos by placing covert Tactical Air Navigation (TACAN) stations at strategically located sites. The equipment provided fixed geographic reference points by broadcasting continuous radio signals to establish bearing and distance relative to the station. These stations required rotations of sheep-dipped U.S. Air Force technicians for routine maintenance.

A TACAN station at Lima Site 85 in northeastern Laos 160 miles west of Hanoi upgraded in 1967 to include a bombing-control radar system for direct support to *Rolling Thunder* missions over North Vietnam. By early 1968, the site was the target of a communist offensive. The U.S. Air Force struck back with fighter-bombers from bases in Thailand and Vietnam. Although the site's vulnerability was recognized, the belief any attack could be held at bay by available forces and air strikes long enough to allow evacuation proved fatal. On March 11, the North Vietnamese attacked Thai and Hmong defensive positions, while a group of perhaps 20 Hmong defectors attacked from the rear after scaling a vertical cliff. Air America helicopters evacuated the two on-site CIA advisers, the FAC, and five U.S. Air Force technicians (one of whom died on the trip to Udorn); 11 Americans died in the battle for Lima Site 85.[16]

Ebb and Flow

Following the successes of the DRV-Pathet Lao forces during the November–May 1964 dry season, the air power and mobility provided by the covert U.S. air force allowed the Hmong and government forces to launch a counteroffensive across the Plain of Jars during the June–October monsoon season. This seasonal ebb and flow in the fighting characterized the war in Laos for the next several years.

Vang Pao launched his most successful campaign in August 1969. His forces severed the overextended supply lines of the North Vietnamese and pushed them out of the Plain of Jars. But a strong dry season offensive from the militarily superior North Vietnamese came when Vang Pao's Hmong were approaching exhaustion. The limited supply of military age and capable Hmong had been stretched thin by years of warfare. In an effort to break up the North Vietnamese advance, President Nixon in February 1970 approved B-52 strikes. These strikes were hardly covert, brought mixed reactions from U.S. legislators, and did not stop the North Vietnamese advance. By March, Vang Pao's stronghold at Long Tieng was under attack. Only reinforcements, including Thai volunteers, brought from other areas prevented its evacuation and gave the Hmong general the opportunity to regain some of the lost ground. After 1971, the Hmong were no longer able to launch major offensive operations, but simply tried to hold on to some of what was left of their homeland.

Nearing the End

The Paris Agreement of January 27, 1973, signed by the United States, North Vietnam, the Saigon government, and the Viet Cong's National Liberation Front, was followed by its counterpart in Laos. The Laotian ceasefire in February essentially accepted the military status quo, leaving DRV forces in control of large segments of Laos.

In April 1974, the Vientiane government agreed with the Pathet Lao on the formation of the Provisional Government of National Union (PGNU). By mid-1974, the Thai mercenaries had been withdrawn and the irregular Lao and minority forces, which had carried the fighting in central and southern Laos, were being integrated into the Laotian army. Surrounded by North Vietnamese and Pathet Lao forces in Long Tieng, Gen. Vang Pao and his family were evacuated to Thailand on May 14, 1975, and eventually resettled in the United States. By December 1975, the Pathet Lao had converted itself into the governing body of the Laotian People's Democratic Republic. Facing retribution from the communists, Hmong and ethnic Lao escaped across the border into Thailand. Refugee camps became the stopping place for tens of thousands of Hmong. Washington eventually relaxed the obstacles to entry of the Hmong, and close to a quarter of a million Hmong now live in the United States.

The Congo

As President Kennedy was preparing to take office, new troubles were brewing in the Congo. Former deputy prime minister Antoine Gizenga formed a breakaway government in Stanleyville. Moise Tshombe, with a substantial force of mercenaries, was in control in Katanga Province and its capital Elisabethville. And Albert Kalonji had reasserted the independence of his diamond-rich state in southern Kasai province. The new administration continued overt and covert support to the Congolese government, and pushed for greater UN involvement. Cyrile Adoula became prime minister in a coalition government in August 1961, a result for which CIA operatives had worked behind the scenes.[17]

One-by-one the rebellions were overcome through the combined (although uncoordinated) efforts of the Congolese National Army (ANC) and a UN multinational force. In December 1961, ANC commander in chief Joseph Mobutu's troops captured southern Kasai Province. Gizenga's rebel government in Stanleyville fell to Mobutu's army in mid-January 1962. In late December 1962, using material and personnel prepositioned by U.S. Air Force transport aircraft (see sidebar, *Military Support to UN Forces in the Congo*), the UN forces launched the decisive operation in Katanga. In January 1963, Tshombe capitulated to the UN forces in exchange for amnesty and exile.

Military Support to UN Forces in the Congo

"The US is supporting the UN Congo effort regularly with airlift, sealift, and equipment. Approximately 65,000 UN personnel have been airlifted in and out of the Congo, and 33,000 have been sealifted. Over 8,000 tons of equipment have been airlifted, including Swedish jet aircraft, and 30,000 tons sealifted. US equipment furnished includes communications gear, munitions, transport aircraft, and helicopters."

Source: "Memorandum from the Joint Chiefs of Staff to Secretary of Defense McNamara," dated December 21, 1962, *FRUS, 1961–1963*, *XX*, *Congo Crisis*, Document 382.

New Troubles

In January 1964, a rebellion broke out in Kwilu Province under the leadership of Pierre Mulele. In political exile since 1962, Mulele had visited China and acquired a patina of Maoist rhetoric and some training in guerrilla warfare. This insurgency was slowly beaten back over the next year and a half. A much more urgent threat came from uprisings in the eastern provinces of Kivu and Orientale. Several insurgent groups were loosely affiliated with the Comité Nationale de Liberation, headed by Christopher Gbenye. The best known of the groups was the "Simbas" (Swahili for "Lions") whose attacks on Westerners, civil servants, and local notables were ferocious.

In July, President Kasavubu brought Moise Tshombe back from exile, and made him prime minister. In August, Simba forces captured Stanleyville. Two dozen Americans, including three CIA and two State Department officers, became the rebels' prisoners, while nearly 2,000 other Westerners and non-Congolese became real or potential hostages.[18] Washington supported a covert operation to reinforce the fragile Congolese army. Tshombe brought back his Katangan gendarmerie and white mercenary forces that had taken refuge in Angola. Mike Hoare led the most prominent of the mercenary units, the English-speaking 5 Commando. Paying for the mercenaries was either through CIA covert channels or regular military assistance.

A Congolese Air Force

In early 1963, the U.S. Defense Department arranged for Italy to donate six World War II vintage AT-6 fighter-trainers to the Congo to provide a symbolic "Congolese air force." These planes were initially unarmed, but eventually were reconfigured with weapons. They and other aircraft that followed them provided tactical support to UN peacekeeping forces, the Congolese army, and mercenaries fighting the rebels. Over time, the Defense Department replaced the AT-6s with 13 T-28 fighter-bombers, 7 B-26 bombers, 2 C-45 and 3 C-46 transports, 3 Bell helicopters, and a Beech twin-engine aircraft. The covert program's aviation component arranged for the pilots and maintenance personnel. Between 1963 and the phasing out of CIA support for the air program in late 1967, six CIA officers supervised in-country operations, working with 125 contract maintenance personnel and 79 foreign contract pilots. The officers supervised air activities from forward airfields throughout the Congo. In 1965, one such forward base, located near the town of Bunia in northeast Congo, was staffed by a unit chief, a logistics officer, a radio operator, two Cuban pilots, and a couple of mechanics. The pilots, employed by an air proprietary company, flew T-28 fighter-bombers armed with 30-caliber machineguns. These and the other aircraft were used for attacks on concentrations of Simba fighters, close air support of ground forces, interdiction of rebel supply lines, forward reconnaissance, and psychological warfare. The covert air operations were integral to eventually suppressing the insurgency.[19]

Retaking Stanleyville

Negotiations for the release of Western captives in Stanleyville went nowhere. In addition, threatening rhetoric coming from Simba leaders and tales of ritualistic killing fed fears about the safety of the hostages.

On November 24, 1964, in an operation (DRAGON ROUGE) preceded by strafing runs from CIA B-26s, a battalion of Belgian Paracommandos dropped into Stanleyville from U.S.-piloted C-130s. The Simbas killed as many as 50 hostages before the others were freed. Congolese ground forces, spearheaded by Hoare's 5 Commando, moved in to take control of the area. Included in Hoare's motorized column was a CIA paramilitary team of an American, William "Rip" Robertson, and 17 or 18 Cuban exiles, with the task of rescuing the U.S. consular officials. Two days later, U.S.-piloted C-130s dropped the Paracommandos into Paulis (Operation DRAGON NOIR), northwest of Stanleyville, to free over 300 European hostages. The Simbas killed more than 20 hostages before fleeing into the bush.[20]

A Congolese Navy

The Simba Rebellion did not end at Stanleyville and Paulis. The brutal war continued into the next year. Just as covert air support was critical to the success of the mercenary-enhanced Congolese army, CIA assistance was instrumental in reducing the arms and other supplies coming to the rebels.

By the spring of 1965, the rebels' main supply line ran from Tanzania across Lake Tanganyika. Strafing by the Cuban-piloted aircraft was only an occasional hazard for gunrunners. Washington provided a maritime patrol capability by cutting a half dozen Swift patrol boats into sections, flying them to the Congo, and reassembling them. The 50-foot-long Swift boats carried modern navigation and communications equipment and were armed with heavy machine guns and other heavy weapons. The CIA contracted with Cuban exiles to serve as boat crews and trainers for recruits from 5 Commando. A Navy SEAL headed the unit.[21]

Cubans versus Cubans

In April 1965, Che Guevara and a small group of Cubans crossed Lake Tanganyika and joined rebels associated with Laurent Kabila. The Cubans eventually numbered about 200 soldiers. Guevara attacked Hoare's commandos with 100 Cubans and 200 Simba soldiers at the town of Bendera in June 1965. They were beaten badly, at least partially because of air support from the CIA's anti-Castro Cubans. Things went from bad to worse for Guevara's command as the Congolese army and 5 Commando pushed the Simba forces into ever more limited territory.

By October 1965, the largest rebel forces were in the mountainous area of Fizi-Baraka above Lake Tanganyika. There were some 5,000 rebel combatants and perhaps 100 Cubans holed up in terrain that favored the defense. Hoare launched a two-pronged ground attack and an amphibious landing in the enemy's rear, with air cover provided by the Cuban exiles. The exiles in the Swift boats shelled shore defenses and provided cover for the landing. The Congolese offensive kept the rebels waging a conventional defensive war, maximizing the effect of the government's control of the airspace over the battlefield. The result was a punishing defeat for the rebels and their Cuban compatriots. The surviving Simbas faded into the countryside where, as roving gangs, they remained a problem but were no longer a serious threat to the central government. The Cubans escaped and fled back to Tanzania.[22]

Tibet

In the Congo, the United States supported counterinsurgency forces, but in Tibet, U.S resources went to the insurgents.[23] By early 1960, the Chinese People's Liberation Army had negated the CIA's use of covert airdrops inside Tibet. Thereafter, support for the Tibetans focused on cross-border operations from the isolated Mustang region of Nepal.

Kennedy viewed the Tibetan operation as the kind of unconventional warfare that was needed to counter communist expansion. Despite U.S. ambassador to India John Kenneth Galbraith's vehement opposition, the president approved renewed covert assistance to the rebels to establish bases inside Tibet. In March 1961, Air America pilots airdropped arms and radio operators to a party of Tibetans from Mustang. The plan was for small guerrilla units to attack isolated Chinese military camps and disrupt traffic on the highway running from Xinjiang/Sinkiang to Lhasa. Although one such raid produced an intelligence windfall, support in Washington was tenuous. Help for sustaining the operation came from clashes between China and India along the Himalayan border. In October 1962, a Chinese attack resulted in a humiliating defeat for the Indians.

India now came to view the Tibetans as an asset, and became a covert partner in organizing and maintaining activities at Mustang. By early 1964, a collaborative effort between the CIA and Indian intelligence—the Combined Operations Center—had been established in New Delhi to assume direction of guerrilla operations at Mustang. As the CIA officer most closely associated with the Center describes its operation:

> The U.S. underwrote the costs of the operations, trained the agents, provided the radios and other gear, and contributed operational guidance and its presumed expertise. The Tibetans provided the manpower for the missions. But the Indians controlled the territory and thereby the operations.[24]

The Indians also moved to make use of the Tibetan refugees for their own purposes. With CIA logistic and training support, the Indians developed their own tactical guerrilla force of Tibetans—the Special Frontier Force (SFF)—to guard India's northern border and conduct cross-border reconnaissance in the Himalayans. SFF teams later reportedly penetrated into China to place sensors for detecting nuclear and missile tests as well as signals intelligence instruments for intercepting PRC military communications.[25]

Despite increased U.S.-Indian cooperation with regard to the Tibetans, few cross-border raids took place after 1964, and support in Washington for continuing the project began to recede. By late 1968, CIA program managers had decided the Tibetan force of 1,800 was oversized for any use given Chinese border control and travel restrictions. Even the radio-equipped road watch teams, infiltrated with Indian assistance into other areas of Tibet, found it nearly impossible to locate safe haven among the local population.

The administration of President Richard Nixon (1969–1974) faced issues of force reduction and resettlement. Further complicating matters, the Indian domestic environment had changed and the CIA and Indian intelligence relationship was fraying. In September 1969, Nixon approved a CIA plan for reducing the Tibetan paramilitary program. CIA resettlement funds of $2.5 million were used to establish carpet-weaving factories and a hotel in the Nepalese city of Pokhara and a carpet factory and a trucking and taxi company in the capital of Kathmandu. In time, the carpet-weaving industry became a major employer in Nepal. Although some Tibetans transferred to India's SFF, others insisted on continuing armed struggle against the Chinese. The Nepalese in early 1974 ordered the remaining Tibetans to disarm and move out. In July, a recording of the Dalai Lama asking the fighters to surrender their arms was carried to the Tibetan camps. Most of the fighters laid down their weapons, a small number committed suicide, and the last leader of the guerrilla force, Wangdu, went down fighting in a Nepalese ambush.[26]

Revelations

Programs using the CIA as a conduit for covert subsidies to private organizations competing internationally with similar Communist-funded organizations began in the late-1940s. Until the mid-1960s, the programs attracted only occasional public attention. In the spring of 1966, a furor followed the publication by *Ramparts* magazine of a story about a Michigan State University project from 1957 to 1962 that included $25 million from the CIA for assistance in training South Vietnamese police.[27]

The March 1967 issue of *Ramparts* revealed both CIA subsidies to the National Student Association and the methodology—the use of private foundations, some real and others CIA proprietaries—through which the funds passed.[28] Condemnation came from all sides of the political spectrum, with only an occasional mention that four presidents had approved the programs. President Lyndon Johnson (1963–1969) established a committee to review the relationships. Acting Secretary of State Nicholas Katzenbach headed the group, with Secretary of Health, Education, and Welfare John Gardner and DCI Richard Helms as the other members. In March 1967, the committee recommended—and the president approved—a prohibition against covert financial assistance to American educational and private voluntary organizations. Existing programs were phased out by the end of the year, although several organizations received forward funding. The Katzenbach Committee concluded that Radio Free Europe (RFE) and Radio Liberty (RL) did not fall within the prohibited category. The International Broadcasting Act of 1973 (Public Law 93–129) created a new federal oversight body, the Board for International Broadcasting (replaced by the Broadcasting Board of Governors in 1994), through which RFE and RL receive funding from open Congressional appropriations.[29]

As for charges that CIA dictated what organizations receiving covert funding could do, the evidence suggests that the assessment by the head of the CIA's Covert Action Staff, Cord Meyer, remains generally accurate. He argued that the leaders of the private organizations, who chose to cooperate with their government, "jealously guarded their independence and organizational integrity."[30]

Chile

Concern about the political climate in Chile began in 1958 when the candidate of the Communist-Socialist popular front, Salvador Allende Gossens, ran a strong campaign. For the Kennedy administration, a presidential election in Chile scheduled for 1964 called for action against the potential for increased communist influence or even power (a "second Cuba") in Chile.[31]

1964 Presidential Election

In 1962, the administration approved financial assistance to presidential candidate Eduardo Frei's centrist Christian Democratic Party. The CIA launched a multimedia anticommunist propaganda campaign. "Black" propaganda, fake material seemingly coming from the target audience, was distributed to cause dissention between socialists and communists in Allende's coalition. The CIA spent $3 million on the September 1964 election that went handily in Frei's favor.[32] From 1964 until 1970, the CIA maintained low-key covert influence operations. In Chile's congressional elections in 1965 and 1969, covert financial support was provided to individual candidates. In 1969, CIA also supported a splinter Socialist Party to drain votes away from Allende's *Unidad Popular* (UP) electoral alliance.

1970 Presidential Election

In 1970, with Frei ineligible for another term, Chile's presidential election became a three-way affair. Allende led a UP coalition of Marxist and non-Marxist parties. Opposing him were former president Jorge Alessandri of the conservative National Party and Christian Democratic nominee Radomiro Tomic. The Nixon administration did not support the non-Marxist candidates directly, but late in the game initiated an anti-Allende "spoiling campaign." Images equating an Allende victory with the 1968 Soviet invasion of Czechoslovakia and Cuban firing squads figured prominently in the work of CIA-financed propaganda. CIA assets placed anti-Allende material in radio commentaries and newspaper editorials, particularly in the influential daily *El Mercurio*.[33] When the other main candidates split the non-Marxist votes, Allende won a plurality in the September 4, 1970, presidential election. Absent a candidate with a majority, the Chilean Constitution provided for Congress to select a president from the first-place (Allende) and second-place (Alessandri) finishers. The U.S. goal became to prevent Allende's selection given the Chilean Congress's history of taking the leading vote getter on such occasions.

September–October 1970

In mid-September 1970, the CIA was tasked with managing two separate covert operations. One operation, undertaken at the direction of the National Security Council, continued anti-Allende propaganda and political action activities. This came to be termed *Track I*. The second operation was ordered by President Nixon, and is known as *Track II*. On September 15, the president instructed DCI Richard Helms to do what was necessary to stop Allende from becoming president of Chile. Nixon said the operation was not to be coordinated with the departments of State or Defense, and the Ambassador in Chile was not to be told.[34]

The CIA established contacts with military officers and former officers. Those who might consider initiating a coup were assured of U.S. support.

The insistence of Chilean commander in-chief Gen. René Schneider that the military remain apolitical was an obstacle. Two days before Congress was to meet, a group associated with a former general tried to kidnap Schneider preparatory to a coup. That effort fell apart when Schneider was killed. The record is clear that the CIA was not complicit in the bungled kidnap attempt. Allende was easily confirmed as president on October 24 and inaugurated on November 3, 1970.[35]

Allende's Presidency

Having failed to prevent Allende's election, the United States proceeded—overtly and covertly—to make his tenure as difficult as possible. (See sidebar, NSDM 93.)

NSDM 93

"The President has decided that (1) the public posture of the United States will be correct but cool . . . ; but that (2) the United States will seek to maximize pressures on the Allende government to prevent its consolidation and limit its ability to implement policies contrary to U.S. and hemisphere interests."

Source: National Security Council, *National Security Decision Memorandum 93*, November 9, 1970, at: http://www.fas.org/irp/offdocs/nsdm-nixon/nsdm-93.pdf.

Washington ended economic aid, refused to advance credits, and enlisted the cooperation of international financial institutions and private banks to tighten multilateral financing and credit for Chilean projects.

Between 1970 and 1973, the administration approved $7 million for covert operations in Chile, with more than half going to maintain opposition political parties. Other funding went to sustain opposition newspapers and radio stations. However, the coup that overthrew Allende on September 11, 1973, did not come from the political parties but from the Chilean military. There is no credible evidence that any U.S. entity had a direct role in the 1973 coup. Nevertheless, the efforts to subvert Allende's government, the encouragement (intended or not) that plotters attributed to their U.S. contacts, and the hostility of Washington to Allende certainly contributed to the environment that produced the 1973 coup.[36]

Notes

1. See Don Bohning, *The Castro Obsession: U.S. Covert Operations against Cuba, 1959–1965* (Washington, DC: Potomac Books, Inc., 2005); the CIA's post-

mortem on the Bay of Pigs, prepared by Inspector General Lyman Kirkpatrick, *Inspector General's Survey of the Cuban Operation and Associated Documents*, dated October 1961, at: http://www.foia.cia.gov/sites/default/files/document_conversions/89801/ DOC_0000129914.pdf; and the rejoinder from Deputy Director for Plans Richard Bissell, *An Analysis of the Cuban Operation*, dated January 18, 1962, at: http://www. foia.cia.gov/sites/default/files/document_conversions/89801/DOC_0000129913.pdf. Four volumes of the CIA's internal history of the Bay of Pigs, written in the 1970s, by Jack B. Pfeiffer, *Official History of the Bay of Pigs Operation*, are at: http://www.gwu. edu/~nsarchiv/NSAEBB/NSAEBB355. See also, *FRUS, 1958–1960, Vol. VI, Cuba*, at: https://history.state.gov/historicaldocuments/frus1958-60v06.

2. See *FRUS, 1961–1963, X, Cuba, 1961–1962*, "Report by Grayston Lynch of the Central Intelligence Agency," dated May 4, 1961, Document 109; and "After Action Report," dated May 4, 1961, Document 110.

3. Ibid., Documents 169, 174–176, 187, 193, 199–200, 209–210, 218–219, 221, 229, and 230–234.

4. Ibid., Document 270; and U.S. Congress, Senate, Select Committee to Study Governmental Operations with Respect to Intelligence Activities [Church Committee], *Interim Report: Alleged Assassination Plots Involving Foreign Leaders*, 94th Congress, 1st Session, S. Report No. 94–465 (Washington, DC: GPO, 1975), pp. 71–190, at: http://www.intelligence.senate.gov/pdfs94th/94465.pdf.

5. On CIA covert operations in Vietnam, see Thomas L. Ahern Jr., *CIA and the House of Ngo: Covert Action in South Vietnam 1954–63* (Washington, DC: Center for the Study of Intelligence, Central Intelligence Agency, 2000), at: http://today. ttu.edu/wp-content/uploads/2009/03/02-cia-and-the-house-of-ngo.pdf; and *The Way We Do Things: Black Entry Operations into North Vietnam* (Washington, DC: Center for the Study of Intelligence, Central Intelligence Agency, 2005), at: http://today. ttu.edu/wp-content/uploads/2009/03/05-the-way-we-do-things.pdf. On the military's covert and special operations in Vietnam, see John L. Plaster, *SOG: The Secret Wars of America's Commandos in Vietnam* (New York: Simon and Schuster, 1997); and Richard H. Shultz Jr., *The Secret War against Hanoi: Kennedy and Johnson's Use of Spies, Saboteurs, and Covert Warriors in North Vietnam* (New York: HarperCollins, 1999).

6. Plaster, *SOG*, pp. 123–38; and Shultz, *Secret War*, pp. 128–73.

7. Plaster, *SOG*, pp. 30–62 and 78–122; and Shultz, *Secret War*, pp. 204–65.

8. Brig. Gen. LeRoy J. Manor, provides a first-hand account at http://www. sontayraider.com/history.htm. See also, John Gargus, *The Son Tay Raid: American POWs in Vietnam Were Not Forgotten* (College Station, TX: Texas A&M University Press, 2007); and Benjamin F. Schemmer, *The Raid* (New York: Harper & Row, 1976).

9. See Thomas L. Ahern Jr., *CIA and Rural Pacification in South Vietnam* (Washington, DC: Center for the Study of Intelligence, Central Intelligence Agency, 2001), pp. 40–62, at: http://today.ttu.edu/wp-content/uploads/2009/03/03-cia-and-rural-pacification.pdf; Richard A. Hunt, *Pacification: The American Struggle for Vietnam's Hearts and Minds* (Boulder, CO: Westview, 1995); and Mark Moyar, *Phoenix and the Birds of Prey: The CIA's Secret Campaign to Destroy the Viet Cong* (Annapolis, MD: Naval Institute Press, 1997).

10. See *FRUS, 1958–1960, XVI, East Asia-Pacific Region; Cambodia; Laos*, Documents 479–498.

11. Text of the Geneva Accords is at: http://treaties.un.org/doc/Publication/ UNTS/Volume%20456/volume-456-I-6564-English.pdf.

12. See Thomas L. Ahern Jr., *Undercover Armies: CIA and Surrogate Warfare in Laos, 1961–1973* (Washington, DC: Center for the Study of Intelligence, Central Intelligence Agency, 2006), at: http://today.ttu.edu/wp-content/uploads/2009/03/06-undercover-armies.pdf; Victor B. Anthony and Richard R. Sexton, *The United States Air Force in Southeast Asia: The War in Northern Laos, 1954–1973* (Washington, DC: Center for Air Force History, United States Air Force, 1993), at: http://www.gwu.edu/~nsarchiv/NSAEBB/NSAEBB248/war_in_northern_laos.pdf; and James E. Parker Jr., *Codename Mule: Fighting the Secret War in Laos for the CIA* (Annapolis, MD: Naval Institute Press, 1995).

13. See William M. Leary, "CIA Air Operations in Laos, 1955–1974," *Studies in Intelligence* (Winter 1999–2000), at: https://www.cia.gov/library/center-for-the-study-of-intelligence/csi-publications/csi-studies/studies/winter99-00/art7.html.

14. Michael E. Haas, *Apollo's Warriors: U.S. Air Force Special Operations during the Cold War* (Maxwell AFB, AL: Air University Press, 1997), pp. 177–88. On Aderholt, see Warren A. Trest, *Air Commando One: Heinie Aderholt and America's Secret Air Wars* (Washington, DC: Smithsonian Institution Press, 2000).

15. See Christopher Robbins, *The Ravens: The Men Who Flew in America's Secret War in Laos* (New York: Crown, 1987); and Ralph Wetterhahn, "Ravens of Long Tieng," *Air & Space/Smithsonian*, October–November 1998, at: http://www.airspacemag.com/military-aviation/ravens.html.

16. See Timothy N. Castle, *One Day Too Long: Top Secret Site 85 and the Bombing of North Vietnam* (New York: Columbia University Press, 1999); and James C. Linder, "The War in Laos: The Fall of Lima Site 85," *Studies in Intelligence* 38, no. 5 (1995): 79–88, at: https://www.cia.gov/library/center-for-the-study-of-intelligence/kent-csi/vol38no5/pdf/v38i5a09p.pdf.

17. Larry Devlin, *Chief of Station, Congo: A Memoir of 1960–67* (New York: Public Affairs, 2007), pp. 157–59, 170, 176, and 195. FRUS, *1964–1968, XIIIX, Congo, 1960–1968*, provides primary source material about CIA activities in the Congo.

18. David Robarge, "CIA's Covert Operations in the Congo, 1960–1968: Insights from Newly Declassified Documents," *Studies in Intelligence* 58, no. 3 (September 2014): 6, at: https://www.cia.gov/library/center-for-the-study-of-intelligence/csi-publications/csi-studies/studies/vol-58-no-3/cia2019s-covert-operations-in-the-congo-196020131968-insights-from-newly-declassified-documents.html.

19. Ibid., p. 5; Devlin, *Chief of Station*, pp. 208–9, 225; Richard L. Holm, *The American Agent: My Life in the CIA* (London: St. Ermin's Press, 2003), pp. 28–33; and Jeffrey H. Michaels, "Breaking the Rules: The CIA and Counterinsurgency in the Congo 1964–1965," *International Journal of Intelligence and CounterIntelligence* 25, no. 1 (Spring 2012), pp. 137–43.

20. Michaels, "Breaking the Rules," pp. 143–45; Thomas P. Odom, *Dragon Operations: Hostage Rescues in the Congo, 1964–1965* (Ft. Leavenworth, KS: Combat Studies Institute, U.S. Army Command and General Staff College, 1988), at: http://usacac.army.mil/cac2/cgsc/carl/download/csipubs/odomLP14.pdf; and Fred E. Wagoner, *DRAGON ROUGE: The Rescue of Hostages in the Congo* (Washington,

DC: National Defense University, Research Directorate, 1980), at: http://www.dtic. mil/cgi-bin/GetTRDoc?AD=ADA094969. Hoare tells the story of "a truck load of Cubans" and their leader in Mike Hoare, *Congo Mercenary* (Boulder, CO: Paladin Press, 2008), p. 118.

21. Michaels, "Breaking the Rules," pp. 145–46; and Frank R. Villafana, *Cold War in the Congo: The Confrontation of Cuban Military Forces, 1960–1967* (New Brunswick, NJ: Transaction, 2009), pp. 149–50. See Felix I. Rodriguez and John Weisman, *Shadow Warrior: The CIA Hero of a Hundred Unknown Battles* (New York: Simon & Schuster, 1989), pp. 125, 133.

22. Jon Lee Anderson, *Che Guevara: A Revolutionary Life* (New York: Grove Press, 1997), pp. 640–69; Ernesto ("Che") Guevara, *The African Dream: The Diaries of the Revolutionary War in the Congo*, trans., Patrick Camiller (New York: Grove Press, 2001); Sean Kelly, *America's Tyrant: The CIA and Mobutu of Zaire* (Washington, DC: American University Press, 1993), pp. 162–65; Michaels, "Breaking the Rules," pp. 146, 149; *Time*, "The Congo: The Road to Fizi," October 15, 1965, at: http://www.time.com/time/magazine/article/0,9171,834492,00.html; Villafana, *Cold War in the Congo*, pp. 147–48, 151–53, 157–63.

23. On the U.S./CIA relationship with the Tibetan supporters of the Dalai Lama from 1961 to 1972, see John Kenneth Knaus, *Orphans of the Cold War: America and the Tibetan Struggle for Survival* (New York: Public Affairs, 1999), pp. 236–310. See also, Kenneth Conboy and James Morrison, *The CIA's Secret War in Tibet* (Lawrence: University Press of Kansas, 2002), pp. 145–253; and Mikel Dunham, *Buddha's Warriors: The Story of the CIA-Backed Tibetan Freedom Fighters, the Chinese Invasion, and the Ultimate Fall of Tibet* (New York: Penguin, 2004), pp. 351–84.

24. Knaus, *Orphans of the Cold War*, p. 276.

25. Ibid., pp. 265–66, 271–73; and Ken Conboy and Paul Hannon, *Elite Forces of India and Pakistan* (Botley, UK: Osprey Publishing, 1992), pp. 23, 27.

26. See Knaus, *Orphans of the Cold War*, pp. 249, 276, 292–310; FRUS, 1969–1972, XVII, China, Documents 273, 274, 278, and 280.

27. Warren Hinckle, Robert Sheer, and Sol Stern, "The University on the Make," *Ramparts* 4 (April 1966), pp. 11–22.

28. Sol Stern, "A Short Account of International Student Politics & the Cold War with Particular Reference to the NSA, CIA, Etc.," *Ramparts* 5, no. 9 (March 1967), pp. 29–38. See also, Hugh Wilford, *The Mighty Wurlitzer: How the CIA Played America* (Cambridge, MA: Harvard University Press, 2008), pp. 232–48.

29. FRUS, 1964–1968, XXXIII, Organization and Management of Foreign Policy; United Nations, "Editorial Note," Document 260; and A. Ross Johnson, *Radio Free Europe and Radio Liberty: The CIA Years and Beyond* (Palo Alto, CA: Stanford University Press, 2010), pp. 202–18.

30. Cord Meyer, *Facing Reality: From World Federalism to the CIA* (New York: Harper & Row, 1980), p. 109.

31. Church Committee, *Staff Report: Covert Action in Chile: 1963–1973* (Washington, DC: GPO, 1975), at: http://www.intelligence.senate.gov/pdfs94th/94chile.pdf; and U.S. Central Intelligence Agency, *CIA Activities in Chile*, September 18, 2000, at: https://www.cia.gov/library/reports/general-reports-1/chile/index.html.

32. Church Committee, *Covert Action in Chile*, p. 1.

33. Ibid., pp. 14, 17–22.

34. For the notes Helms took in the meeting with President Nixon on September 15, 1970, see Church Committee, *Alleged Assassination Plots*, p. 227.

35. Church Committee, *Covert Action in Chile*, pp. 25–26. For DCI Helms's recounting, see Richard Helms with William Hood, *A Look over My Shoulder: A Life in the Central Intelligence Agency* (New York: Random House, 2003), pp. 403–08. On Schneider's death, see Church Committee, *Alleged Assassination Plots*, pp. 225–54.

36. Church Committee, *Covert Action in Chile*, pp. 26–39. See also, Nathaniel Davis, *The Last Two Years of Salvador Allende* (Ithaca, NY: Cornell University Press, 1985).

CHAPTER 7

New Rules, New Challenges: 1974–1981

The period from the end of the Vietnam War to the dissolution of the Soviet Union was a difficult one for U.S. Presidents and their use of covert operations. For 200 years, with only a few challenges along the way, Congress had acceded broad deference to the president in the management of matters involving foreign affairs and national security. After passing the National Security Act of 1947, the House and the Senate delegated the responsibility for intelligence oversight to special subcommittees of their respective Appropriations and Armed Services committees. Working in what today would be viewed as a remarkably nonpartisan manner, the relationship of the subcommittees with intelligence officials tended to be collegial and supportive, with trust generally dominating interactions. Widespread allegations of abuses of power by the military, the Federal Bureau of Investigation, the National Security Agency, and the Central Intelligence Agency (CIA) led both the Senate and House of Representatives to establish special committees to investigate intelligence activities. Covert operations came in for a fair share of the investigators' attention. Assassination plots, efforts to destabilize the regime of Chilean president Salvador Allende, and other covert operations became headline news. Congress reacted by instituting new rules on the approval and reporting of covert actions.

Hughes-Ryan Amendment

By the mid-1970s, the widespread public antipathy to the just-ended wars in Southeast Asia coupled with the resignation of the disgraced President Richard Nixon in the wake of the Watergate scandal had aroused concerns about presidents making warlike decisions and open-ended commitments without recourse to consultations with Congress. This concern became particularly vivid when Senate hearings in the early 1970s publicized the direct involvement of U.S. military aircraft and personnel in the covert bombing of Cambodia and Laos. Congress acted to provide for enhanced legislative involvement in covert operations by passing the Hughes-Ryan Amendment to the Foreign Assistance Act, signed by President Ford on December 30, 1974. Named for its coauthors Democratic senator Harold Hughes of Iowa and Democratic representative Leo Ryan of California, the amendment prohibited the expenditure of any funds by the CIA for covert operations until the president "finds" that such operations are "important to U.S. national security" and "reports" this to the Congress "in a timely fashion." Intelligence collection activities were excluded from the scope of this injunction.[1] (See sidebar, *Hughes-Ryan Amendment*.)

Hughes-Ryan Amendment

"Limitation on Intelligence Activities.—(a) No funds appropriated under the authority of this or any other Act may be expended by or on behalf of the Central Intelligence Agency for operations in foreign countries, other than activities intended solely for obtaining necessary intelligence, unless and until the President finds that each such operation is important to the national security of the United States and reports, in a timely fashion, a description and scope of such operation to the appropriate committees of the Congress, including the Committee on Foreign Relations of the United States Senate and the Committee on Foreign Affairs of the United States House of Representatives."

Source: Section 32, Adding Section 662, Foreign Assistance Act of 1961, "Limitation on Intelligence Activities," Foreign Assistance Act of 1974 (Public Law 93–559), December 30, 1974.

Although it gets much less attention than the work of Congressional committees in 1975–1976, the Hughes-Ryan Amendment initiated a major change in the way the U.S. Government approves covert operations. It established the basic framework within which Congress has since operated in fulfilling its constitutionally based oversight function regarding intelligence matters and covert operations. The core concepts of presidential accountability and notification of Congress contained in Hughes-Ryan remain in effect. The requirement for the reporting of a "presidential finding" to Congress meant that covert operations now belonged to the president who ordered them. Presidents' "plausible deniability" for covert operations virtually disappeared, as they could no longer disclaim knowledge of a specific covert operation. Absence of such knowledge meant the president had not approved the operation, and the spending of appropriated dollars on an unapproved operation would represent a misappropriation of government funds—a criminal offense.

The Hughes-Ryan Amendment opened the door for legislative committees or even individual members of Congress to have what amounts to veto power over a proposed operation. In addition to exercising its budgetary authority as a tool for influencing policy (no funding, no operation), the real or implied threat by a committee or a member to take opposition into the public arena—as in a leak to the media—is probably sufficient to stop operational planning in its tracks. Other options for Congress include negotiating with the president over the nature or scope of a proposal or, in the case of a disagreement internal to a committee, taking the dispute to the floor of the relevant chamber in secret session (whether anything could remain covert in this situation is doubtful). At the same time, the Hughes-Ryan Amendment represented formal acknowledgement by Congress that the president does indeed use the CIA to conduct covert operations in foreign countries. And inclusion of the legislative committees in the covert operations process, if only because notification must be made, also raises the opportunity to acquire additional support for the proposed activity.

In 1988, Hughes-Ryan's vague "timely" reporting requirement was replaced by a mandate that presidential findings be reported to the appropriate committees within 48 hours of their signing. However, presidents could still report findings retroactively in emergency situations. Initially, Hughes-Ryan meant reporting proposed covert operations to six committees, a number that rose to eight after the Senate and House each established intelligence oversight committees. In other words, the number of individuals "witting," that is, knowledgeable, about covert operations increased enormously (to include not just the legislators but certain staff personnel as well) from the days when the CIA needed to tell only a handful of senior legislators what was being done. In 1991, the number of committees that had to be informed finally was reduced to the two oversight committees.

The Church Committee

The relationship between the executive and legislative branches was further tested during the course of 1975. On December 22, 1974, the *New York Times* carried a front-page story by Seymour M. Hersh with the headline "Huge C.I.A. Operation Reported in U.S. against Antiwar Forces, Other Dissidents in Nixon Years." Thus 1975, which came to be known as "The Year of Intelligence," began with a flurry of newspaper and television exposés that ranged beyond the initial focus on domestic abuses of power. President Ford tried to head off congressional involvement by appointing an executive branch intelligence review commission under Vice President Nelson Rockefeller. This ploy was unsuccessful. In a direct challenge to the prerogatives of the president and an early indication that this would become a fight between the two branches, the Senate and the House each created special committees to delve into the misdeeds of the Intelligence Community. The best known and most often quoted of the two congressional committees is the Senate Select Committee to Study Governmental Operations with Respect to Intelligence Activities, better known as the Church Committee after its chairman, Democratic senator Frank Church of Idaho. The House Select Committee on Intelligence is generally referred to as the Pike Committee after its second chairman, Democratic representative Otis Pike of New York. The House committee's deliberations became so embroiled in controversy that its final report was never officially released. Consequently, it is sometimes spoken of as "that other committee."[2]

The Church Committee eventually published 14 volumes of materials from its investigation. In addition to the discussion of covert operations contained in Book I of the Final Report, *Foreign and Military Intelligence*, two volumes dealt specifically with the subject. One report, *Alleged Assassination Plots Involving Foreign Leaders*, focused on allegations of CIA assassination planning and plots against (1) Congolese leader Patrice Lumumba; (2) Cuban leader Fidel Castro; (3) Dominican dictator Rafael Trujillo (contact with dissidents was maintained, but no evidence exists that United States instigated assassination); (4) South Vietnamese president Ngo Dinh Diem and his brother, Ngo Dinh Nhu (United States encouraged the coup but was not involved in the assassinations); and (5) Chilean army commander in chief Gen. René Schneider. Another volume contains the hearings before the committee on covert action generally, and includes a staff case study of covert activities in Chile.[3] The committee concluded that over time the use of covert operations had become too much of a routine method for influencing foreign governments and exercising power. Although it considered proposing a total ban on all types of covert operations, the Church Committee decided that the United States needed to keep the covert option open against future needs in response to some as-yet-unknown threat to national security. Instead, the focus shifted to calling for the executive branch to strengthen its review process for covert operations and for greater legislative oversight of intelligence activities in the interest of ensuring accountability.[4]

The work of the Church Committee produced action and reaction from both the executive and legislative branches. In an effort to get out ahead of Congress, President Ford issued Executive Order (EO) 11905 on February 18, 1976. Focused primarily on rearranging the bureaucratic management and coordination of the Intelligence Community (the old 40 Committee was renamed the Operations Advisory Group (OAG) and its membership expanded), EO 11905 dealt with the issue of assassination with a blanket prohibition on "political assassination":

> [Sec. 5] *(g) Prohibition of Assassination.* No employee of the United States Government shall engage in, or conspire to engage in, political assassination.[5]

On the legislative side, the Senate moved relatively quickly to establish a permanent oversight committee specifically for intelligence—the Senate Select Committee on Intelligence (SSCI). Perhaps burned by the controversies surrounding the Pike Committee, the House took another year to get to the same conclusion, finally establishing the House Permanent Select Committee on Intelligence in July 1977. Intelligence in general and specifically covert operations now had to operate within a much more formalized regime of legislative oversight.

Angola

While the debate was continuing in Congress and the media over the role of—and even the need for—covert operations, the Ford administration was preparing for a covert intervention in the former Portuguese colony of Angola.

The government that took power in Portugal after the April 1974 overthrow of Marcello Caetano, successor to longtime dictator António Salazar, simply did not want to add dealing with the indigenous independence movements in Angola to its long list of other problems. In the end, it walked away from the situation, with Angola scheduled to gain its independence in November 1975. However, the major lines for conflict had been well established before that point. An Angolan nationalist insurgency had begun in the early 1960s. It gave birth to three separate, tribal-based independence movements, each with its own army and sources of external support:

- Holden Roberto led the National Front for the Liberation of Angola (*Frente Nacional de a Libertação de Angola,* FNLA). Operating from bases in Zaire, the FNLA was heavily dependent on the support of Zairian president Mobutu. It also received both nonmilitary supplies and a low level of monetary support from the CIA beginning in the 1960s. In January 1975, the 40 Committee approved a $300,000 program of political action support for Roberto. After 1973, the FNLA forces also received some equipment, as well as training by over 100 military advisors, from the People's Republic of China.

- Agustinho Neto headed the Popular Movement for the Liberation of Angola (*Movimento Popular de Libertação de Angola*, MPLA), with its base of operations during the insurgency in Zambia. Strongly Marxist in orientation, the MPLA received material and training support from the Soviet Union, Cuba, Soviet-bloc countries in Eastern Europe, and African and Third World states that tended to line up against the West on international issues. Washington came to regard the MPLA as a Soviet surrogate. Preventing its assumption of government power in Angola became the primary aim of the U.S. covert operation.
- Jonas Savimbi formed the National Union for the Total Independence of Angola (*União Nacional para a Independência Total de Angola*, UNITA) as an offshoot of the FNLA in the mid-1960s. UNITA initially operated out of Zambia, but by the late 1960s had established an enclave inside Angola. Early in the insurgency against Portugal, Savimbi had the support of the PRC; but he later moderated his revolutionary Marxist views.

Talks between the three movements and Portugal in January 1975 in the Portuguese town of Alvor led to an agreement (the "Alvor Accords") for a transitional government incorporating all three factions. Less than a month later, an armed power struggle pitting the FNLA and UNITA against the MPLA began. The FNLA and UNITA forces lost, and by July 1975 had been pushed out of the capital. This brought the transitional government to an end, and set the stage for the MPLA to be recognized by the Soviet Union and others in November 1975 as the legitimate government of Angola.

At the White House, the decision-making process with regard to Angola revolved around what today can be seen as Cold War issues (essentially a fear of the Soviet Union gaining a communist foothold in this part of Africa), and was driven to a considerable extent by Secretary of State Henry Kissinger. The program was controversial from the beginning, with Assistant Secretary of State for African Affairs Nathaniel Davis resigning in protest when the choice was made not to pursue a diplomatic-political solution but rather to initiate a covert intervention so circumscribed that it could not effect real change in the situation in Angola and yet too large to remain covert.[6]

On July 18, 1975, as required by the Hughes-Ryan Amendment, President Ford sent a "finding" to Congress communicating his decision to initiate unspecified covert activities in an unnamed African country. The finding launched the U.S. covert intervention in Angola. The program provided funding and arms to Roberto's FNLA and Savimbi's UNITA. The arms moved from CIA stocks by air and sea to Zaire where they were transshipped to the FNLA and UNITA forces, used to replace supplies donated by Mobutu to the Angolan factions, or served as an incentive for Mobutu to continue his support to the covert paramilitary effort.[7] In the same general timeframe,

Cuban advisors—and eventually combat forces—began arriving in Angola in greater numbers than previously to support the MPLA; additional Soviet arms were delivered to the MPLA by air and sea; Mobutu sent ever-increasing numbers of Zairian troops into northern Angola to bolster the severely flagging FNLA forces; and South Africa, creating a de facto alliance (some allege with U.S. encouragement), initiated its not-so-covert assistance to both the FNLA and UNITA. Over the next several months, the Cuban forces grew into several thousand (and would increase even more as Cuba's long-term commitment in Angola continued). In coordination with Neto's MPLA forces, the more numerous, well-trained, and better equipped Cubans were able to stop and reverse the movement toward Luanda of a South African force pushing out of southern Angola and routed a Zairian-FNLA movement from the north.

It seems clear that in Angola Washington policy makers turned to a covert operation in the absence of a willingness to either ignore or take more direct action to confront what they saw as Soviet proxy forces. As Ambassador Davis had warned, the program proved to be too small to be effective and too large to remain covert. Exposure in the American news media took place incrementally between September and mid-December 1975. The story of U.S. assistance to groups that were also being aided by apartheid South Africa undercut the credibility of the U.S. involvement. It was at this juncture (and possibly with the Vietnam disaster still raw in their minds) that Congress chose to flex its muscles in the field of foreign policy and covert operations. The funding for the Angola operation had come from the CIA's Contingency Reserve Fund. When that fund was depleted in November 1975, the administration had to go to Congress for additional money, and Congress proved unwilling to provide it. With the funding already in the pipeline and some reprogramming, it was possible for the CIA to project continued support to the FNLA and UNITA for some months—but not indefinitely. In December 1975, the Senate passed an amendment introduced by Democratic senator John Tunney of California to the defense appropriations bill that in January 1976 became law as the Defense Appropriations Act (P.L. 94-212) when passed by the House of Representatives and signed by President Ford. The Tunney Amendment terminated funding for the ongoing covert assistance to the anti-MPLA forces in Angola. Later that year, an amendment sponsored by Democratic senator Dick Clark of Iowa to what became the International Security Assistance and Arms Export Control Act of 1976 (P.L. 94-329) made the ban on assistance to and activities in Angola permanent, except for humanitarian purposes. The two actions by Congress are known collectively as the Clark-Tunney Amendment. (See sidebar, *Clark-Tunney Amendment*.)

Clark-Tunney Amendment

"SEC. 404. (a) Notwithstanding any other provision of law, no assistance of any kind may be provided for the purpose, or which would have the effect, of promoting or augmenting, directly or indirectly, the capacity of any nation, group, organization, movement, or individual to conduct military or paramilitary operations in Angola unless and until the Congress expressly authorizes such assistance by law enacted after the date of enactment of this section. . . .

(c) The prohibition contained in subsection (a) does not apply with respect to assistance which is furnished solely for humanitarian purposes."

Source: "Limitation on Assistance to and Activities in Angola," International Security Assistance and Arms Export Control Act of 1976 (P.L. 94–329), June 30, 1976.

During 1976, the increased supply of heavy weapons and aircraft from the Soviet Union and the growing contingent of Cuban combat troops turned the military situation in Angola almost completely in favor of the MPLA. As the FNLA disintegrated early in the year, Mobutu withdrew the Zairian forces that had been the backbone of the war in the north. What remained of the FNLA reverted to conducting isolated guerrilla activities in the north. At the same time, South Africa began to pull its troops back from contact with the MPLA-Cuban forces and by March had retreated out of Angola. With South Africa's departure (although armed incursions continued), Savimbi's UNITA was reduced to holding an enclave in the Angolan interior from which it launched guerrilla operations. In the United States, the Clark-Tunney prohibition on covert assistance to Angola remained in effect until it was repealed in 1985 when the situation in Angola resurfaced as a matter of concern in Washington.[8]

Changing Attitude

It is broadly accepted that James Earl "Jimmy" Carter arrived at the presidency (1977–1981) with a bias against—even a moral objection to—the use of covert operations as an instrument of foreign and national defense policy. Nevertheless, it did not take him long to realize that having options between diplomacy and military force was not just useful but even necessary in the management of America's interaction with the rest of the world. By the end of his term in office, Carter had launched an ill-fated, high-risk military special operation and begun the largest covert paramilitary operation since the end of the Vietnam War.

In organizing his administration to coordinate covert activities, Carter's EO 12036[9] replaced Ford's OAG with the senior-level Special Coordination Committee (SCC) as the focal point in the National Security Council (NSC) for the review and approval of proposed covert operations before being presented to the president for final approval. Establishing such a central review entity was in keeping with the precedents set by his post–World War II predecessors. Truman had placed the review function in the 10/12 and 10/13 Committees; the similar group under Eisenhower was called the 5412 Committee; Kennedy created his Special Group and Special Group (Augmented); the Johnson administration utilized the 303 Committee; and Nixon and Ford used the 40 Committee, until Ford rearranged the NSC's coordination of the Intelligence Community and created the OAG.

Early in his administration, Carter's deep commitment to a broadly defined notion of human rights presented him with a dilemma in seeking to confront what he saw as the Soviet Union's failure to live up to its obligations under international agreements to which it was a signatory. At the urging of National Security Adviser Zbigniew Brzezinski, Carter approved a series of CIA covert propaganda and political action operations targeting opinion within the USSR. One such activity involved smuggling forbidden books and other written material into the USSR, while another provided support for the publication and dissemination of the underground writings (*samizdat*) of dissidents inside the Soviet Union and in exile in Western Europe. Brzezinski's long-standing interest in the non-Russian nationalities that made up the Soviet empire was reflected in the covert infiltration of written materials about their history and culture into areas where the minorities lived. When the Soviets launched a propaganda campaign in Western Europe against the planned deployment of the neutron bomb, Carter countered by approving the provision of covert financial assistance for some Western groups and journalists.

In early 1979, the radical Marxist government of the People's Democratic Republic of Yemen (PDRY or South Yemen) attacked the neighboring Yemen Arab Republic (YAR or North Yemen). Washington was immediately concerned about the possibility of Soviet, Cuban, and/or Ethiopian involvement and the potential that the PDRY leader would seek to foment a Marxist revolution throughout the Arabian Peninsula. Covert assistance to the YAR was agreed upon at an April SCC meeting and President Carter gave his approval in a July 1979 finding. Also, in mid-1979, the influx of arms and other material from Cuba into Sandinista-controlled Nicaragua led Carter to approve funding and political assistance to the regime's opponents. A similar finding authorized covert support to El Salvador as it faced a Marxist insurgency that was receiving Cuban arms and material support by way of Nicaragua. Another July 1979 finding focused on a propaganda and political action operation against the Marxist, pro-Cuban regime of Maurice Bishop in Grenada. When the Senate Select Committee on Intelligence (SSCI) objected to this proposal, it was dropped. However, events in Iran and Afghanistan in 1979 moved President Carter out of such relatively low-risk activities into more active measures.[10]

Crisis in Iran

Throughout 1978, Washington watched as the Shah's control over his country deteriorated. In mid-January 1979, the Shah fled Iran for haven in Egypt (he later moved on to several other countries but ended up in Egypt at the end). On February 1, 1979, Shiite cleric and revolution leader Ayatollah Khomeini returned to Tehran from exile, swept aside the old order, and replaced it with a theocratic state. In an instance of "the covert road not taken," Carter had rejected Brzezinski's suggestion of seeking to encourage a military coup in Iran, the outcome of which would have been doubtful and which probably would have resulted in a bloodbath. In October 1979, Carter decided to allow the Shah, ailing from malignant lymphoma, to enter the United States for medical treatment. On November 4, 1979, the event took place that would consume and perhaps determine the remainder of Carter's stint as president—a mob of several thousand radical "students" stormed the U.S. Embassy in Tehran, taking 66 (including three at the Foreign Ministry) Americans hostage. Planning for a military-style rescue operation began within days, although Carter focused for some months on a diplomatically negotiated resolution.[11]

Help from Friends

In addition to the 53 hostages (reduced from 66 when the Iranian government released women and minority-group members) held at the Embassy, six members of the American diplomatic community avoided being captured and took refuge in the residences of Canadian ambassador Kenneth Taylor and his chief immigration officer John Sheardown. While planning (which eventually included CIA participation) went forward for a larger rescue operation, President Carter gave DCI Stansfield Turner the task of rescuing the Americans in hiding with the Canadians. Despite certain Hollywood-style embellishments (such as, a chase scene that never happened) and less attention to the Canadians than they deserve, individuals who have seen the critically acclaimed (three Oscars, including Best Picture) and commercially successful movie *Argo* have a good picture of how this covert exfiltration operation was planned and carried out.

The CIA's Office of Technical Services (OTS) developed a fictitious motion picture production company, "Studio Six Productions." A Hollywood consultant came up with a script incorporating science fiction, mythological, and Middle Eastern elements, which became the basis for the fictitious *Argo*. Canadian cooperation in the venture included the provision of the alias passports under which the six checked out of Tehran. OTS specialists forged the requisite personal documentation, fine-tuned individual cover stories, and created the light disguises necessary for the perilous task of exfiltrations from hostile territory. The overall cover story for the operation was that the group—the six Canadian "houseguests" and the two CIA officers who traveled to Tehran to prepare the group for their escape and then accompanied them out of Iran—was an advance party working on identifying appropriate locations for filming a movie. Airport control procedures and the manner in which they were being conducted were technically one of the most critical items in creating the false documentation. Collection of current information on airport controls included debriefing intelligence officers and agents traveling in and out of Iran in support of the planning for a mission to rescue the hostages being held at the Embassy and the Foreign Ministry. The travel documentation with the forged Iranian visas and entry cachets, cover story outlines for the six to memorize in all their detail, "pocket litter" (such items as match books and business cards) to match their cover stories, and disguise materials went in a Canadian pouch from Ottawa to Tehran. Presented with options of Canadian or U.S. passports, group or individual exfiltration, and two cover possibilities other than the Studio Six story, the six chose to go with the plan that we now know as *Argo*. On the morning of January 28, 1980, they flew out of Tehran to Zurich, beneficiaries of one of the classic covert exfiltration operations of our time.[12]

Failure in the Desert

It is interesting, and perhaps instructive, that when President Carter told the U.S. military establishment to prepare contingency plans for a military extraction of the American hostages in Tehran, no one apparently informed him that in the post–Vietnam era the military had no mechanism for managing and conducting such a complex special operation. Stated simply, neither the Defense Department nor the JCS had a standing joint counterterrorism task force, and the individual services had come close to eliminating Special Operations Forces from the active force. The Joint Task Force, headed by Army Major General James B. Vaught, that oversaw the development of Operation EAGLE CLAW (also known as Operation RICE BOWL) was a makeshift or, in gentler terms, an ad hoc body within the JCS.

And therein can be found many of the problems that eventually destroyed this brave endeavor.

Planning, training, and rehearsals for an armed rescue of the hostages went forward from early November 1979 over the next five months of on-again-off-again negotiations with the Iranians. However, there were no full-scale rehearsals that brought all the elements together for a coordinated exercise; instead, rehearsals took place within each segment separately.[13] By March 1980, all efforts to negotiate had proved fruitless, and President Carter's patience was exhausted. The decision to act was made on April 11, and a final review with the president was done on April 16. By this point, each of the military services had achieved its desire to have a piece of the EAGLE CLAW action. The assault team that was to go into the Embassy and rescue the hostages was drawn from the army's newly created Delta Force, headed by Col. Charles Beckwith. Air Force Col. James H. Kyle led the fixed wing contingent, and Marine Lt. Col. Edward Seiffert led the force of Marine pilots flying navy helicopters.

The plan for Operation EAGLE CLAW represented an audacious and high-risk undertaking with little room for error. Step one of the plan called for a nighttime rendezvous of airplanes and helicopters in the desert south of Tehran. The CIA had earlier landed a small plane at the proposed site to verify that the area would support the aircraft that would be landing there. Six U.S. Air Force C-130 Hercules transport aircraft, three carrying the assault team and three carrying fuel bladders, would fly out of Oman's Masirah Island. The intermediate desert site—designated Desert One—was necessitated by the choice of the RH-53D Sea Stallion helicopter for transporting the assault forces to a daytime hiding site closer to Tehran. The RH-53D, normally a minesweeping helicopter, lacked in-flight refueling capability and would have to be refueled while on the ground. Eight helicopters would fly from the USS *Nimitz* in the Straits of Hormuz to the Desert One site where they would be refueled prior to moving the assault force.

On the night of April 24, 1980, the six C-130s and six of the eight RH-53D helicopters made it to the Desert One site. One helicopter was abandoned en route because of mechanical problems and a second was forced to return to the *Nimitz* after becoming lost in a desert sandstorm and showing cockpit control lights indicating equipment failures. Therefore, only six helicopters made it to Desert One, and a failed hydraulic pump on one of those made the helicopter inoperable. The mission profile called for a minimum of six helicopters to proceed. After the decision to abort was confirmed by the White House, calamity befell the now terminated mission. The departure from Desert One was forever marred when a C-130 and a helicopter, both loaded with fuel, collided. The lives of eight U.S. servicemen were lost in the ensuing conflagration. The remaining C-130s were loaded with the remaining members of the task force and returned safely to Masirah. The helicopters were left behind, some of which still contained classified material pertinent to the unfulfilled aspects of the mission.[14]

The Department of Defense convened a Special Operations Review Group, known as the Holloway Commission, after its chairman, former chief of naval operations Adm. J. L. Holloway III. The Review Group found significant command-and-control problems arising out of the ad hoc nature of the task force and an excessive degree of security that led to a debilitating level of compartmentalization of the individual elements away from each other. In addition, the absence of an existing central coordinating body for such a joint special operations endeavor meant that the planners themselves were doing all the reviews of the plans. What the Commission did not say directly but can certainly be gleaned from its conclusions is that, while the operation was feasible, the Department of Defense and the JCS were ill-prepared for the assignment they were given. In the wake of the drawdown from the Vietnam War, the special operations capabilities of the individual services had been allowed to atrophy to such an extent that neither the necessary pieces nor the organizational structure existed for what they needed to do.[15] In many ways, certain members of Congress understood this conclusion better than the services; and as the 1980s progressed, a framework for rebuilding U.S. special warfare capability began to emerge.

Notification of Congress

Neither Argo nor EAGLE CLAW was briefed to Congress until after the fact. The president decided that this level of secrecy was necessary even though the Hughes-Ryan requirement for providing "timely notice" to eight Congressional committees of covert operations remained the law. In the main, members of Congress understood, and some were even sympathetic; but it was also suggested that in the future, a smaller number of members might be given foreknowledge of such plans to ensure at least some level of legislative oversight.[16]

The requirement of how many members of Congress need to be notified of a projected covert operation was modified later in 1980. The Intelligence Oversight Act of 1980 amended Hughes-Ryan to require that notice only had to go to the two intelligence committees, thereby eliminating the requirement to notify six other committees. In addition, the president was given the option in exceptional circumstances of providing "timely notice" only to specific members—the majority and minority leaders in each chamber and the chair and ranking minority member of the two intelligence committees—rather than the full committees. This configuration became known as the "gang of eight." (See sidebar, *Gang of Eight*.)

Gang of Eight

"[T]he Director of Central Intelligence and the heads of all departments, agencies, and other entities of the United States involved in intelligence activities shall—(1) keep the Select Committee on Intelligence of the Senate and the Permanent Select Committee on Intelligence of the House of Representatives (hereinafter in this section referred to as the 'Select Committees') fully and currently informed of all intelligence activities which are the responsibility of, are engaged in by, or are carried out for or on behalf of, any department, agency, or entity of the United States, including any significant anticipated intelligence activity, except that (A) the foregoing provision shall not require approval of the Select Committees as a condition precedent to the initiation of any such anticipated intelligence activity, and (B) if the President determines it is essential to limit prior notice to meet extraordinary circumstances affecting vital interests of the United States, such notice shall be limited to the chairmen and ranking minority members of the Select Committees, the speaker and minority leaders of the House of Representatives, and the majority and minority leaders of the Senate."

Source: Intelligence Oversight Act of 1980, Enacted as Intelligence Authorization Act for Fiscal Year 1981, Pub. L. No. 96–450, sec. 407(a), 94 Stat. 1975 (1980).

Afghanistan

America's long-running involvement in what has been called the "graveyard of empires" began in the last years of the Carter administration. Early in 1979, the president and his senior advisers were considering whether to extend covert assistance to the tribally based Afghan resistance movement (lumped together under the term *mujahedeen*) that was waging an insurgency against the Soviet-supported central government. An important piece of the puzzle was that both Pakistan and Saudi Arabia had indicated a willingness to participate in helping the United States support the *mujahedeen* forces. In early July, the president signed a finding (properly briefed to Congress) providing for covert nonmilitary support—propaganda and other psychological operations, cash payments, and nonlethal supplies. Funding was set at just over $500,000. All the previous planning was upended when the Soviet Union, seeking to stabilize the deteriorating situation in the country, launched an air and land invasion of Afghanistan on Christmas Eve and Christmas Day in 1979. The Carter administration responded strongly in both the overt and covert arenas. The president signed a new finding in January 1980 authorizing the CIA to supply weapons to the *mujahedeen*. Both intelligence committees supported the operation. Within a year, covert assistance grew to tens of millions of dollars for military weaponry, communications equipment, and other supplies needed for waging guerrilla warfare against the Soviet military invaders. In keeping with the covert nature of the activity, the CIA moved to acquire Soviet weapons through third parties, including China and Egypt. Saudi Arabia promised to match the U.S. funding dollar-for-dollar, and equipment and supplies were funneled through Pakistan. Thus, as the U.S. presidency passed into new hands in January 1981, the essential elements of a complex, CIA-managed covert operation that would evolve over the next eight years were in place.[17]

Notes

1. Section 32, Adding Section 662, Foreign Assistance Act of 1961, "Limitation on Intelligence Activities," Foreign Assistance Act of 1974 (Public Law 93–559), December 30, 1974, at: http://www.gpo.gov/fdsys/pkg/STATUTE-88/pdf/STATUTE-88-Pg1795.pdf. For a discussion of the impact of the Hughes-Ryan Amendment, see William J. Daugherty, *Executive Secrets: Covert Action and the Presidency* (Lexington: University Press of Kentucky, 2004), pp. 92–98.

2. See Seymour M. Hersh, "Huge C.I.A. Operation Reported in U.S. against Anti-War Forces, Other Dissidents in Nixon Years," *New York Times*, December 22, 1974, pp. 1, 26. On the work of the Church Committee, see Loch K. Johnson, *A Season of Inquiry: The Senate Intelligence Investigation* (Lexington: University Press of Kentucky, 1985). On the controversies surrounding the Pike Committee, see Gerald K. Haines, "The Pike Committee Investigations and the CIA," *Studies in Intelligence* (Winter 1998–1999): 81–92, at: https://www.cia.gov/library/center-for-the-study-of-intelligence/kent-csi/vol42no5/pdf/v42i5a07p.pdf.

3. See U.S. Congress, Senate, Select Committee to Study Governmental Operations with Respect to Intelligence Activities [Church Committee], *Final Report: Book I, Foreign and Military Intelligence*, 94th Congress, 1st Session, S. Report No. 94–755 (Washington, DC: GPO, 1976), pp. 141–61, 475–555, 563–65, at: http://www.intelligence.senate.gov/pdfs94th/94755_I.pdf; *Interim Report: Alleged Assassination Plots Involving Foreign Leaders*, 94th Congress, 1st Session, S. Report No. 94–465 (Washington, DC: GPO, 1975), at: http://www.intelligence.senate.gov/pdfs94th/94465.pdf; and *Hearings, Vol. 7, Covert Action*, 94th Congress, 1st Session (Washington, DC: GPO, 1976), at: http://www.intelligence.senate.gov/pdfs94th/94intelligence_activities_VII.pdf. *Staff Report: Covert Action in Chile: 1963–1973*, is "Appendix A" in Vol. 7, pp. 144–204, and at: http://www.intelligence.senate.gov/pdfs94th/94chile.pdf.

4. Church Committee, *Foreign and Military Intelligence*, pp. 153, 159.

5. Gerald R. Ford, Executive Order 11905, *United States Foreign Intelligence Activities*, February 18, 1976, at: https://www.fas.org/irp/offdocs/eo11905.htm.

6. See Nathaniel Davis, "The Angola Decision of 1975: A Personal Memoir," *Foreign Affairs* 57, no. 1 (Fall 1978): 109–24; John Prados, *Safe for Democracy: The Secret Wars of the CIA* (Chicago: Ivan R. Dee, 2006), pp. 439–55; John Stockwell, *In Search of Enemies: A CIA Story* (New York: Norton, 1979); and Gregory F. Treverton, *Covert Action: The Limits of Intervention in the Postwar World* (New York: Basic Books,

1987), pp. 148–60. On Kissinger's position see, for example, *FRUS, 1969–1976, XXVIII, Southern Africa,* "Memorandum for the Record," dated July 14, 1975, Document 115, and "Memorandum of Conversation," dated July 17, 1975, Document 117.

7. *FRUS, 1969–1976, Southern Africa,* "Report Prepared by the Working Group on Angola," dated February 20, 1976, Document 181.

8. See Edward George, *The Cuban Intervention in Angola, 1965–1991: From Che Guevara To Cuito Cuanavale* (London: Frank Cass, 2005); and Robert David Johnson, "The Unintended Consequences of Congressional Reform: The Clark and Tunney Amendments and U.S. Policy toward Angola," *Diplomatic History* 27, no. 2 (April 2003): 215–43. For a CIA assessment of the impact of the Tunney Amendment on the Angolan Covert Action Program, see *FRUS, 1969–1976, Southern Africa,* "Letter from Director of Central Intelligence Bush to the Chairman of the House Appropriations Subcommittee on Defense (Mahon)," dated March 18, 1976, Document 183.

9. Executive Order 12036, January 24, 1978, at: https://www.fas.org/irp/offdocs/eo/eo-12036.htm. For the president's signing statement, see Jimmy Carter, "United States Foreign Intelligence Activities Statement on Executive Order 12036," January 24, 1978, at: http://www.presidency.ucsb.edu/ws/?pid=31111.

10. See Daugherty, *Executive Secrets,* pp. 185–92; and Robert M. Gates, *From the Shadows: The Ultimate Insider's Story of Five Presidents and How They Won the Cold War* (New York: Simon & Schuster, 1996), pp. 143, 149–53, 176–79.

11. See Jimmy Carter, *Keeping Faith: Memoirs of a President* (New York: Bantam Books, 1982), pp. 468–528. See also, Zbigniew Brzezinski, *Power and Principle: Memoirs of the National Security Advisor, 1977–1981* (New York: Farrar, Straus, and Giroux, 1983), pp. 376–98.

12. See Antonio J. Mendez and Matt Baglio, *Argo: How the CIA and Hollywood Pulled Off the Most Audacious Rescue in History* (New York: The Viking Press, 2012); and Antonio J. Mendez, with Malcolm McConnell, *The Master of Disguise: My Secret Life in the CIA* (New York: Morrow, 1999), pp. 267–305. See also, Jean Pelletier and Claude Adams, *The Canadian Caper: The Inside Story of the Daring Canadian Rescue of Six American Diplomats Trapped in Iran* (New York: Morrow, 1981); and Robert Wright, *Our Man in Tehran* (New York: Other Press, 2011).

13. See Charlie A. Beckwith and Donald Knox, *Delta Force* (New York: Harcourt Brace Jovanovich, 1983). Colonel Beckwith was ground force commander for EAGLE CLAW. The book's "Prologue" covers the White House briefing prior to the launch of EAGLE CLAW. See also, James H. Kyle and John Robert Eidson, *The Guts to Try: The Untold Story of the Iran Hostage Rescue Mission by the On-Scene Desert One Commander* (New York: Orion Crown Publishers, 1990). Colonel Kyle commanded the fixed-wing contingent for EAGLE CLAW.

14. See Mark Bowden, "The Desert One Debacle," *The Atlantic,* May 2006, at: http://www.theatlantic.com/magazine/archive/2006/05/the-desert-one-debacle/304803/; and Charles T. Kamps, "Operation Eagle Claw: The Iran Hostage Rescue Mission (English Version)," *Air & Space Power Journal en Español* 18, no. 3 (2006), at: http://www.airpower.maxwell.af.mil/apjinternational/apj-s/2006/3tri06/kampseng.html.

15. For the unclassified version of the Holloway Commission report, see Department of Defense, Special Operations Review Group [Holloway Commission], *Rescue Mission Report* (August 1980), at: http://www2.gwu.edu/~nsarchiv/NSAEBB/NSAEBB63/doc8.pdf.

16. Carter, *Keeping Faith*, pp. 521, 528; Frank J. Smist Jr., *Congress Oversees the United States Intelligence Community, 1947–1994* (Knoxville: University of Tennessee Press, 1994), pp. 120–22; L. Britt Snider, "The Iranian Rescue Operations: 1979–80," in *The Agency and the Hill: CIA's Relationship with Congress, 1946–2004* (Washington, DC: Central Intelligence Agency, Center for the Study of Intelligence, 2008), pp. 282–83, at: https://www.fas.org/irp/cia/product/snider.pdf; and Stansfield Turner, *Burn Before Reading: Presidents, CIA Directors, and Secret Intelligence* (New York: Hyperion Books, 2005), p. 179.

17. Gates, *From the Shadows*, pp. 143–49; Snider, "Afghanistan: 1979–87," in *The Agency and the Hill*, pp. 283–85.

CHAPTER 8

Agreements and Disagreements: 1981–1989

Ronald Reagan's anticommunist credentials were well established before he became U.S. president (1981–1989), and this bias punctuated his rhetoric and actions. With George H. W. Bush, whose résumé included a stint as director of Central Intelligence (DCI), as his vice president, and William J. Casey, an old Office of Strategic Services hand, as DCI, Reagan had an activist team that, on the surface at least, understood intelligence matters.[1] Covert operations became the administration's tool for countering the Soviet Union on its own turf and Marxist-leaning regimes beyond the Warsaw Pact.

Poland: The Rise of Solidarity

The volatile situation in communist Poland was an inherited crisis in the making. On July 1, 1980, the Polish government announced it was raising the prices of food and other consumer goods. The next day, widespread strikes for matching wage increases erupted. Similar protests had occurred in 1970 and in 1976 when the government sought to increase food prices. These events were marked by violence in the ensuing police and military crackdown. In this instance, the government chose to negotiate; but as soon as an agreement was reached at one enterprise, another strike broke out elsewhere. On August 14, 1980, the Lenin Shipyards in Gdansk—the site of the worst violence during the 1970 uprising—went on strike. Lech Walesa emerged from this strike as one of the leaders of what became the Solidarity (*Solidarność*) trade union movement. Much of the first year of the Reagan administration was spent watching the ebb and flow of confrontations between the government and Solidarity. But events inside Poland and discussions within the U.S. government all took place against the backdrop of potential Soviet military action to crush the unrest being generated by Solidarity and other dissident groups.

Martial Law Declared

Prodded for over a year by the Soviet Union to take decisive action, Polish prime minister Gen. Wojciech Jaruzelski on December 13, 1981, imposed martial law and outlawed Solidarity. The military and police arrested the leaders and thousands of members of Solidarity, including Walesa. The dissidents who avoided "internment" went into hiding and prepared to wage clandestine political warfare against the government's repressive measures.[2]

Even before the imposition of martial law, the American Federation of Labor and Congress of Industrial Organizations (AFL-CIO) on the initiative of its leader Lane Kirkland had been active in raising funds for its fellow trade unionists in Poland; and the Carter administration had begun a modest level of covert assistance to Solidarity-support groups outside of Poland. After the declaration of martial law, what emerged over the next year was a three-headed covert effort involving the CIA, the AFL-CIO, and the Polish-born Pope John Paul II to keep alive Poland's underground political movement. This was not a centrally coordinated tripartite arrangement; each element had its own ideas about what was needed and its own lines of communication into and inside Poland. However, there were consultations between U.S. government officials (White House, State Department, and CIA) and Kirkland and other AFL-CIO representatives. And after Reagan's meeting with the Pope on June 7, 1982, there were regular closed-door meetings at the Vatican between the Pope and American intermediaries, particularly DCI Casey and Ambassador-at-large Vernon Walters. The CIA's covert support to Solidarity was funneled through third-party groups and took the form of money and the equipment and supplies needed to wage underground political warfare. As an underground organization, Solidarity was

> supplied, nurtured and advised largely by the network established under the auspices of Reagan and John Paul II. Tons of equipment—fax machines (the first in Poland), printing presses, transmitters, telephones, shortwave radios, video cameras, photocopiers, telex machines, computers, word processors—were smuggled into Poland via channels established by priests and American agents and representatives of the AFL-CIO and European labor movements. Money for the banned union came from CIA funds, the National Endowment for Democracy, secret accounts in the Vatican and Western trade unions.[3]

Throughout the 1980s, the underground opposition engaged in antigovernment and anti-Soviet activities. Solidarity organized mass demonstrations on key dates in Polish history. When riot police using clubs and water cannons broke up such events, headlines around the world were generated, since pictures and reports of police brutality were communicated out of the country on Western-supplied and Solidarity-controlled communications equipment.

The printing presses, ink, and paper smuggled in from the West made pos-sible a vigorous opposition press. Some underground newspapers reached tens of thousands of readers. The impact of reports of government misbehav-ior published in the underground press was magnified when they were read over Western international broadcast services, especially Radio Free Europe. A CIA-supplied transmitter gave the underground the capability to break into government television programs with audio and visual messages, includ-ing calls for strikes and demonstrations.[4] In his memoirs, former DCI Robert M. Gates provided concrete examples of CIA propaganda support to the Pol-ish opposition in 1985:

> In March, we printed and smuggled into Poland forty thousand postcards with a photograph of Father Popieliusko (the Polish priest . . . beaten to death by the security services) and the texts from some of his sermons.
>
> In May, we arranged a pro-Solidarity demonstration at a soccer match between Poland and Belgium, including a twenty-foot wide banner that was clearly seen on Polish (and international) television.
>
> In June, the CIA obtained a copy of the map used by Hitler's For-eign Minister, Joachim von Ribbentrop, and Soviet Foreign Minister V.M. Molotov during their meeting in Moscow in September 1939 that resulted in the partition of Poland. We made hundreds of miniaturized copies and arranged for their infiltration into Poland. On the reverse side of the map, we printed, in Polish, the text of the secret protocols of the meeting.[5]

The covert support from the CIA and Western labor groups helped sus-tain the opposition in Poland all the way to Solidarity's eventual victory. In April 1989, after General Secretary of the Communist Party of the Soviet Union Mikhail Gorbachev signaled his acceptance that Solidarity's participa-tion was necessary to the governing of Poland, Walesa and Interior Minister Czeszlaw Kiszczak signed a pact legalizing Solidarity and agreeing to hold free parliamentary elections. By the end of August, a Solidarity-led government was in place. In December 1990, Lech Walesa became president of Poland's first freely elected noncommunist government since World War II.

Afghanistan

Afghanistan was another ongoing covert operation that transitioned from Carter to Reagan. Over Reagan's first three years, commitments to the strug-gle of the *mujahedeen* against the Soviet invaders increased incrementally. By 1984, more sophisticated weaponry was being funneled covertly to the *mujahedeen* through Pakistan's Inter-Services Intelligence, and U.S. funding had reached $60 million, a sum being matched by Saudi Arabia.[6]

During 1984–1985, the level of U.S. and associated support to the *muja-hedeen* began to change dramatically. The Saudis proposed increasing their contribution to $75 million in 1984 and $100 million in 1985 if the United States would match those amounts. Then, there was the intervention of flamboyant Democratic Congressman Charles Wilson of Texas. A member of the defense subcommittee of the House Appropriations Committee, Wilson arranged to add an extra $40 million to the Afghan program. Much of the increase was to be spent on providing the *mujahedeen* with the Swiss-made Oerlikon antiaircraft gun. This enhancement to the weapons program went forward even though neither the CIA nor the Defense Department believed the Oerlikon, a high-tech, rapid-fire weapon that required continuing main-tenance, was appropriate for use in the environment of Afghanistan.[7] Wil-son's activities provide an indication that covert operations were no longer the exclusive property of the executive branch. In October 1984, DCI Casey took a proposal, first, to the congressional committees and after approval, to the Saudis to increase U.S. funding for the *mujahedeen* to $250 million in 1985. Casey's proposal signaled that the administration's thinking was mov-ing from a strategy of "making the Soviets bleed" to one of waging a surrogate war focused on "winning." The shift to a strategy of winning was formalized in March 1985 when National Security Decision Directive 166 (NSDD-166) declared that the goal of U.S. policy in Afghanistan was to drive the Soviet Union out. (See sidebar, *NSDD-166*.)

NSDD-166

"The Soviet war in Afghanistan is now well into its sixth year. The two princi-pal elements in our Afghanistan strategy are a program of covert action support to the Afghan resistance, and our diplomatic/political strategy to pressure the Soviet Union to withdraw its forces from Afghanistan and to increase interna-tional support for the Afghan resistance forces. This directive establishes the goals and objectives to be served by these programs. . . . The ultimate goal of our policy is the removal of Soviet forces from Afghanistan and the restoration of its independent status."

Source: Ronald Reagan, "National Security Decision Directive 166: U.S. Policy, Programs and Strategy in Afghanistan," March 27, 1985, at: http://www.fas.org/irp/offdocs/nsdd/nsdd-166.pdf.

A Turning Point

The shift in U.S. policy toward a strategy of winning added emphasis to the discussion of how best to arm the *mujahedeen*. The arms being supplied now included heavy machineguns, the Oerlikon, and Soviet-made SA-7 and British-made Blowpipe ground-to-air missiles. CIA and military personnel began to provide sophisticated communications equipment and associated training in Pakistan. Previously, the weapons had been non-U.S.-produced, taken either from CIA stockpiles of Soviet weapons and ammunition or purchased from third parties, including Egypt and China. The issue now was whether to provide the Afghan fighters with the shoulder-fired, U.S.-made Stinger ground-to-air missile. Relatively easy to use, the infrared homing Stinger offered significant advantages of portability over the Oerlikon and of dependability over the SA-7 and Blowpipe. Discussion revolved around military concerns about potential technology transfer and CIA objections to the loss of "plausible deniability" with the introduction of American weaponry into an ostensibly covert paramilitary operation.

In March 1986, acting on the basis of President Carter's original finding, President Reagan approved sending the Stinger missiles to the *mujahedeen*. By September 1986, the *mujahedeen* had the Stinger missiles in the field. The effect was to force the Soviets into nighttime operations; but within months, the CIA had developed a new sighting system that improved the Stingers' effectiveness in the dark. Soviet and Afghan government aircraft began flying higher to avoid the missiles, thereby reducing the effectiveness of bombing missions and ground-support activities. By the end of 1986, the Soviet leadership had concluded that the war in Afghanistan had to end. They first replaced their anointed leader of Afghanistan, Babrak Karmal, with Mohammed Najibullah, head of Afghan intelligence. Gorbachev announced in February 1988 that the Soviet troop withdrawal would begin in May and be finished by March 15, 1989. The withdrawal was completed on February 15, 1989, when General Boris Gromov became the last Soviet soldier to leave Afghanistan. After the general crossed the bridge that connects the Soviet Union and Afghanistan, the CIA chief in Pakistan sent a brief message to CIA Headquarters "We won."[8]

Reviving Special Forces

While the CIA was busy in Afghanistan, the American military establishment was agonizing over where special operations forces (SOF) fit into the collective and individual orders of battle. The calamitous conclusion of Operation EAGLE CLAW at Desert One was a visible manifestation of how far special operations had declined since the end of the Vietnam War. The disdain for and even distrust of SOF within the conventional military had been accompanied by significant funding cuts for special operations. The U.S. invasion of Grenada (Operation URGENT FURY) in 1983 further exposed the inability of the individual services to coordinate their activities and communicate across

service lines. Slow to change internally and resistant to change from outside, the Joint Chiefs of Staff (JCS) and the individual services soon found
themselves playing catch up behind a Congress determined to make them
work together and to nurture the forces needed for a robust special operations
capability.[9]

At this point, operational control of the small number of special operations
units left over from Vietnam was dispersed across the individual services. The
units included the army's Delta Force (activated in 1977), Rangers, Special
Forces (Green Berets), and Task Force 160, from which other army SOF drew
their helicopter and light aviation support; the air force's First Special Operations Wing; and the Navy SEALs. By the mid-1980s, Congress had grown
impatient with waiting for the secretary of defense, the Joint Chiefs, and
the armed services to overcome parochial interests and address the needs for
organizational reform. If the U.S. military establishment would not reform
itself, reform would come from outside. On October 1, 1986, President Reagan signed into law the Goldwater-Nichols Department of Defense Reor-
ganization Act (Pub. L. 99–433) mandating the principle of "jointness" in
armed forces organization and operations. Named for its sponsors, Republican
Senator Barry Goldwater of Arizona and Democratic Representative William
Nichols of Alabama, the Goldwater-Nichols Act remodeled the U.S. military
command structure.

The Goldwater-Nichols Act was quickly followed by a special operations
specific amendment to the National Defense Authorization Act of 1987,
sponsored by Republican Senator William S. Cohen of Maine and Democratic Senator Sam Nunn of Georgia. Congress was reaching deeply into what
many believed were the prerogatives of the executive branch. The Cohen-
Nunn Act (PL 99–661), signed into law by the president in November 1986,
created a unified combatant command—U.S. Special Operations Command
or USSOCOM—for all U.S. special operations forces based in the continental United States. A four-star officer reporting directly to the chairman of
the JCS would head the new command. To strengthen its bureaucratic clout,
USSOCOM was provided independent authorities for budgeting, training,
and equipping, matters usually reserved for departments. The act also established the position of Assistant Secretary of Defense for Special Operations
and Low-Intensity Conflict (ASD SO/LIC), and created a Board for Low-
Intensity Conflict within the National Security Council (NSC).[10]

Neither the president nor the Pentagon was in a hurry to implement the
new legislation. USSOCOM was not formally activated at MacDill Air Force
Base in Florida until April 1987. It was January 1988 before the ASD SO/LIC
was formally established in the Office of the Under Secretary of Defense for
Policy and six months later before a candidate for the position was confirmed.
Although confronting multiple obstacles (most involving turf and money),

USSOCOM continued to have the support of Congress. At a time of diminishing resources for the military in general, USSOCOM and its component commands were able to grow their personnel totals and obtain increased funding for modernizing and upgrading equipment, more extensive training, and other necessities.[11]

Angola Redux

When the Clark-Tunney Amendment of 1976 cut off American covert assistance to the noncommunist factions in Angola, the country's civil war did not end. Soviet military aid to the Marxist Popular Movement for the Liberation of Angola (*Movimento Popular de Libertação de Angola*, MPLA), which had established a government in the capital of Luanda, continued. Soviet assistance included Hind helicopter gunships, combat aircraft, and heavy battle tanks. In addition, by 1985, there were as many as 40,000 Cuban troops fighting alongside the MPLA. On the other side, Jonas Savimbi's National Union for the Total Independence of Angola (*União Nacional para a Independência Total de Angola*, UNITA) was holding on to territory in the Angolan interior with military support from South Africa.

President Reagan tended to see the Soviet activities and Cuban presence in Angola as an effort to establish a communist foothold in southern Africa. Supporting Savimbi's "freedom fighters" fit firmly within the so-called Reagan Doctrine with its espousal of aiding anticommunist resistance movements in order to break the grip of Soviet-backed communist governments.[12] Concern about the Soviet and Cuban intervention in Angola led Congress to repeal the Clark Amendment in August 1985, opening the door to renewed covert assistance to Savimbi and UNITA. In November 1985, a presidential finding authorized lethal covert assistance for UNITA. A CIA-managed airlift of weapons and military equipment was promptly initiated; it would expand significantly over the next two years. (See sidebar, *CIA in Angola*.) Early in 1986, Savimbi made the first of several visits to Washington to meet with the president and argue his case to Congress. To counter the Soviet-Cuban-MPLA use of helicopters, combat aircraft, and heavy tanks, the decision was made in February 1986 to provide UNITA with Stinger antiaircraft missiles and TOW (tube-launched, optically tracked, wire-guided) antitank weapons.[13]

CIA in Angola

"CIA formed a special task force to administer the program. . . . We sent a man to Jamba [UNITA's headquarters] to serve as liaison with Savimbi, and a CIA representative would remain there, living in a thatch hut, for the next several

> years. Our airlift was a masterpiece of logistical planning as we often used a single C-130 to ferry goods from our staging base [in Zaire] to Jamba—where the plane would remain on the ground only a few minutes while being quickly unloaded."
>
> ——————
>
> *Source:* Robert M. Gates, *From the Shadows: The Ultimate Insider's Story of Five Presidents and How They Won the Cold War* (New York: Simon & Schuster, 1996), p. 347.

With all the weapons and outside assistance that had been poured into Angola, it was perhaps inevitable that a large-scale (and some argue decisive) battle would take place. In July 1987, the Angolan government and Cuban forces launched a concerted and initially successful drive against UNITA-held territory. South Africa rushed troops to Savimbi's aid. In a series of set-piece battles involving ground-support aircraft, tanks, and heavy artillery in October and November, the South African forces put Angolan forces into disorderly flight. The Angolans took up a defensive position behind a river in the small town of Cuito Cuanavale, where they were reinforced by Cuban troops. The siege of Cuito Cuanavale continued until March 1988. After a final UNITA–South African assault failed to dislodge the Angolans, the South Africans pulled back. The Angolans, Cubans, and the South African National Congress claimed Cuito Cuanavale as a victory for their side, which was disputed by supporters of the South African military. In a way, it may have been a victory for all sides, including the United States, as it seemed to spur the warring parties (except UNITA, which would fight on) toward one of the main goals of the United States—getting the Cubans out of Angola. Since early in the Reagan administration, Assistant Secretary of State for African Affairs Chester Crocker had been pursuing a negotiated political settlement to the Angolan situation. A series of agreements that began in May 1988 culminated in a trilateral (Angola, Cuba, and South Africa) agreement that ended South African military support to UNITA, and called for the phased withdrawal of Cuban forces from Angola by July 1, 1991, and South Africa's withdrawal from Namibia. Although both South Africa and Cuba met the requirements of this agreement and U.S. covert assistance apparently ended in the early 1990s, neither this nor follow-on agreements ended the civil war in Angola. Savimbi fought on until his death in battle in 2002.[14]

Aiding the Contras

After the Sandinista National Liberation Front (*Frente Sandinista de Liberación Nacional* or FSLN) overthrew Nicaraguan dictator Anastasio Somoza in July 1979, it did not take long before the Sandinistas' Marxist rhetoric, close relations with Cuba and the Soviet Union, and support for the Marxist guerrillas in El Salvador to arouse concerns in Washington. President Carter signed a finding in the fall of 1979 authorizing a covert political action program to support the democratic, anti-Sandinista elements in Nicaragua. At the same time, Carter issued a finding providing for covert training by U.S. Special Forces and material support to El Salvador in resisting the Salvadoran insurgents. The covert operation in Nicaragua included money to individuals and groups and even newsprint to an opposition newspaper. In 1980, the president doubled the financial commitment to the covert program, and right before leaving office suspended further U.S. aid to Nicaragua.[15]

President Reagan terminated the remainder of the aid package to the Sandinista government and signed a finding for additional covert support to El Salvador in interdicting the flow of arms from Nicaragua. In December 1981, Reagan issued a new finding on Nicaragua, authorizing the CIA to provide paramilitary training to Nicaraguan exile groups and to support and conduct paramilitary operations against Nicaragua. The anti-Sandinista groups came to be collectively referred to as the *Contras*, a derivative from counterrevolutionaries, although to the president they were always freedom fighters. A multimillion-dollar budget was established for training a force of 500 Contras. The rationale stated to Congress for covert support to the Contras was to assist Honduras in interdicting the flow of arms from the Sandinistas to the Salvadoran rebels. The conflict between this justification and the Contras' core objective of overthrowing the Sandinista government haunted the covert operation from its beginning.

The initial group to receive funding and arms, the Nicaraguan Democratic Force (*Fuerza Democrática Nicaragüense* or FDN), was already in existence. Argentine military intelligence was funding the group in southern Honduras. At this point, the FDN consisted of former Somoza National Guardsmen (Somocistas) and anti-Somozo exiles also opposed to the Sandinistas. A small group of indigenous Miskitos who had fled across the border to escape the Sandinistas' effort at forced collectivization was also available for training. Much of the training for the Contras and for the Salvadoran military's counterinsurgency units came from U.S. special operations personnel either on detached assignment or acting under Defense Department aid programs.[16]

Progress and Problems

The first full year of the covert operation against the Sandinistas was marked by successes in organizing, training, and utilizing the Contra forces but serious problems on the political front. In mid-March 1982, the Contra guerrillas launched their first cross-border attack into northern Nicaragua, blowing two bridges on the Pan-American Highway. Other similar small-scale incursions into Nicaragua followed. The Contra cause was further bolstered in April when former Sandinista hero, Eden Pastora (whose revolutionary name was Comandante Zero), publicly announced his defection, denounced the regime, and began building his own guerrilla force with CIA assistance. However, supporting Pastora had an awkward downside. His forces were located in Costa Rica to the south of Nicaragua, and arguing that they were part of interdicting the arms flow to El Salvador was a thin reed on which to hang justification for the covert support.

By later 1982, the Contra force had grown to some 3,700–4,200 (including 900 Miskitos) based in Honduras and 500 with Pastora in Costa Rica and southeastern Nicaragua. The numbers of the Contra forces continued to grow over the years as Sandinista policies, especially rural collectivization, drove peasants off their land. On the other hand, the covertness of the operation was mostly gone as the *Washington Post*, the *New York Times*, and other national media began reporting in February and March 1982 on the administration's decision to direct a paramilitary operation at Nicaragua. Washington's relationship with the Contras became in many respects an "overt covert" operation, while members of Congress grew increasingly uneasy about activities in Central America. The problem was not just Nicaragua. The horrors perpetrated by right-wing "death squads" in El Salvador raised concerns about the millions of dollars going to that country to fight its war against left-wing guerrillas. However, Congressional concerns focused in particular on the disconnect between the administration's arms interdiction justification and the seemingly clear intent of the Contras to overthrow the Sandinista regime.[17]

Conflict with Congress

By the fall of 1982, trust between the administration and the Congress had eroded to such an extent that Congress put boundaries around the relationship with the Contras. On December 21, 1982, President Reagan signed into law as part of the Defense Appropriations Act of 1983 the first of a series of legislative actions collectively known as the Boland Amendments (after Democratic Representative Edward Boland of Massachusetts). The Amendment prohibited the CIA or the Defense Department from furnishing military equipment, training, advice, or other support for persons seeking to overthrow the Nicaraguan government.[18]

In practice, the first Boland Amendment did little to interfere with aid to the Contras, as the administration continued to maintain that the purpose of its assistance was to hamper the flow of Soviet and Cuban arms from Nicaragua to the Salvadoran Marxist rebels. By the spring of 1983, members of

Congress were questioning the legality of the CIA's support to the Contras and the increasingly aggressive attacks into Nicaragua. The president issued a new finding in September 1983, which portrayed the administration's goals as interrupting the flow of arms, diverting the Sandinistas' attention and resources away from fomenting violence beyond their borders, and pressuring them into negotiations aimed at changing their behavior. After an effort to cut off all funding for the Contras was turned back in the Senate, Congress capped funding for the war at $24 million (well below the administration's request) in the Intelligence Authorization Act for fiscal year 1984. The act also barred the CIA from using its contingency reserves to cover the difference between the administration's request and the approved amount.

Even while Contra forces in both the north and south continued to grow in size and operational sophistication, events during 1984 seriously undermined support in Congress for the Nicaragua project. In January and February, the CIA mined Nicaraguan harbors on both the Atlantic and Pacific coasts. Although originally presented as a Contra operation, the actual mining was planned and implemented by the CIA using contract operatives and U.S.-owned vessels to infiltrate the harbors and lay the mines. Even the mines involved were special CIA creations designed to produce mostly noise and flash rather than the destruction associated with the more powerful military mines. In early April, the story of the CIA's direct involvement broke publicly. Many members of Congress from both parties viewed the mining as almost an act of war, but the effect was perhaps greatest on Republican Senator Barry Goldwater of Arizona, chairman of the Senate Select Committee on Intelligence and a stanch supporter of the administration and the CIA. The senator believed the committee had not been informed in advance of the operation as required by law. The record substantiated Casey's argument that he had done so (if in less than clear terms), but the damage had been done. Not only did the CIA not get the supplemental funding it was seeking for the Contras but Congress also enacted in October 1984 what is known as the "full Boland Amendment" that prohibited the CIA, the Defense Department, or any other U.S. agency or entity involved in intelligence activities from providing, directly or indirectly, military or paramilitary assistance to the Contras. As a result, large numbers of CIA and Defense Department personnel were withdrawn from Central America. This created a void in White House policy that the NSC staff proceeded to fill.[19]

Going "Off the Books"

Even before Congress cut off funding for the Contras, President Reagan had made his determination to keep the Contras' activities alive plain to those around him. The White House decided to initiate its own covert operation to try to fill the gap between the $24 million in appropriated funding and the additional $10–15 million in supplemental funds needed to maintain operations for the remainder of the fiscal year. This covert operation hearkened back to the country's early history; it would be managed right out of the White House. The operation would be run out of the NSC, and would be so covert that Congress would not know about it. The operational point person for the NSC endeavor was Marine Lt. Col. Oliver North, a member of National Security Advisor Robert "Bud" McFarlane's staff.

This was essentially an "off-the-books" operation involving an effort to identify funding from private donors and third countries. In seeking support from outside the purview of Congress, the seeds of half of what became known as Iran-Contra were sown. McFarlane in March 1984 secured a commitment from Saudi Arabia of $1 million a month for the Contras for "humanitarian purposes." The money was deposited directly into an offshore bank account. Early in 1986, Saudi Arabia doubled its contribution to $2 million a month. It was 1987 before the intelligence committees were told of the Saudi contribution. The NSC operation included a privately run pipeline to move money from donors to the Contra leaders and to assist them in making weapons purchases. Instead of the CIA and armed forces personnel who had previously provided training and technical assistance, former military and intelligence personnel were recruited as private citizens to work with the Contras.[20]

For fiscal year 1986, Congress approved $27 million in nonlethal humanitarian aid—food, medicine, and clothing—for the Contras with the stipulation that neither the CIA nor the Defense Department could manage the aid. A special State Department unit, the Nicaraguan Humanitarian Assistance Office, was created for this purpose. At the same time, the NSC staff focused on beefing up the Contras' military activities, including opening a second front from Costa Rica in the south. A private logistics infrastructure (the "Enterprise") to provide airlift capability—planes, pilots, crew, and maintenance facilities—was set up to purchase and ferry arms, ammunition, and other material to the Contras. The funding came in part from money diverted from arms sales to Iran in the second of the NSC's off-the-books covert operations. The private air supply operation was terminated in October 1986 after one of its airplanes was shot down in southern Nicaragua. Three crewmembers were killed but one survived and was captured. All of the crew had documentation in their pockets linking them directly to Southern Air Transport, a former CIA proprietary airline. In addition, the surviving crewmember, Eugene Hasenfus, told the Sandinistas that he believed he was working for the CIA. In essence, the NSC staff had been arranging for precisely what Congress had refused to fund—the supply of military equipment to Contra forces. (See sidebar, *House-Senate Conclusion*.)

House-Senate Conclusion

"[F]or more than 2 years, the NSC staff had secretly achieved what Congress had openly disapproved in the Boland Amendment—an extensive program of military support for the Contras. The Boland Amendment operated as a restraint on disclosure, not on action, as the NSC staff placed policy ends above the law."

Source: U.S. Congress, *Report of the Committees Investigating the Iran-Contra Affair, with Supplemental, Minority, and Additional Views*, S. Rept. No. 100–216, H. Rept. No. 100–433, 100th Congress, First Session (Washington, DC: Government Printing Office, 1987), p. 59.

In June 1986, the House approved an administration request for $100 million in assistance for fiscal year 1987—$30 million in humanitarian aid and $70 million unrestricted, that is, paramilitary, aid. The new money brought about a renewed level of Contra pressure on the Sandinista government. Cease-fire talks began in late 1987. Mediation efforts by Central American leaders, coupled with the end of CIA paramilitary assistance in February 1988 (political action support to moderate political groups and the opposition newspaper continued), led to an agreement whereby the Contras would demobilize in return for free elections. The elections in February 1990 surprised many observers by replacing the Sandinista president, Daniel Ortega, with the head of a wide-ranging, anti-Sandinista coalition, Violeta Chamorro.[21]

More "Off the Books"

In mid-1985, at the same time it was covertly privatizing support to the Contras, the NSC staff initiated a second off-the-books covert operation.

Congress had embargoed arms sales to Iran in November 1979, but the staffers devised a plan to sell weapons (initially using Israel as an intermediary) to Iran in return for that country's assistance in freeing American hostages being held in Lebanon. It is generally accepted that President Reagan approved the sale in August 1985. This endeavor was undertaken in the face of clearly articulated policy that the United States would not negotiate with terrorists. Hostage taking in Lebanon by the Iranian-sponsored Hezbollah had begun in 1984 and included the CIA's chief of station in Beirut, William Buckley, as well as private American and foreign citizens living or working in Lebanon. Because use of the CIA would have required a presidential finding and notification of Congress, the NSC staff sought to manage this complex (some suggest bizarre) covert operation through private third parties, some of who were of doubtful reliability. Stymied on how to transport the weapons—mostly U.S.-made TOW antitank missiles and HAWK antiaircraft missiles—the White House staffers turned to the CIA and one of its proprietaries to handle the logistics of getting the weapons into Iran. A retroactive finding eventually authorized the CIA involvement, but the finding also ordered that Congress not be informed. (See sidebar, *Retroactive Finding.*) The finding was finally sent to Congress 10 months after Reagan signed it.[22]

Retroactive Finding

On December 5, 1985, President Reagan signed a presidential finding stating: "I direct the Director of Central Intelligence not to brief the Congress of the United States, . . . until such time as I may direct otherwise. . . . All prior actions taken by U.S. Government officials in furtherance of this effort are hereby ratified."

Source: U.S. Congress, *Report of the Committees Investigating the Iran-Contra Affair, with Supplemental, Minority, and Additional Views*, S. Rept. No. 100–216, H. Rept. No. 100–433, 100th Congress, First Session (Washington, DC: Government Printing Office, 1987), pp. 186, 195.

The first shipment of TOW missiles to Iran took place in August 1985. Fifteen months later, on November 3, 1986, after multiple shipments of TOW and HAWK missiles and the release of only three hostages, the story of the arms sales broke in a Lebanese magazine. *Al-Shiraa* was given the story by individuals in the Iranian government opposed to interacting with the Americans. The story provided such details as the trip to Tehran in May 1986 by former national security advisor McFarlane and a delegation to negotiate further exchanges of arms for hostages. The members of the group traveled unofficially—a potentially dangerous gesture since the country they were entering was clearly hostile to America. And they traveled in what they perceived to be the best covert tradition, using false passports, aliases, and pseudonyms. The group took a pallet of HAWK parts with them on the aircraft. The secretary of state was not advised of the trip. Similarly, the chairman of the JCS was not told about the arms sales. The day after the story broke in Lebanon, it was headline news in the U.S. media.

The NSC staff and others sought to conceal as many of the details of the arms sales as possible. Public denials, including from the president, became the norm. False and misleading statements were made to Congressional committees. Documents were altered and destroyed. Much of that effort was also directed at preventing the discovery of the linkage between the arms sales and aid to the Contras. As early as November 1985, the managers of the Iranian initiative had decided that by overcharging the Iranians for the weapons, profits could be generated that would benefit both the private entrepreneurs promoting the deal and the cash-strapped Contras. The funds that went toward supporting the Contras are referred to as the "diversion." Following revelation of the arms-for-hostages deal, Attorney General Edwin Meese noted discrepancies in the administration's public statements and testimony to Congress about the arms sales. He recommended that his office gather the facts on the situation. The president agreed. During his investigation, the "diversion" was uncovered. On November 25, 1986, the resignation of National Security Advisor John Poindexter and the reassignment of North to the Marine Corps were overshadowed by a statement from President Reagan and a press conference by Meese acknowledging the diversion of funds to the Contras from the arms sales to Iran.[23] In the end, the series of rapid exposures—under-the-table funding of the Contras, arms sales to Iran, inflating prices for a profit—added a taint of impropriety and even illegality to the whole affair.

Pursuing Terrorists

The 1970s and early 1980s saw numerous acts of international terrorism; but a succession of violent acts in 1985, combined with the taking of Western hostages by Hezbollah terrorists in Lebanon, seemed to bring the issue into greater focus for U.S. policy makers. Of particular note were the hijacking of TWA Flight 847 in June by Lebanese terrorists, in which a U.S. Navy diver who was onboard was murdered; the hijacking of the *Achille Lauro* cruise ship in October by Palestinian terrorists, highlighted by the murder of a Jewish-American tourist, the dumping of his body overboard, and the contrived escape of the terrorists with the collaboration of the Italian and Egyptian governments; and on December 27, terrorists of the Abu Nidal Organization (ANO) attacked the flight terminals at the airports in Vienna and Rome, wounding hundreds and killing 18 people including 5 Americans, one of whom was an 11-year-old girl.

In July 1985, the president established a task force under the vice president and led by Adm. James L. Holloway III, to study implementation of a counterterrorism strategy. The task force's recommendations were formalized in NSDD 207, of January 20, 1986, which declared terrorism to be a potential threat to U.S. national security that the government would use all legal means to combat.[24] (See sidebar, *NSDD 207*.) In February, the president reinforced those sentiments with a finding that authorized CIA covert operations against terrorists worldwide. At the same time, the CIA created a new cross-directorate, multidiscipline Counterterrorism Center (CTC). The original concept of the CTC proposed the organizing of "action teams" to capture terrorists wherever they were. However, the relationship between the legislative and executive branches was such that it was not difficult for members of Congress to see the nascent groups as "hit teams" that violated the ban against assassination. Congressional opposition moved the CTC into a different direction.

NSDD 207

"The U.S. Government considers the practice of terrorism by any person or group a potential threat to our national security and will resist the use of terrorism by all legal means available. . . . The entire range of diplomatic, economic, legal, military, paramilitary, covert action, and information assets at our disposal must be brought to bear against terrorism."

Source: Ronald Reagan, "National Security Decision Directive 207: The National Program for Combating Terrorism," January 20, 1986, at: http://www.fas.org/irp/offdocs/nsdd/nsdd-207.htm.

The CTC was organized into subunits that focused on different terrorist groups. One of the larger branches targeted Abu Nidal (born Sabri al-Banna) and the organization (ANO) he had built up following his break from al-Fatah in 1974. An agent within the ANO and the work of analysts from the CIA's Directorate of Intelligence allowed the CTC to develop a detailed picture of Abu Nidal's extensive commercial network. The decision was made that publicly revealing that network would put pressure on those countries in Eastern and Western Europe directly and indirectly collaborating in his activities. The CTC arranged the publication of *The Abu Nidal Handbook*, a detailed accounting of the ANO's crimes and accomplices with names and addresses. This was sufficient for even Poland and East Germany to terminate their dealings with the ANO.

At the same time that it was working to deny the ANO safe harbors outside of its home bases in southern Lebanon and Libya, the CTC began a program that essentially played on the paranoia intrinsic to many who live a high-risk, clandestine life. CTC case officers began making recruitment pitches to ANO personnel in various countries, both in the hopes of acquiring another agent and as a means of sowing dissension among the organization's ranks. Those who reported being approached by the CIA were not hailed as loyal followers but were, instead, tortured and killed. Aware that the CIA was targeting him, Abu Nidal turned his terror tactics to his own organization and essentially destroyed it from within. During 1987, hundreds of ANO follow-ers were slaughtered (in one case, 170 on a single night) in southern Lebanon and Libya. Defections from the ANO snowballed as more insiders were killed or simply disappeared, and by the end of the 1980s, Abu Nidal and the ANO were no longer major players among international terrorist organizations.[25]

Notes

1. See Nicholas Dujmovic, "Reagan, Intelligence, Casey, and the CIA: A Reap-praisal," *International Journal of Intelligence and CounterIntelligence* 26, no. 1 (2013): 1–30.

2. Robert M. Gates, *From the Shadows: The Ultimate Insider's Story of Five Pres-idents and How They Won the Cold War* (New York: Simon & Schuster, 1996), pp. 161–69, 226–37; and Douglas J. MacEachin, *US Intelligence and the Confrontation in Poland, 1980–1981* (University Park: Penn State University Press, 2002).

3. Carl Bernstein, "The Holy Alliance," *Time*, February 24, 1992, at: http://content.time.com/time/magazine/article/0,9171,159069,00.html.

4. Ibid.; and Arch Puddington, "How American Unions Helped Solidarity Win," at: http://www.videofact.com/help_for_solidarity.html.

5. Gates, *From the Shadows*, p. 358.

6. See Milt Bearden and James Risen, *The Main Enemy: The Inside Story of the CIA's Final Showdown with the KGB* (New York: Random House, 2003), pp. 205–96, 308–18, 331–67; Steve Coll, *Ghost Wars: The Secret History of the CIA, Afghanistan, and Bin Laden, from the Soviet Invasion to September 10, 2001* (New York: Penguin, 2004); and George Crile, *Charlie Wilson's War: The Extraordinary Story of the Largest Covert Operation in History* (New York: Atlantic Monthly, 2003).

7. On Charlie Wilson and the Oerlikon, see Gary J. Schmitt, "My War with Charlie Wilson," *Daily Standard*, December 28, 2007, at: http://www.aei.org/article/foreign-and-defense-policy/regional/asia/my-war-with-charlie-wilson. See also, Bob Woodward, *Veil: The Secret Wars of the CIA, 1981–1987* (New York: Simon & Schus-ter, 1987), pp. 356–59.

8. See Bearden, *The Main Enemy*, pp. 358–59; Steve Coll, "Anatomy of a Vic-tory: CIA's Covert Afghan War," *Washington Post*, July 19, 1992, p. A1, and "In CIA's Covert Afghan War, Where to Draw the Line Was Key," *Washington Post*, July 20, 1992, p. A1; Gates, *From the Shadows*, pp. 349–50, 429–32; and L. Britt Snider, "Chapter 9: Oversight of Covert Action—Afghanistan: 1979–87," *The Agency and the Hill: CIA's Relationship with Congress, 1946–2004* (Washington, DC: Central Intelligence Agency, Center for the Study of Intelligence, 2008), pp. 283–85.

9. See John T. Carney Jr., and Benjamin F. Schemmer, *No Room for Error: The Covert Operations of America's Special Tactics Units from Iran to Afghanistan* (New York: Presidio Press, 2001), pp. 184–89; *United States Special Operations Command: History*, 6th ed. (MacDill Air Force Base, FL: United States Special Operation Command, 2008), at: http://www.socom.mil/Documents/history6thedition.pdf; and Lucien S. Vandenbroucke, *Perilous Options: Special Operations as an Instrument of U.S. Foreign Policy* (New York: Oxford University Press, 1993), pp. 171–73.

10. See William G. Boykin, *The Origins of the United States Special Operations Command* (MacDill Air Force Base, FL: United States Special Operation Command, n.d.), at: http://www.afsoc.af.mil/Portals/1/documents/history/AFD-051228-009.pdf. The Goldwater-Nichols Act of 1986 (U.S. Code, Title 10, Subtitle A, Part I, Chapter 5) is at: http://www.au.af.mil/au/awc/awcgate/congress/title_10.htm. See also, James R. Locher, *Victory on the Potomac: The Goldwater-Nichols Act Unifies the Pentagon* (College Station: Texas A&M University Press, 2002).

11. Vandenbroucke, *Perilous Options*, p. 174.

12. See Stephen S. Rosenfeld, "The Reagan Doctrine: The Guns of July," *Foreign Affairs* 65 (Spring 1986), at: http://www.foreignaffairs.com/articles/40801/stephen-s-rosenfeld/the-reagan-doctrine-the-guns-of-july.

13. Gates, *From the Shadows*, pp. 346–48; John Prados, *Safe for Democracy: The Secret Wars of the CIA* (Chicago: Ivan R. Dee, 2006), p. 503; and Snider, "Angola and South Africa: 1985–88," *The Agency and the Hill*, pp. 286–87.

14. Ibid., pp. 433–34; and Prados, *Secret Wars of the CIA*, pp. 503, 575, 579–80. See also Chester A. Crocker, *High Noon in Southern Africa: Making Peace in a Rough Neighborhood* (New York: W. W. Norton, 1992). On Cuba's involvement in the Angolan civil war, see Edward George, *The Cuban Intervention in Angola, 1965–1991: From Che Guevara to Cuito Cuanavale* (London: Frank Cass, 2005).

15. U.S. Congress, *Report of the Committees Investigating the Iran-Contra Affair, with Supplemental, Minority, and Additional Views*, S. Rept. No. 100–216, H. Rept. No. 100–433, 100th Congress, First Session (Washington, DC: Government Printing Office, 1987), p. 27. See also, Woodward, *Veil*, pp. 110–12.

16. See Duane R. ("Dewey") Clarridge, with Digby Diehl, *A Spy for All Seasons: My Life in the CIA* (New York: Scribner's, 1997), pp. 196–210, 221; Gates, *From the Shadows*, pp. 242–45; and Snider, "Central America: 1979–86," *The Agency and the Hill*, pp. 287–89. The December 1, 1981, finding is available at: http://www.brown.edu/Research/Understanding_the_Iran_Contra_Affair/documents/d-all-45.pdf; the accompanying NSDD-17, dated January 4, 1982, is available at: http://www.reagan.utexas.edu/archives/reference/Scanned%20NSDDS/NSDD17.pdf.

17. Clarridge, *Spy for All Seasons*, pp. 218–25; and Gates, *From the Shadows*, pp. 245–47. Early newspaper coverage includes Don Oberdorfer and Patrick E. Tyler, "Reagan Backs Action Plan for Central America," *Washington Post*, February 14, 1982, pp. A1, A4; Patrick E. Tyler and Bob Woodward, "U.S. Approves Covert Plan in Nicaragua," *Washington Post*, March 10, 1982, pp. A1, A6; and Leslie H. Gelb, "U.S. Said to Plan Covert Actions in Latin Region," *New York Times*, March 14, 1982, pp. 1, 12.

18. On the Boland Amendment, see P.L. 97–377, Stat. 1865. Sec. 793, cited in U.S. Congress, Senate, *Senate Report, Iran-Contra Investigation, Appendix C, Chronology of Events*, S. Rept. No. 100–216, 100th Congress, First Session (Washington, DC: Government Printing Office, 1987), p. 2. See also the report of the Independent Counsel: Lawrence E. Walsh, "Part I: The Underlying Facts," *Final Report of the Independent Counsel for Iran-Contra Matters, Vol. 1: Investigations and Prosecutions* (Washington, DC: United States Court of Appeals for the District of Columbia Circuit, August 4, 1993), available at: http://www.fas.org/irp/offdocs/walsh.

19. Gates, *From the Shadows*, pp. 298–301, 306–11; U.S. Congress, Senate, *Chronology of Events*, pp. 4, 5, 6, 7, 8, 9, 12, 16; Woodward, *Veil*, 308–10, 338–39,

361–70, 402–4. See also, David Rogers, "U.S. Role in Mining Nicaraguan Harbors Reportedly Is Larger than First Thought," *Wall Street Journal*, April 6, 1984, p. A9.

20. U.S. Congress, *Report of the Committees*, pp. 31, 39–40, 43, 44. See also, Gates, *From the Shadows*, 390–403. For detailed accounts with varying viewpoints, see William S. Cohen and George J. Mitchell, *Men of Zeal: A Candid Inside Story of the Iran-Contra Hearings* (New York: Viking Penguin, 1988); Theodore Draper, *A Very Thin Line: The Iran-Contra Affair* (New York: Hill and Wang, 1991); and Peter Kornbluh and Malcolm Byrne, eds., *The Iran-Contra Scandal: The Declassified History, A National Security Archive Documents Reader* (New York: New Press, 1993).

21. U.S. Congress, *Report of the Committees*, pp. 59–72, 99; Gates, *From the Shadows*, pp. 434–36; Prados, *Secret Wars*, pp. 570–571, 581.

22. U.S. Congress, *Report of the Committees*, pp. 166–68, 175–77, 185, 186, 195.

23. Ibid., pp. 168, 179, 221, 237, 247, 280, 305, 309–10, 316–17.

24. Ronald Reagan, "National Security Decision Directive 179: Task Force on Combating Terrorism," July 20, 1985, at: https://www.fas.org/irp/offdocs/nsdd/nsdd-179.htm; and "National Security Decision Directive 207: The National Program for Combating Terrorism," January 20, 1986, at: http://www.fas.org/irp/offdocs/nsdd/nsdd-207.htm.

25. Clarridge, *Spy for All Seasons*, pp. 331–36; Coll, *Ghost Wars*, pp. 137–144; and Mark Perry, *Eclipse: The Last Days of the CIA* (New York: Morrow, 1992), pp. 189–93.

CHAPTER 9

New Presidents, New Rules: 1989–2001

It was well into the presidency of George H. W. Bush (1989–1993) before Congress completed its renegotiation with the White House of the ground rules governing the executive-legislative relationship concerning covert operations. Many of the legislatively enacted changes had been put in place by presidential directive, but Congress wanted the changes to have the effect of law.

New Rules

The Intelligence Authorization Act of 1991 embodied the effort to reinforce legislative oversight of covert operations and to circumscribe future short-circuiting of the finding process. The Act, signed by President Bush on August 14, 1991, requires that:

- The President determine that a covert operation by any U.S. Government entity (not just the CIA) supports "identifiable foreign policy objectives" and is important to U.S. national security.
- Findings be in writing. In an emergency, a written finding must be produced within 48 hours of the decision. With that exception, no finding may be retroactive.
- The finding identify any U.S. Government entity or "third party" (such as, a foreign government) that may be involved in funding or otherwise participating in the covert operation.
- The Director of Central Intelligence (changed to Director of National Intelligence in 2004) and the head of any U.S. Government entity involved keep the intelligence committees "fully and currently" informed.
- Findings be reported to the intelligence committees prior to initiating a covert operation. In extraordinary circumstances, the report may be limited to the House

Speaker and minority leader, the Senate majority and minority leaders, and the chairs and ranking minority members of the intelligence committees (the "Gang of Eight").

- When a finding is not reported prior to initiation of a covert operation, the President must still inform the committees in a "timely fashion" of the finding and provide a statement as to why prior notice was not given.
- The President ensure that any significant change to a previously approved covert operation is reported to the committees or, if necessary, the specified members of Congress.[1]

In his statement on signing the Intelligence Authorization Act of 1991, President Bush expressed concerns about the new law:

> Several provisions in the Act requiring the disclosure of certain information to the Congress raise constitutional concerns. These provisions cannot be construed to detract from the President's constitutional authority to withhold information the disclosure of which could significantly impair foreign relations, the national security, the deliberative processes of the Executive, or the performance of the Executive's constitutional duties.[2]

A Changing Dynamic

The world scene changed dramatically during George H. W. Bush's four years in the Oval Office. These changes affected the number, nature, and targets of new covert operations. Several long-running covert operations were being wrapped up as the Reagan years ended, but carrying them to conclusion became the responsibility of Bush and his national security team.

In Afghanistan, the Soviet Union completed its withdrawal on February 15, 1989. However, the Soviets and the United States continued to support their respective sides until the end of 1991. A grouping of tribal warlords overthrew Najibullah the next year, but was in turn displaced by the Taliban in 1996.

By the end of August 1989, a Solidarity-led government was in place in Poland, and overt support to the growth of freedom there replaced covert operations. Similarly, as the Berlin Wall fell to sledgehammers in the hands of German citizens on November 9–10, 1989 and the other Communist governments in Eastern Europe—Bulgaria, Czechoslovakia, Hungary, Romania—surrendered to the will of their people, the role of covert operations disappeared. An effort based on diplomacy and new, overt organizations to assist the East European countries in making the transition to democratic institutions took the place of the old Cold War covert methods.

In Angola, Bush continued covert aid to the UNITA faction in the war for the first two years of his administration, but that support appears to have ended with the withdrawal of Cuban forces by July 1991. Nonetheless, Jonas Savimbi and UNITA fought on until Savimbi's death in 2002.

In Nicaragua, the termination of CIA paramilitary assistance in early 1988 added a sense of urgency to the Contras' participation in mediation efforts with the Sandinista government. For their part, the Sandinistas were experiencing economic difficulties (exacerbated by the U.S. embargo) and a slowdown in Soviet military and financial aid. An agreement brokered by Central American political leaders led to the demobilization of the Contras in December 1989. Free elections followed in February 1990, and the Sandinistas lost to a multiparty coalition led by Violeta Chamorro, who had headed the anti-Somoza and anti-Sandinista newspaper *La Prensa* since her husband's murder in 1978.

The most far-reaching change to the international environment occurred on December 25, 1991, when the red flag of the Union of Soviet Socialist Republics (USSR) was replaced on the Kremlin with the tricolor flag of Russia. The dissolution of the Soviet Union concluded an often hidden struggle that had reached so many corners of the world. As the president most versed in covert affairs since Eisenhower, Bush found himself turning less to covert operations than to the overt use of military power.

The Noriega Problem

Among the ongoing issues on the administration's to-do list was Manuel Noriega. The Panamanian dictator had been indicted by a U.S. grand jury in 1988 on drug trafficking and racketeering charges. Noriega was a problem for Bush, since he had met with the Panamanian leader on multiple occasions, both as director of Central Intelligence (DCI) and, as recently as 1983, as vice president. During both the Republican primaries and the presidential election campaign, Bush faced probing questions about the relationship.[3]

From the late-1950s through his rise in the ranks of the Panamanian Defense Forces (PDF), Noriega probably was a paid source of intelligence for the CIA. By the 1970s, Noriega was the head of Panamanian military intelligence under strongman Omar Torrijos. Noriega's reputation was already sufficiently tainted that former DCI Stansfield Turner (1977–1981) reportedly said he had Noriega dropped from the ranks of U.S. paid informants, only to hear that the relationship had been restarted in the Reagan administration.[4] After Torrijos died in a plane crash in 1981, Noriega emerged as the successor and consolidated his hold on both the PDF and the civilian government. During the early to mid-1980s, Noriega and Panama played a significant role in supporting the war against the Sandinista government in Nicaragua and the guerrilla forces in El Salvador. However, questions continued to be raised in Congress and the media about Noriega's relationship with Cuba, his ties to drug smuggling and money laundering, and the internal brutality of his regime.

Following Noriega's indictment in February 1988, presidential findings in April and May authorized covert political assistance—propaganda, a low-power mobile radio transmitter, and other nonlethal support—to opposition groups in Panama. After Noriega rejected a State Department initiative for him to step down, a new finding directed the CIA to work with disaffected PDF members to remove Noriega from office. Because a military coup could result in Noriega's death, the Senate Select Committee on Intelligence (SSCI) objected and the finding was withdrawn. Meanwhile, covert financial and other support to the groups organizing for a Panamanian national election increased. An anti-Noriega coalition of parties won the May 1989 election; but Noriega nullified the results, declaring them a fraud by the U.S.-backed candidates. The broadcasting on American television of a vicious attack by Noriega supporters on the opposition candidates for president and vice president increased public pressure on President Bush to "do something" about Noriega. An ill-conceived coup attempt by a group of PDF officers in October 1989, undertaken without U.S. support, was brutally put down. U.S.-Panama relations continued on a downward spiral as pro-Noriega forces increased incidents of harassment and violence against American civilians and military personnel. Then on December 15, Noriega "declared war," if just verbally, on the United States. Since it was now clear that covert operations would not force Noriega into giving up the reins of power, Washington turned to the direct use of U.S. military power.[5]

Invading Panama

The U.S. invasion of Panama—Operation JUST CAUSE—gave the new Joint Special Operations Command its first test under fire. A Joint Special Operations Task Force (JSOTF) was formed to plan, coordinate, and oversee the participation of multiple special operations units. Overall, the U.S. Special Operations Forces (SOF) were used in an appropriate manner (rather than being thrown in to augment conventional forces); and the operation was marked by improved but not perfect coordination among the various special operators and between those forces and conventional forces.

Operation JUST CAUSE was launched in the morning of December 20. It began with simultaneous assaults by special operations forces on key PDF installations. The JSOTF commander divided his forces into five task forces, each with its own objectives:

- Task Force RED, primarily troops from the 75th Infantry Regiment (Ranger), conducted airborne assaults against Rio Hato Military Base and Omar Torrijos International Airport and the adjacent Tocumen Military Airfield (Torrijos-Tocumen Airport), the latter a critical objective.

- Task Force BLACK was based on Southern Command's 3rd Battalion, 7th Special Forces, reinforced by a Special Forces company. On day one, it seized control of the Pacora River Bridge and took Panamanian TV Channel 2 and Radio Nacional's AM and FM transmitters off the air.
- Task Force WHITE, with Navy SEALs and Special Boat units, conducted operations in Panama City, Balboa Harbor, and Colón Harbor. One SEAL team landed from the sea near Punta Paitilla Airfield where in heavy fighting they destroyed Noriega's personal jet. Another SEAL unit sank a Panamanian patrol boat in Balboa Harbor by affixing demolition charges on its hull.
- The Army Special Forces of Task Force GREEN rescued an American businessman arrested while running a covert anti-Noriega radio operation and imprisoned in the Carcel Modelo near the PDF headquarters compound, *La Comandancio*.
- Task Force GREEN and Task Force BLUE (Navy SEALs) were prepared to rescue any hostages taken by the Noriega regime.

The main attack came when U.S conventional forces entered Panama City, secured the U.S. Embassy, and, in a three-hour firefight, captured the PDF headquarters. Army Special Forces' attack helicopters supported the attack on *La Comandancio*. With the loss of central command and control capabilities and the absence of Noriega, organized resistance began to diminish. However, pockets of resistance remained, and marauding members of the so-called Dignity Battalions, Noriega's paramilitary supporters, remained an issue for some time. Noriega evaded capture and sought asylum in the papal *Nunciatura*. He remained there until January 3, 1990, when he surrendered to the U.S. military and was handed over to agents of the Drug Enforcement Agency and transported to Homestead Air Force Base.[6]

Operation Desert Shield/Desert Storm

Iraq invaded Kuwait on August 2, 1990. By August 7, acting on the request of King Fahd, President Bush had launched Operation DESERT SHIELD, with U.S. fighter squadrons and ground troops from the 82nd Airborne Division deploying to Saudi Arabia. Special operations personnel from the navy, air force, and army followed.

Although special operations forces were involved in multiple aspects of the multiphased Operation DESERT SHIELD/DESERT STORM, it is generally accepted that the U.S. Central Command commander in chief, Gen. H. Norman Schwarzkopf, neither liked nor trusted unconventional forces, a fairly common attitude at the time among long-serving infantry officers. Throughout the buildup to DESERT STORM, Schwarzkopf seemed to keep special operations on a short leash, requiring that he personally approve all cross-border operations.[7] Much of the work of the army and navy special operations personnel involved specialized training for and coordination with the forces of Saudi

Arabia, Kuwait, Egypt, and others of the more than 30 coalition partners. Saudi and special operations units were placed along the border in order to act as a "trip wire" for U.S. intervention should Iraq invade Saudi Arabia.

On November 29, 1990, UN Security Council Resolution 678 set a deadline for Iraqi withdrawal from Kuwait of January 15, 1991. When Iraq failed to meet that deadline, President Bush initiated the first phase of Operation DESERT STORM—an aerial bombing campaign involving fixed-wing aircraft, helicopters, and Tomahawk cruise missiles. This became the first war televised "live," as millions watched as CNN broadcast images of the air attack on Baghdad. An initial attack by Army AH-64 Apache helicopters to take out Iraqi antiaircraft radar installations and clear an air corridor into western Iraq was led by Air Force Special Operations MH-53 Pave Low helicopters. A number of fixed Scud missile sites in western Iraq, identified by satellite and other intelligence, were destroyed in the early bombing attacks, but the Iraqis retained a large number of mobile Scud missile launchers. The first wave of what became more than 30 Iraqi Scuds was launched against Israel on January 17. Other Scuds were fired at Saudi Arabia. Teams of Delta Force operators supported by Army Rangers and 160th SOAR (A) helicopters were covertly inserted deep into Iraq to aid in locating and destroying Scud sites.

As the time for beginning the ground campaign neared, there was an increase in reconnaissance penetrations into Iraq by special operations forces to check potential routes for heavy armor. At the same time, Navy SEALs and Special Boat personnel conducted operations that were part of Central Command's deception plan to convince the Iraqis there would be a sea-based assault. Other special forces reconnaissance teams were infiltrated deep behind enemy lines to monitor potential routes for counterattack.[8]

The ground war began on February 24, 1991 (Washington time), with army, Marines, and coalition forces moving into Iraq and Kuwait. By February 26, U.S. and Allied forces controlled Kuwait City. Members of the underground Kuwaiti Resistance greeted the liberating forces. Internal resistance to the Iraqi occupation initially included armed attacks on Iraqi forces, but harsh reprisals forced the resistance into activities more focused on gathering intelligence and communicating that intelligence to the coalition. U.S. special operators also were involved in helping to reconstitute both the Kuwaiti army and navy.[9] When President Bush announced a cease-fire on February 27, Iraq had been soundly defeated and its forces had fled in disorder out of Kuwait.

Among the contributions made by American special operations forces to the coalition victory in Operation DESERT SHIELD/DESERT STORM was a lengthy and substantial psychological operations (PSYOPS) campaign. Led by the 4th Psychological Operations Group (Airborne), coalition PSYOPS encompassed leaflet, radio, and loudspeaker activities that continued throughout the air and ground phases of the conflict. The target was the morale of Iraqi troops. By the war's end, almost 30 million leaflets, ranging from black-and-white to four-color flyers, had been air dropped, mostly by MC-130 Combat Talon aircraft. (See sidebar, *Leaflet Exemplars.*) The Voice of the Gulf radio network went on the air on January 19, 1991 and broadcast on both AM and FM frequencies through March. The operation utilized fixed transmitters sited in Saudi Arabia, as well as EC-130 aircraft, to carry the message of "surrender or die" to the Iraqi troops. That message was reinforced by the deployment of tactical PSYOPS loudspeaker teams with major ground units. The loudspeaker teams included Arabic speakers and broadcast instructions on how to surrender. Although the intensive bombing campaign probably was the primary reason for the virtual collapse of many Iraqi units, the PSYOPS campaign can also be credited with convincing Iraqi soldiers that it was safe to desert, defect, or surrender when the ground assault began. Many of those defecting or surrendering met the coalition forces with "safe conduct" leaflets in hand.[10]

Leaflet Exemplars

For bombing campaign: "Warning! . . . This could have been a real bomb. We have no desire to harm innocent people, but Saddam is leading you to certain death and destruction. . . . [T]he Multi-National Forces have the ability to strike anywhere . . . and at anytime! Warning!"

With image of stealth bomber: "This location is subject to bombardment. Escape now and save yourselves."

Targeting specific units: "The 16th Infantry Division will be bombed tomorrow. The bombing will be heavy. . . . Save yourselves and head toward the Saudi border, where you will be welcomed as a brother."

Daisy Cutter bombs: "You have just experienced the most powerful conventional bomb dropped in the war. It has more explosive power than 20 SCUD missiles. You will be bombed again soon. . . . Flee south and you will be treated fairly."

Safe conduct passes: "The bearer of this card is permitted to cross the borders to the Joint Forces. . . . He will receive good treatment so that he reaches the nearest Joint Forces Headquarters in complete safety without being exposed to any danger. He will be treated according to the Geneva Convention."

Source: 4th Psychological Operations Group (Airborne), "Leaflets of the Persian Gulf War" (Ft. Bragg, North Carolina, 1991), at: http://www.psywar.org/psywar/reproductions/ LeafletsPersianGulfWar.pdf.

In the wake of the chaotic situation following Iraq's defeat, the Shiites in the south and the Kurds in the north of the country revolted against the central authority of Baghdad. Although his army had fled Kuwait in total dis-array, absent U.S. intervention, Saddam Hussein retained sufficient military might in his Revolutionary Guards to brutally put down these challenges to his rule. Saddam Hussein and his regime would remain a target for U.S. covert operations, and eventually military force, for two more administrations.

New Leadership Arrives

When William Jefferson Clinton (1993–2001) moved into the Oval Office, the basic dynamic of America's national security policy was evolving out of a Soviet-centric model to a more diverse version. Covert and special opera-tions would move from a concentration on countries and geographic "blocs" to more amorphous issues, such as terrorism, organized crime, and prolifera-tion of weapons of mass destruction. R. James Woolsey summed up the chal-lenge well in testimony to the SSCI in early 1993 prior to his confirmation as DCI: "We have slain a large dragon. But we live now in a jungle filled with a bewildering variety of poisonous snakes. And in many ways, the dragon was easier to keep track of."[11]

Woolsey's look into the future was made at the same time that the downsiz-ing of the country's military and of its covert and special operations capabili-ties, which had begun under the Bush administration, was gaining momentum under the rubric of the "peace dividend." The end of the Cold War brought with it a lessened number of findings during the Bush administration, and this trend continued under Clinton. Nevertheless, several existing covert opera-tions, some with findings dating back to the Reagan years, continued.

Imbroglio in Somalia

America's ever-deepening involvement in Somalia in the early 1990s began with what President Bush believed would be a relatively brief humanitarian intervention coordinated with the United Nations. Even before the deploy-ment of U.S. troops to Somalia, personnel from the 5th Special Forces Group (Airborne) had been providing security for UN humanitarian flights from Kenya to the chaotic and famine-stricken country. In the interim between President Bush's decision to take a leadership role in the UN's relief efforts (Operation RESTORE HOPE) and the landing of U.S. Marines on December 9, 1992, Navy SEALs and a Special Boat Unit conducted hydrographic recon-naissance to map the beaches on which the Marines would be landing. The Marines' amphibious landing, targeted on securing the Mogadishu airport, went smoothly. It was met not with hostile fire but the news media. The absence of local opposition has been attributed to the negotiations with Somali warlords by a small team of CIA officers dispatched to Mogadishu to restart intelligence collection activities that had been closed down by budget cuts.[12]

The presence of the American troops improved the effort to distribute food and other supplies in the country. A Joint Psychological Operations Task Force (JPOTF) supported the military's armed component in this endeavor. The JPOTF used native Somali speakers on contract to produce Somali language radio broadcasts, a newspaper (*Rajo*), and millions of copies of leaflets, handbills, and posters. Nevertheless, the internal security situation continued to deteriorate. Between March and May 1993, a UN multinational force (UN Operations Somalia or UNOSOM II) replaced many of the U.S. forces. At the same time, in a classic case of "mission creep," the UN objective in Somalia grew from a humanitarian relief activity into an effort to restore some version of a viable Somali state. In June, forces of Somali warlord Mohammed Farah Aideed ambushed and killed 24 Pakistani soldiers from the UN contingent. The UN response included putting a price on Aideed's head, ground assaults against Aideed's strongholds in Mogadishu, and combat missions by U.S. Air Force AC-130 gunships of the Air Force Special Operations Command. Although the attacks resulted in driving Aideed into hiding, the level of violence only increased.

Continuing attacks by Aideed's supporters on UN and U.S. forces and installations brought on the deployment by President Clinton and Defense Secretary Les Aspin of a JSOTF in August 1993. Task Force Ranger's mission was to capture Aideed and his main lieutenants. An incursion by the Task Force into Aideed-controlled territory on October 3 resulted in an overnight urban battle known as the Battle of Mogadishu or, more popularly, as Black Hawk Down after the title of a best-selling book and movie.[13] Operating under increasingly heavy fire from Aideed's forces, the combined Ranger and Special Forces assault team was initially successful in capturing two dozen Somalis. However, things turned increasingly negative after a rocket-propelled grenade shot down one of the covering MH-60 Black Hawk helicopters. Shortly after, a second Black Hawk was shot down, its occupants killed by a Somali mob, and the pilot taken captive (later released). Two of the special operations defenders at the second crash site were posthumously awarded the Medal of Honor. The troops isolated near the first crash site were rescued the next day by a ground force combining Rangers, Navy SEALs, a Quick Reaction Force from the 10th Mountain Division, Pakistani tanks, and Malaysian armored personnel carriers, with cover provided by U.S. Army helicopters. Task Force Ranger lost 16 members killed while the 10th Mountain had two killed. Graphic images on American television of the bodies of U.S. casualties from the second helicopter crash being dragged through the streets by Somali crowds was more than the U.S. body politic could stand. President Clinton immediately provided armored reinforcements to the U.S. forces in Somalia and also began planning to withdraw U.S. troops. Most of the American forces were out of Somalia by March 25, 1994.

More Trouble in Iraq

Saddam Hussein's Iraq was another holdover covert operation from the Bush administration. Although Bush decided against having the coalition forces push on to Baghdad after evicting the Iraqis from Kuwait, he signed a finding in May 1991 for a covert operation to encourage Iraqi government and military officials and other individuals and groups, inside and outside Iraq, to take action to remove Saddam from power. To this end, the CIA began developing relationships with Iraqi exile groups and other dissidents, particularly the Kurdish minority in northern Iraq. With the CIA's encouragement, Iraqi opposition leaders created an umbrella group, the Iraqi National Congress (INC), and elected Ahmed Chalabi, a secular Iraqi Shiite living in exile, as its chairman. Using American money, Chalabi opened an office in Kurdish-controlled northern Iraq in 1992. He also established media outlets there, including radio and television broadcasting.

Difficulties arose early in the CIA-Chalabi relationship. As the CIA experienced in its early days, working with exile groups had distinct drawbacks. For one thing, they tend to have their own agendas. Chalabi was adept at end runs when CIA decisions did not fit his interests, going straight to Congress to lobby for additional support. Such groups also tend to be less than careful stewards of the largesse bestowed upon them, leaving government organizations (in this case the CIA's Iraq Operations Group) with concerns about how the U.S. money is being spent. And they are prone to penetration and become counterintelligence nightmares.

Using the Kurdish forces that controlled an enclave in northern Iraq as a launch pad for overthrowing Saddam made sense geographically, but the two major Kurdish armed groups—the Kurdish Democratic Party and Patriotic Union of Kurdistan—expended too much of their energy fighting each other. A plan, involving the Kurdish forces and Shia groups and military units inside Iraq, to topple Saddam's regime was undercut when Washington learned Chalabi was trying to sell it to the Iranians on the basis of U.S. military support. This was accompanied by an uproar at the National Security Council (NSC) over reports that a U.S. representative had said he wanted to kill/assassinate Saddam. Chalabi went forward with the plan without U.S. support. The early March 1995 "uprising" only generated a low-level series of attacks and went nowhere. Over the following 18 months, CIA covert operations to overthrow Saddam were largely destroyed. In June 1996, Iraqi security forces arrested and executed as many 100 army officers and other anti-Saddam dissidents associated with the Iraqi National Accord, another CIA-funded group based in Jordan. Then, in August, Saddam Hussein sent his military forces into northern Iraq and decimated the INC when the White House chose not to use U.S. airpower to interdict the Iraqi forces. The remnants of the INC fled the country, and perhaps as many as 5,000 Kurds and Iraqis were evacuated.[14]

In late 1996, the Clinton administration decided to cease funding the INC; and by February 1997, the CIA had terminated its relationship with Chalabi. However, continued lobbying of sympathetic members of Congress by Chalabi and other Iraqi exiles paid off. In a clear example of an overt commitment to wage covert war, Congress passed the Iraq Liberation Act of 1998 (Public Law 105–338). Reluctantly signed by the president on October 31, 1998, the act declared U.S. support for efforts to remove Saddam Hussein from power and authorized assistance (capped at $97 million) to support a transition to democracy in Iraq. The president gave responsibility for administering the funds to the State Department. In early 1999, the president named the INC as one of seven approved groups; but disputes in Congress over whether the money should go to organizations inside or outside Iraq delayed the release of funds until after the George W. Bush (2001–2009) administration was in place.[15]

Congress and "Covertness"

With passage of the Iraq Liberation Act and its public declaration of support for "regime change" in another country, Congress reinforced an emerging trend that had arguably drained the concept of "covert operations" of much of its previous meaning. The details of what was being done may be hidden, but not the fact of the target and certainly not the activity's sponsor.

Congress's action in 1998 had been foreshadowed almost three years earlier. House Speaker Newt Gingrich, who had publicly espoused the need for covert operations to oust the Iranian regime, inserted an additional $18 million in classified funding in the Intelligence Authorization Act for Fiscal Year 1996 (Public Law 104–93) for a CIA covert program designed to "change the behavior" of the Iranian government. The president, the Senate leadership, and the CIA all opposed the plan as likely to be ineffective and a waste of funds. CIA officials also worried that launching a covert operation at the direction of Congress rather than the president would place the Agency in a vulnerable position in the executive-legislative battles that had characterized much of the Clinton administration. Although Gingrich's "add" to the CIA budget was within the classified portion of the bill, it was leaked into the media even before the bill was passed at the end of December 1995. Passage of the act left the CIA under a mandate to launch a covert operation it did not believe was feasible and the "covertness" of which was already blown.[16]

The Disintegration of Yugoslavia

The breakup of Yugoslavia, expected since the death of Josip Broz Tito in 1980, began in earnest 10 years later. Slovenia and Croatia each declared independence on June 25, 1991. Bosnia-Herzegovina followed in May 1992. Warfare in Croatia between Croatian and Serbian forces continued until 1995, and from 1992 saw the intervention of some 14,000 UN troops (United Nations Protection Force or UNPROFOR) to separate the warring sides. However, it was the horrific ethnic war being waged by Serbs in Bosnia-Herzegovina that finally forced the United Nations and the North Atlantic Treaty Organization (NATO) into a more concerted action.

The Bush administration basically had chosen to leave the issue in the hands of Europe. However, the reluctance of the European Community to intervene saw the killing continue. The Clinton administration began advocating a "lift and strike" policy, that is, lifting the arms embargo that was penalizing the Bosnian Muslims and striking Bosnian Serb targets from the air. In April 1993, NATO began enforcing a no-fly zone over Bosnia-Herzegovina (Operation DENY FLIGHT). U.S. Air Force special operations forces from the 16th Special Operations Wing and the 352nd Special Operations Group initially provided search and rescue capability for NATO air operations and later close air support to UNPROFOR. Finally, in February 1994, NATO, with the UN secretary-general's approval, gave the green light to air strikes against Serbian aggressive activity. In the latter part of 1994 and the first half of 1995, NATO conducted limited air strikes against Bosnian Serb military targets when those forces violated UN Security Council Resolutions. The Srebrenica massacre of mid-July 1995 shocked world opinion and then on August 28, 1995, a Bosnian Serb mortar shell dropped into a Sarajevo market, killing 38 civilians and injuring 85 more. Two days later, NATO launched a sustained air campaign—Operation DELIBERATE FORCE. Combined with an offensive from Croatian, Bosnian Croatian, and Bosnian Muslim forces, the airstrikes brought about a cease-fire in October and led to the Dayton Peace Accords in November and the Paris Peace Agreement a month later. Implementation of the peace agreement was the responsibility of NATO's Implementation Force (IFOR)—Operation JOINT ENDEAVOR.

There were few military challenges to the division-level U.S. military presence in Bosnia that, along with contingents from Britain and France, was the underpinning of the peace agreement. However, U.S. SOF were called upon to play a role other than combat action, undertaking a series of liaison, coordination, and civil action activities. As part of IFOR, U.S. Army Special Forces personnel from the 10th Special Forces Group (Airborne) deployed to Bosnia in December 1995. For the next year, they and limited numbers of U.S. Air Force Special Operations Tactical Air Control operators served as liaison and coordination elements to the IFOR troops from non-NATO countries. In December 1996, IFOR transitioned to the Stabilization Force (SFOR)—Operation JOINT GUARD—and Army Special Forces took over Joint Commission Observer (JCO) operations from British special operations personnel. JCO teams of six to eight men (drawn from an Army Special Forces A-Team augmented by air force special operators and/or Navy SEALs) lived in specific neighborhoods with ready access to the local population and leaders. Their job was to report back the "ground truth" to the Combined Joint Special Operations Task Force at SFOR Headquarters and to work to diffuse local tensions as they arose. By eating at local restaurants, moving in relatively small groups, and wearing other than full combat gear, JCO teams openly intermingled with the local population, building access, and winning trust and sometimes cooperation. Despite some grumbling from the more traditional military establishment, the JCO mission continued until 2001.[17]

An NSC Covert Operation?

During Washington's deliberations in 1994 about what to do in Bosnia, the CIA found itself in the middle of what looked like another Iran-Contra—a rogue covert operation initiated from within the NSC and the State Department and not reported to the congressional oversight committees. The incident gained public attention following an article in the *Los Angeles Times* in April 1996 accusing President Clinton of allowing covert Iranian arms shipments to Bosnian forces in contravention of the UN arms embargo to the region.

In early 1994, Croatian president Franjo Tudjman asked U.S. ambassador Peter W. Galbraith for the U.S. reaction to moving weapons through Croatia to the Bosnians. Acting on explicit orders from the White House and the State Department, Galbraith told Tudjman that he had "no instructions" concerning such smuggling operations, essentially saying there would be no U.S. protest to the covert shipments. The existing low-level flow of small arms through Croatia grew into a substantial airlift of weaponry, other military equipment, and eventually Iranian Revolutionary Guard advisors. At the same time, however, the administration chose not to advise the CIA, the Joint Chiefs of Staff, or U.S. ambassadors elsewhere of the change in U.S. support for the UN embargo. CIA reporting from the field expressed concerns that the United States was covertly engaged in violating the embargo. A review by the president's Intelligence Oversight Board, initiated when DCI R. James Woolsey took the agency's evidence of embargo violations to the White House, concluded that the administration's actions did not constitute an illegal covert action. Consequently, no presidential finding or congressional notification was required.[18]

When the *Los Angeles Times* story broke, the congressional intelligence committees opened investigations. The House Permanent Select Committee on Intelligence found that there had been no covert action within the legal meaning of the term (see sidebar, *Legal Definition*) by administration officials to arm the Bosnian Muslims. However, the Committee stated firmly that the "no instructions" approach constituted a major change in policy and should have been shared with appropriate members of Congress and communicated clearly to the CIA, Defense Department, and other U.S. government organizations. The SSCI agreed with the House that Congress should be informed of significant secret policy changes in U.S. foreign policy. The SSCI noted that the unusual level of secrecy surrounding the "no instructions" decision left Congress "dangerously ignorant" at the same time it was considering legislation on enforcing the embargo. The committee could not reach agreement on whether a covert action had occurred, although it did conclude that the "no instructions" interchange between Galbraith and Tudjman was not "traditional diplomatic activity," as it is generally understood.[19]

Legal Definition

A "covert action" is defined in 50 U.S.C. 413b(e) as "an activity or activities of the United States Government to influence political, economic, or military conditions abroad, where it is intended that the role of the United States will not be apparent or acknowledged publicly, but does not include . . . traditional diplomatic or military activities or routine support to such activities."

Source: 50 U.S.C. 413b(e).

Back to the Balkans

In 1989, the regime of Slobodan Milošević in Serbia reduced the autonomy of Kosovo province and began a decade of repression of ethnic majority Albanians. By 1996, the Kosovo Liberation Army (KLA; *Ushtria Clirimtare Kosova* or UCK in Albanian) had begun guerrilla or terrorist attacks, depending on the prevailing point of view, on Serbian police and army troops. The Milošević government responded with an even more indiscriminate counterinsurgency campaign—with attendant massacres and ethnic expulsions—resulting in a humanitarian crisis in the neighboring areas of Albania and Macedonia. By early 1999, the international community's inability to negotiate an end to the conflict led NATO to launch a military operation. The bombing campaign in Serbia and Kosovo (Operation ALLIED FORCE) began on March 24, 1999, and lasted until June 11, 1999.

The U.S. SOF deployed to Albania in support of Operation ALLIED FORCE had a range of missions. Prohibited from entering Kosovo, some 20-plus soldiers of the 10th Special Forces Group (Airborne) colocated with the KLA at their base camps near the Albanian border with Kosovo. These forces served as a conduit for targeting and battle damage assessment information collected inside Kosovo by the KLA guerrillas. The establishment of the relationship between Special Forces personnel and KLA fighters was perhaps enhanced by the alleged presence of covert CIA paramilitary officers who may have been in touch with the KLA inside Kosovo until pulled out before the bombing campaign began.[20] SOF Civil Affairs units coordinated large-scale humanitarian relief efforts—food, water, and medical care for thousands of Kosovar refugees—with U.S. government agencies and international relief organizations. PSYOPS personnel used EC-130E Commando Solo aircraft to broadcast Serbian-language radio and television programs into the area, while other aircraft dropped propaganda leaflets telling the Serbian population that Milošević was destroying their country. Special Forces' AC-130 Spectre gunships participated directly in the bombing campaign by attacking Serbian positions. And SOF combat search and rescue teams successfully evacuated the pilots of the only two U.S. aircraft shot down during Operation ALLIED FORCE.

After Slobodan Milošević accepted the removal of his forces from Kosovo, the NATO-led Kosovo Force (KFOR) peacekeeping mission deployed into Kosovo on June 12, 1999 in Operation JOINT GUARDIAN. Within days, SOF units had entered Kosovo and begun to conduct missions similar to those they had handled in Bosnia and Albania. They quickly launched into civil affairs and psychological operations. SOF liaison teams also worked directly with Polish and Russian contingents in KFOR. A Special Forces detachment with Arabic-language skills served as the liaison between KFOR and units from Jordan and the United Arab Emirates until they were fully integrated into KFOR.[21]

The humanitarian postconflict missions assumed by U.S. SOF in the Balkans typified the nonoffensive roles asked of them by their civilian and military leaders in the 1990s following Operation DESERT STORM.

Notes

1. U.S Congress, *Intelligence Authorization Act, Fiscal Year 1991*, Public Law 102–88, August 14, 1991, at: http://www.intelligence.senate.gov/laws/pl102-88.pdf. See also David C. King and Kirsten Lundberg, *Congressional Oversight and Presidential Prerogative: The 1991 Intelligence Authorization Act (Teaching Note to Case 1605.2)* (Cambridge, MA: John F. Kennedy School of Government, 2002).

2. George H. W. Bush, *Statement on Signing the Intelligence Authorization Act, Fiscal Year 1991* (Washington, DC: Office of the Press Secretary, 1991), at: http://www.presidency.ucsb.edu/ws/?pid=19899#axzz2jRq4379N.

3. See Steven Engelberg, with Jeff Gerth, "Bush and Noriega: Examination of Their Ties," *New York Times*, September 28, 1988.

4. *United Press International*, "CAMPAIGN '88: Former CIA Chief Says Bush Rehired Noriega," *Los Angeles Times*, October 1, 1988.

5. See L. Britt Snider, "Chapter 9: Oversight of Covert Action—Noriega and the SSCI: 1988–89," *The Agency and the Hill: CIA's Relationship with Congress, 1946–2004* (Washington, DC: Central Intelligence Agency, Center for the Study of Intelligence, 2008), pp. 299–301, at: https://www.fas.org/irp/cia/product/snider.pdf. See also, Mark Perry, *Eclipse: The Last Days of the CIA* (New York: Morrow, 1992), pp. 104–35, 251–85, 293–95.

6. Ronald H. Cole, *Operation Just Cause: The Planning and Execution of Joint Operations in Panama, February 1988–January 1990* (Washington, DC: Joint History Office, Office of the Chairman of the Joint Chiefs of Staff, 1995), at: http://www.dtic.mil/doctrine/doctrine/history/justcaus.pdf. See also, U.S. Special Operations Command (SOCOM), *History of the United States Special Operations Command*, 6th ed. (Tampa, FL: MacDill Air Force Base, 2008), pp. 36–48, at: http://www.socom.mil/Documents/history6thedition.pdf; and Jerry L. Thigpen, *The PRAETORIAN STARShip: The Untold Story of the Combat Talon* (Maxwell Air Force Base, AL: Air University Press, 2001), pp. 317–36.

7. See Rick Atkinson, *Crusade: The Untold Story of the Persian Gulf War* (Boston: Houghton Mifflin, 1993), p. 369; and Susan L. Marquis, *Unconventional Warfare: Rebuilding U.S. Special Operations Forces* (Washington, DC: Brookings Institution, 1997), pp. 230–31.

8. SOCOM, *History of the United States Special Operations Command*, pp. 49–57. See also, Department of Defense, "Appendix J: Special Operations Forces," *Conduct of the Persian Gulf Conflict: Final Report to Congress* (April 1992), pp. 606–27, at: http://www.dod.mil/pubs/foi/operation_and_plans/PersianGulfWar/404.pdf; and Douglas Waller, "Exclusive—Behind Enemy Lines: The First Combat Photos of Green Beret Commandos on a Secret Mission Deep Inside Iraq," *Newsweek*, October 28, 1991, p. 34.

9. See Ibrahim Al-Marashi, "Saddam's Security Apparatus during the Invasion of Kuwait and the Kuwaiti Resistance," *The Journal of Intelligence History* 3 (Winter 2003), p. 80; Atkinson, *Crusade*, p. 428; Frank Greve, "CIA, Army Said to Be Supporting Kuwait Resistance," *Philadelphia Inquirer*, August 31, 1990; and Michael Wines, "Confrontation in the Gulf: U.S. Is Said to Quietly Encourage a Resistance Movement," *New York Times*, September 1, 1990.

10. Atkinson, *Crusade*, pp. 335–36; 4th Psychological Operations Group (Airborne), "Leaflets of the Persian Gulf War" (Ft. Bragg, NC, 1991), at: http://www.psywar.org/psywar/reproductions/LeafletsPersianGulfWar.pdf.

11. Quoted in Douglas F. Garthoff, "Chapter Twelve: R. James Woolsey: Uncompromising Defender," *Directors of Central Intelligence as Leaders of the U.S. Intelligence Community, 1946–2005* (Washington, DC: Central Intelligence Agency, Center for the Study of Intelligence, 2005), at: https://www.cia.gov/library/center-for-the-study-of-intelligence/csi-publications/books-and-monographs/directors-of-central-intelligence-as-leaders-of-the-u-s-intelligence-community/chapter_12.htm. See also Garthoff's Footnote 1.

12. SOCOM, *History of the United States Special Operations Command*, pp. 59–63; Vernon Loeb, "After-Action Report," *Washington Post*, February 27, 2000, p. W6; John Prados, *Safe for Democracy: The Secret Wars of the CIA* (Chicago: Ivan R. Dee, 2006), pp. 585–91; and Richard W. Stewart, *The United States Army in Somalia, 1992–1994*, CMH Pub 70–81–1 (Washington, DC: U.S. Army Center of Military History, 2002), at: http://www.history.army.mil/brochures/Somalia/Somalia.pdf.

13. Mark Bowden, *Black Hawk Down: A Story of Modern Warfare* (New York: Atlantic Monthly Press, 1999), which was dramatized in an Oscar-winning movie of the same title (2001).

14. U.S. Congress, Senate, Select Committee on Intelligence, *Report on the Use by the Intelligence Community of Information Provided by the Iraqi National Congress together with Additional Views*, September 8, 2006, at: http://www.intelligence.senate.gov/phaseiiinc.pdf; and Snider, "Support for the INC and the Iraq Liberation Act of 1998," *The Agency and the Hill: CIA's Relationship with Congress, 1946–2004*, pp. 283–85. See also Robert Baer, *See No Evil: The True Story of a Ground Soldier in the CIA's War on Terrorism* (New York: Three Rivers Press, 2002), pp. 171–213; *Los Angeles Times*, "U.S. Begins Flying Kurdish Refugees to Guam," September 17, 1996; R. Jeffrey Smith and David B. Ottaway, "Anti-Saddam Operation Cost CIA $100 Million," *Washington Post*, September 15, 1996, pp. A1, A29–30; and Tim Weiner, "Iraqi Offensive into Kurdish Zone Disrupts U.S. Plot to Oust Hussein," *New York Times*, September 7, 1996, pp. A1, A4.

15. U.S. Congress, *Iraq Liberation Act of 1998* (Public Law 105–338) (Washington, DC: GPO, 1998), at: http://www.gpo.gov/fdsys/pkg/PLAW-105publ338/html/PLAW-105publ338.htm. See William J. Clinton: "Statement on Signing the Iraq Liberation Act of 1998," October 31, 1998, at: http://www.presidency.ucsb.edu/ws/?pid=55205. See also, James Risen, "C.I.A. Plan for Covert Iraq Action Was Reportedly Turned Down," *New York Times*, November 5, 1998; and Robin Wright, "U.S. Dispute Holds Up Covert Iraq Operation," *Los Angeles Times*, January 5, 1999.

16. Snider, "The Gingrich 'Add' for Covert Action in Iran: 1995," *The Agency and the Hill: CIA's Relationship with Congress, 1946–2004*, p. 302. See also, James Risen, "Gingrich Wants Funds for Covert Action in Iran," *Los Angeles Times*, December 10, 1995; James Risen, "Congress OKs House Plan to Fund Covert Action in Iran," *Los Angeles Times*, December 22, 1995; and Tim Weiner, "U.S. Plan to Change Iran Leaders Is an Open Secret Before It Begins," *New York Times*, January 26, 1996.

17. Charles T. Cleveland, *Command and Control of the Joint Commission Observer Program: U.S. Army Special Forces in Bosnia* (Carlisle Barracks, PA: U.S. Army War College, 2001), at: http://www.dtic.mil/cgi-bin/GetTRDoc?AD=ADA391195; Ryan C. Hendrickson, "Crossing the Rubicon," *NATO Review* (Autumn 2005), at: http://www.nato.int/docu/review/2005/issue3/english/history.html; SOCOM, *History of the United States Special Operations Command*, pp. 68–73; and U.S. Department of State, Office of the Historian, "The Breakup of Yugoslavia, 1990–1992," at: https://history.state.gov/milestones/1989–1992/breakup-yugoslavia.

18. James Risen and Doyle McManus, "U.S. OK'd Iranian Arms for Bosnia, Officials Say," *Los Angeles Times*, April 5, 1996. See also Snider, "Iranian Arms Shipments to Bosnia: 1996," *The Agency and the Hill: CIA's Relationship with Congress, 1946–2004*, p. 301.

19. U.S. Congress, House, Permanent Select Committee on Intelligence, *Investigation into Iranian Arms Shipments to Bosnia: Report, together with Minority and Additional Views*, House Report 105–804 (Washington, DC: U.S. Government Printing Office, October 9, 1996), at: http://www.gpo.gov/fdsys/pkg/CRPT-105hrpt804/html/CRPT-105hrpt804.htm; U.S. Congress, Senate, Senate Select Committee on Intelligence, "C. Inquiry Into U.S. Actions Regarding Iranian and Other Arms Transfers to the Bosnian Army," *Special Report*, Senate Report 105–1 (Washington, DC: U.S. Government Printing Office, January 22, 1997), at: http://www.gpo.gov/fdsys/pkg/CRPT-105srpt1/html/CRPT-105srpt1.htm. See also Tim Weiner and Raymond Bonner, "Gun-Running in the Balkans: C.I.A. and Diplomats Collide," *New York Times*, May 29, 1996.

20. See Dana Priest, "Kosovo Land Threat May Have Won War," *Washington Post*, September 19, 1999; and Tom Walker and Aidan Laverty, "CIA Aided Kosovo Guerrilla Army," *Sunday Times* (London), March 12, 2000.

21. SOCOM, *History of the United States Special Operations Command*, pp. 72–73. See also Armando J. Ramirez, *From Bosnia to Baghdad: The Evolution of US Army Special Forces from 1995 to 2004* (Monterey, CA: Naval Postgraduate School, 2004), pp. 15–21.

CHAPTER 10

A Changed Game

The administration of George W. Bush (2001–2009) had been in office less than nine months when the terrorist attacks of September 11, 2001 (9/11), pushed American national security policy into a period dominated by waging war on terrorism. Covert and special operations have played a critical role in this war.

The 9/11 attacks on the American Homeland were not the country's introduction to the threat of terrorism directed against U.S. targets. Nor was it America's introduction to Osama bin Laden's al-Qaeda Islamic terrorist group. The first attack on the World Trade Center on February 26, 1993, killed six people and injured more than 1,000. In June 1995, President Clinton tasked the director of Central Intelligence (DCI) with leading "an aggressive program of foreign intelligence collection, analysis, counterintelligence and covert action" targeted on international terrorism.[1] In early 1996, the CIA's Counterterrorism Center (CTC) created a unique subunit (codenamed ALEC) focused on bin Laden. In 1998, the CIA reportedly recruited a group of 15–30 Afghans who were paid to keep track of bin Laden's whereabouts in Afghanistan.[2] The bombings of the U.S. embassies in Kenya and Tanzania on August 7, 1998, in which 12 Americans were killed, were followed by U.S. cruise missile strikes against al-Qaeda sites in Afghanistan and Sudan. Al-Qaeda suicide bombers attacked the guided-missile destroyer USS *Cole* (DDG-67) in the Yemen port of Aden on October 12, 2000, killing 17 and injuring 39 sailors.

In the immediate aftermath of the 9/11 attacks, Congress gave the president authority to:

use all necessary and appropriate force against those nations, organizations, or persons he determines planned, authorized, committed, or aided
the terrorist attacks that occurred on September 11, 2001, or harbored
such organizations or persons, in order to prevent any future acts of international terrorism against the United States by such nations, organizations, or persons.[3]

Back to Afghanistan

President Bush's strong desire to strike back swiftly at the perpetrators of
the 9/11 horror and those who harbored them drove much of Washington's
initial decision-making in the wake of the attacks. After learning the U.S.
military had no contingency plan for attacking the al-Qaeda terrorists and
their Taliban protectors, Bush and his national security team opted for a CIA
proposal based on contacts and planning that had been underway for at least
four years.

The Taliban took power in Kabul in 1996, ousting the *mujahedeen* coalition that had governed since 1992; but areas of armed resistance to the
Taliban regime remained. The most significant opposition was in northeastern Afghanistan under the leadership of Ahmed Shah Masood, a Tajik and
former defense minister. Masood led a grouping of loosely associated, tribally
based forces (largely Tajiks and Uzbeks) collectively known as the Northern Alliance (Shura Nazar). The CIA had maintained contact with and
provided support to Masood in his stronghold in the Panjshir Valley since
1996–1997.

The Plan

The CIA plan called for inserting small paramilitary teams into Afghanistan to renew relationships with the opposition forces, particularly the
Northern Alliance; collect intelligence on the disposition of Taliban forces
and the whereabouts of Osama bin Laden; and obtain agreement from the
Northern Alliance leadership to the deployment of U.S. forces. The goal
was to bring together the disparate parts of the Northern Alliance and
opposition groups elsewhere in the country as a force that with U.S. support
could remove the Taliban from power, destroy al-Qaeda, and capture or kill
Osama bin Laden. One obstacle in the plan was that al-Qaeda had assassi-
nated Masood two days before the attack on the United States, but the CIA's
contacts with the Northern Alliance leadership proved sufficiently robust
to overcome that challenge. The president provided the CIA with broad
authorities for going after al-Qaeda and bin Laden, including the authority
to detain al-Qaeda operatives wherever they were found. Even though its

in-house paramilitary assets had been eroded significantly during the 1990s by budget cuts and retirements, the CIA retained the capability and flexibility to take the lead in America's war against the Taliban and al-Qaeda terrorists.[4]

The initial Northern Alliance Liaison Team—codenamed JAWBREAKER—departed the United States on September 19, 2001. After waiting several days for clearances, the seven-man team staged out of Tashkent, Uzbekistan, and refueled in Dushanbe, Tajikistan. Flying in a refurbished, CIA-owned Soviet Mi-17 helicopter, the group traversed the Hindu Kush Mountains and arrived in the Panjshir Valley on September 26. In addition to personal items, weapons, communications equipment, water, and other supplies, the team carried $3 million in used, nonsequential $100 bills. Over the next 40 days, team leader Gary Schroen dispensed that initial amount plus an additional $2 million to Afghan warlords and tribal leaders prepared to cooperate with the United States. Some of the money went to individuals willing to defect from the Taliban forces. The team immediately set up an intelligence cell to filter the information flow from Northern Alliance radio intercept operations and from individuals who had crossed the relatively static battle lines between the Taliban and Northern Alliance forces. Over the following months, six additional CIA teams were deployed in Afghanistan to work not only with Gen. Mohammad Fahim Khan, who had succeeded Masood as the overall leader of the Northern Alliance but also with other key anti-Taliban commanders with whom contact had been established.

The Bombing Campaign

In preparation for a bombing campaign, the team used GPS mapping to establish the Northern Alliance's front lines. The exact nature of the bombing campaign was a matter of discussion in Washington, as were the questions of what manner of U.S. forces would be deployed and what their role would be. By the time the U.S. military leadership decided to undertake unconventional warfare (see sidebar, *Unconventional Warfare: Definition*) and prepared to deploy SOF teams to Afghanistan, the CIA contacts had cleared the way for a multiagency, multinational effort. Along the way the team had to overcome such hurdles as the Afghan leadership not wanting U.S. troops to be in uniform and opposing the deployment of British troops. After the U.S. Air Force had established Combat Search and Rescue capabilities in Uzbekistan, the initial phase of the bombing campaign began on October 7 (Operation ENDURING FREEDOM). The early impact of the bombing on the Taliban's war-fighting ability was minimal as the strikes were directed at fixed targets and in the south, not on front-line positions in the north.

Unconventional Warfare: Definition

"A broad spectrum of military and paramilitary operations, normally of long duration, predominantly conducted by indigenous or surrogate forces who are organized, trained, equipped, supported, and directed in varying degrees by an external source. It includes guerrilla warfare and other direct offensive, low visibility, covert, or clandestine operations, as well as the indirect activities of subversion, sabotage, intelligence activities, and evasion and escape."

Source: U.S. Department of Defense, *Joint Doctrine Encyclopedia* (July 16, 1997), p. 713, at: http://www.bits.de/NRANEU/others/jp-doctrine/jp-encyclop(97).pdf.

The effects of the bombing improved only after the arrival of Special Forces teams (Task Force Dagger) beginning on October 19 and after Washington made the political decision to focus on Taliban military positions in the north. The Operational Detachments Alpha (ODAs) were based on the 5th Special Forces Group (Airborne), augmented by aviators from the 160th Special Operations Aviation Regiment (Airborne) and air control personnel from the Air Force Special Operations Command (AFSOC). The use of GPS-guided weapons and of SOFLAM (Special Operations Forces Laser Marker) devices for guiding "smart-bombs" to specific targets allowed ODAs to call in close air support to devastating effect against armored vehicles, troop concentrations, command posts, and antiaircraft positions. On the night of October 19–20, U.S. SOF staged two raids deep in Taliban territory in southern Afghanistan, basically just to show that the United States could strike wherever it pleased. In an operation codenamed Objective RHINO, about 200 soldiers from the U.S. Army's 75th Ranger Regiment parachuted onto a desert airfield some 75 miles south of Kandahar, killed several dozen defenders, secured the landing strip, collected intelligence, spent five hours on the ground, and departed, leaving behind propaganda leaflets. The same night, about 100 Delta Force soldiers conducted a helicopter raid (Objective GECKO) on a compound belonging to Taliban leader Mullah Omar on the outskirts of Kandahar. Mullah Omar was not there, but Taliban documents and messages were seized. Also, in October, the CIA began flying armed MQ-1 Predator unmanned aerial vehicles (UAVs), or drones, in Afghanistan. Originally built for reconnaissance work and used in that way in the hunt for Osama bin Laden in Afghanistan since September 2000, the Predator had been modified to carry Hellfire missiles. In Afghanistan, the drone proved effective in locating and destroying small, single-unit targets.

Taking the North

Although there were qualms in Washington about events moving too rapidly in U.S. support for the Tajik-based Northern Alliance forces, the application of air power on the Taliban's front lines quickly proved decisive. In an interesting picture of how in this war old and new ways overlapped each other, the Special Forces ODA that had linked up on October 20 with an in-place CIA team working with Gen. Abdul Rashid Dostum designated targets and called in air strikes while traveling on horseback with Dostum's Uzbek forces as they and the troops of Ostad Atta took Mazar-e Sharif on November 10. Correctly assessing that the bombing had weakened the Taliban front lines in the Shomali Plains north of Kabul, Fahim Khan launched an assault with Northern Alliance forces under Gen. Bismullah Khan on November 13. The defenses of the Taliban and their al-Qaeda foreign fighters (Arab, Chechen, Uzbek, and Pakistani) broke, with the fighters fleeing south toward Kandahar and east to Tora Bora in the White Mountains near Jalalabad. The next day, the Northern Alliance forces liberated Kabul. Concerns about a Tajik on Pashtun bloodbath, pushed by the Pakistanis but shared by some in Washington, proved to be unfounded. In the central northern area, Taloqan fell to Gen. Daoud Khan's forces on November 11, and the Taliban leaders in Konduz surrendered on November 23.[5]

The Taliban fighters that surrendered to Daoud's forces on November 24 were taken to Qala-I Jangi, a 19th-century fortress near Mazar-e Sharif, without being searched. The next day, the prisoners staged a violent uprising. Among those killed in the revolt was CIA paramilitary operations officer Johnny Micheal Spann, the first American killed in combat during Operation ENDURING FREEDOM. The battle for Qala-I Jangi lasted until November 29 and involved U.S. AC-130 Spectre gunships and SOF-directed air strikes. The Northern Alliance forces, supported by tank fire, eventually fought their way into the compound and forced the Taliban fighters to surrender.[6]

Moving South

With the collapse of Taliban opposition in the north, the Northern Alliance controlled about half of Afghanistan. The task became one of pursuing the Taliban and al-Qaeda fighters into their eastern and southern strongholds around Jalalabad and Kandahar, a fight the Northern Alliance was not enthusiastic about undertaking. On November 14, a 6-man CIA team, a 12-man Special Forces ODA, and a 3-man Joint Special Operations Command (JSOC) unit were inserted near the village of Tarin Kowt, 70 miles north of Kandahar, along with Pashtun leader Hamid Karzai and some of his tribal elders. The mission was to work with Karzai and other anti-Taliban leaders in the south to support and supply additional alliances. South of Kandahar, CIA personnel and a Special Forces ODA joined up with Gul Agha Sherzai, the pre-Taliban governor of Kandahar Province. Backed by American arms, food, money, and air support, Karzai's and Sherzai's forces converged on Kandahar. At the same time, a United Nations-sponsored conference in Bonn was in the process of establishing a transitional government for the country. When Karzai was selected to head that government, his new status helped him negotiate the evacuation of the Taliban forces from Kandahar; and on December 7, the city fell to what was now being called the Eastern Alliance. In less than three months after the attacks on the United States, the unique combination of 110 CIA officers, 316 members of the Special Forces, a mixture of JSOC personnel, the forces (mostly tribal militias) of assorted Afghan warlords, and U.S. air power had overthrown the Taliban regime.

By December 2001, many Afghan Taliban and al-Qaeda fighters had been killed, captured, or dispersed back into the population of their home areas. Others, including Osama bin Laden and his Arab and other foreign fighters, had retreated into bin Laden's fortified cave complex at Tora Bora in the White Mountains near the border with Pakistan. Given that time was of the essence in hunting bin Laden and local militia teams were not yet in place, the head of Central Command, Gen. Tommy Franks, was requested to deploy additional U.S. forces. The goal was to block escape routes between Tora Bora and the Pakistan border. Franks decided to keep the American "footprint" small and to rely on the local Afghan forces to wage the fight in the mountains. Although unimpressed with the quality, commitment, or leadership of the local militias in the east (it was Ramadan and the Afghans tended to stop fighting at the end of the day and go home to break their fast), the CIA and SOF elements, consisting of 6 CIA operatives, about 60 Special Forces, and 12 British commandos, worked with the surrogate forces available. Among other feats, a joint five-man team infiltrated deep into the mountains and for the better part of four days used their laser-designation equipment to call in massive air strikes against the fortified caves and tunnels. Hundreds of al-Qaeda operatives were killed, and Osama bin Laden's training camps destroyed. By December 17, al-Qaeda's forces were beaten; but bin Laden had slipped away into the unregulated tribal area of Pakistan.[7]

Early in 2002, intelligence began reporting Taliban and al-Qaeda activity in the Shah-I Khot Valley, in a mountainous region southeast of Gardez in eastern Afghanistan. The size of the al-Qaeda force, estimated as high as 1,000, and their presence in easily defendable terrain suggested that conventional ground combat forces supported by SOF and limited air strikes would be needed. In reality, the al-Qaeda fighters were better armed and dug in than expected. This meant that the force of 600 lightly armed U.S. infantry, nearly 1,000 Afghan troops that had been quickly trained by U.S Special Forces, and 200 special operations forces from allied countries faced different operational circumstances than had been projected. They were, in effect, shocked at the strength and resilience of al-Qaeda's forces. Day one of the operation, March 2, 2002, saw the Afghan forces suffer substantial casualties from al-Qaeda artillery and eventually withdraw from the attack. On the night of March 3–4, U.S. Navy SEALs and Army Rangers had seven killed and six wounded in an effort to take the peak of Takur Ghar, the highest point in the valley. The peak was eventually taken with the aid of Hellfire missiles from a CIA MQ-1 Predator, which took out a bunker on top of Takur Ghar. A CIA Predator previously had destroyed an al-Qaeda command and control facility in the valley. The battle plan now shifted to an air bombardment campaign. After a week of steady air strikes, many targets had been destroyed and the al-Qaeda forces weakened. Additional Afghan forces under Northern Alliance general Gul Huidar were brought in to reinforce the original group. By March 12, most of the al-Qaeda forces had either been killed or fled the valley. Mopping up operations continued for another week on al-Qaeda's last refuge in Afghanistan.[8] (See sidebar, *Evaluating Operation* ENDURING FREEDOM.)

Evaluating Operation ENDURING FREEDOM

"Too much . . . should not be drawn from the easy collapse of the Taliban. The United States had heavy assistance from its Northern Alliance allies, who had their own political aims in mind. They were, in essence, a surrogate ground army that proved quite effective when provided some coordination elements and air power assistance. These circumstances are so unique that one should be leery of applying any 'new model' of warfare wholesale without considering all the unique elements of any other situation."

Source: Richard W. Stewart, *Operation Enduring Freedom: The United States Army in Afghanistan, October 2001–March 2002* (Washington, DC: U.S. Army, Center of Military History, 2004), p. 45, at: http://www.history.army.mil/catalog/pubs/70/70-83.html.

On May 1, 2003, Defense Secretary Donald Rumsfeld "announced the end of major combat operations in Afghanistan. . . . Although 'pockets of resistance' remained, 'the bulk of the country' was secure and U.S. forces would shift their efforts to stabilization and reconstruction."[9] Nevertheless, CIA and Special Forces remained in Afghanistan after that announcement, with both establishing forward operating bases/firebases. Special Forces' missions included training the Afghan military forces and enhancing security along the eastern and southern border with Pakistan. The CIA focused on locating and capturing senior al-Qaeda members for interrogation in the elusive hunt for the next major terrorist act. However, attention in Washington was increasingly on Iraq. This impacted the availability of personnel and resources to be directed to Afghanistan, and particularly the kinds of military units—conventional versus special operations—on the ground. The several hundred SOF available were insufficient for denying movement across the border with Pakistan. By late 2006, the Taliban were increasingly moving out of their sanctuaries and returning to guerrilla warfare in the southern and southeastern parts of Afghanistan where they retained sympathizers.

Taking the Fight to Yemen

One of the central developments in American war-fighting capabilities over recent decades has been the weaponization of UAVs or drones, specifically the MQ-1 Predator and the larger MQ-9 Reaper. Originally designed for intelligence collection, surveillance, and reconnaissance, when these UAVs are armed with the Hellfire missile they become lethal additions to the U.S. arsenal. Their deployment initially was limited to the war zone in Afghanistan, where on October 17, 2001, the Defense Department acknowledged that "armed unmanned drones (Predators equipped with Hellfire missiles) had been used for the first time."[10] They have now developed into the weapon of choice for offensive strike operations in hard-to-reach locations, such as Yemen.

In November 2001, President Ali Abdullah Saleh of Yemen made an official visit to the United States, where he saw President Bush and virtually all the administration's top officials. In a meeting with DCI George Tenet, the discussion centered on improving cooperation in security and intelligence issues. Saleh purportedly left Washington with promises of some $400 million in economic and security assistance. A counterterrorism partnership (but one not without friction) emerged following Saleh's visit.[11] For the United States, the primary target was al-Qaeda in the Arabian Peninsula and its leadership. Saleh allegedly agreed to armed Predator flights and the deployment of a small special-operations team in his country. While some members of the mission's counterterrorism team sought to build up the intelligence on al-Qaeda's activities, Special Forces and Marines focused on training, equipping, and advising the Yemeni military.

Shifting to Iraq

After the 9/11 attacks, the CIA and SOF became growth industries as the antiterrorism war gained traction. This was especially true for special operators across all the services and for the JSOC. Congress and Defense Secretary

Donald Rumsfeld, who had been embarrassed when the CIA was the sole option for early U.S. entry into Afghanistan, drove this development. Rumsfeld was determined that the Pentagon would henceforth take the lead in Washington's war plans—that the military would not again be put in the situation of being the "supporting" element. The defense secretary proceeded to declare U.S. Special Operations Command as the lead element in planning the war on terror, an act that created friction within the national security apparatus.

Turning to the Kurds

By early 2002 the CIA and U.S. Central Command had begun planning for a U.S. invasion of Iraq. President Bush directed the CIA to support the U.S. military in overthrowing Saddam Hussein. Congress approved a budget of $189 million for the first year. The CIA reenergized its Northern Iraq Liaison Element (NILE) that had worked closely with the Kurds in northern Iraq over the years.[12] A survey team covertly entered northern Iraq, reestablished contact with the Kurdish leadership, and prepared the way for the introduction of more direct assistance to the Kurdish *peshmerga*. In March, DCI George Tenet met with the leaders of the two main Kurdish forces in northern Iraq, Massoud Barzani and Jalal Talabani, heads of the Kurdish Democratic Party and the Patriotic Union of Kurdistan, respectively.

On July 10, 2002, an eight-man CIA team crossed into the Kurdish Autonomous Zone in northern Iraq. The team stayed until August, evaluating the situation with the primary Kurdish fighting forces, establishing agent networks to gather intelligence within Iraq, and interviewing Iraqi defectors and refugees. The team returned to northern Iraq in October, accompanied by a second CIA team, Special Forces operators, and boxes containing tens of millions of dollars. The teams confronted a wealth of problems in preparing the way for U.S. military operations. These included recruiting reliable agents inside Iraq, the activities of Iraqi counterintelligence, and the presence of major concentrations of Iraqi troops just across the "Green Line" that separated them from the Kurdish forces. Beyond these issues, the difficulties of moving military personnel, weapons, and supplies into northern Iraq created significant obstacles for the NILE teams. Eventually, with the onset of war on March 20, 2003, "[t]he United States withdrew an offer of $6 billion in aid and $24 billion in loans to Turkey in view of Turkey's refusal to permit the deployment of U.S. troops" from its territory.[13]

CIA and Special Forces personnel created teams of Kurdish *peshmerga* to conduct covert long-range reconnaissance and sabotage operations deep behind Iraq lines. Trained in the use of handheld GPS locators and satellite phones, the Kurdish teams crossed through the Iraqi battle lines days before the air attack began and were in place to call in locations of surface-to-surface missile sites for U.S. airstrikes. Since the Iraqi troops manning the Green Line represented almost 40 percent of Saddam's conventional forces, holding them in place was an important strategic goal for the U.S. planners. The Kurdish teams pinpointed Iraqi troop movements from north to south for air attacks, and sabotaged railroad lines that could be used to move troops in either direction. Because of Turkey's refusal to allow the use of its land and air space for moving the U.S. Army' 4th Infantry Division into northern Iraq, it was March 26, 2003, six days after the start of the war, before almost 1,000 members of the U.S. 173rd Airborne Brigade parachuted from C-17s into Bashur Airfield in Kurdish-controlled territory. The 173rd was the first wave of conventional American forces into the Kurdish Autonomous Zone, which included another 1,200 soldiers, tanks, and other heavy equipment. These forces augmented the Kurdish *peshmerga* and the CIA and SOF that had already begun the process of defeating the increasingly demoralized 1st and 5th Corps of the Iraqi army.

Operation Iraqi Freedom

The invasion of Iraq began earlier than planned when intelligence reports from CIA sources inside Iraq indicated that Saddam Hussein might be attending a meeting at a compound outside Baghdad called Dora Farms. The facility was attacked on March 19 with cruise missiles and "bunker-buster" bombs from F-117 Nighthawk stealth fighters in a "regime decapitation strike." However, neither Saddam nor other senior Iraqi leaders were at the site. Other air attacks based on targets identified by covert teams inserted earlier struck Iraqi air defense and missile sites.

On March 20, the U.S. 3rd Infantry Division launched the main ground attack north into Iraq from Kuwait. At the same time, the 1st Marine Expeditionary Force and the 1st (UK) Armoured Division pushed into southern Iraq to protect the oil fields in the area of Basra and the Al Few peninsula, a major strategic objective. Although the initial phase of Operation Iraqi Freedom (OIF) is generally portrayed as primarily conventional warfare, U.S. and coalition SOF played a significant role. In addition to the critical effort of the Kurdish, CIA, and Special Forces in the north to prevent movement of Iraqi forces southward, the behind-the-lines identification by SOF teams for bombing strikes from U.S. and coalition aircraft of Iraqi fixed and mobile missile targets throughout the western desert and southern Iraq prevented the large-scale use of the weapons as the Iraqis had done in the 1991 war. The few tactical missiles fired against Kuwait were all intercepted by Patriot missile systems. The drive on the oil fields by the Marines and British forces was supported by a psychological operations (PSYOPS) campaign. Radio broadcasts and leaflet drops sought to convince the Iraqi defenders that preventing the destruction of the production and processing facilities was in the best interests of their country. The combination of swift movement by the coalition forces and the PSYOPS campaign restricted Iraqi efforts to repeat the type of widespread destruction that had taken place in 1991.

By the second full day of the invasion, Navy SEALS in collaboration with coalition special forces had seized Iraq's major gas and oil terminals in the northern Persian Gulf. After being captured in an ambush by Iraqi irregular forces, which killed 11 and captured seven soldiers, on March 23, PFC Jessica Lynch of the 507th Maintenance Company was rescued by SOF from a hospital in An Nasiriyah on April 1. Ten days later, the other survivors of the luckless 507th column and two captured helicopter pilots were rescued. Coalition forces reached Baghdad on April 5, and resistance there was over by April 9, as the world watched on television while the enormous statue of Saddam Hussein in al-Firdos Square was toppled. In the north, Kurdish *peshmerga*, the 173rd, and special forces, backed by U.S. air power, liberated Irbil on April 1, Kirkuk and associated airfields and oil fields on April 10, and Mosul the following day. Earlier (March 28–30), the Kurds and Americans had secured the Kurds' rear area by attacking and scattering the terrorist group *Ansar al-Islam* that had controlled a small enclave in the northeast corner of Kurdish territory along the border with Iran. On May 1, 2003, President George W. Bush declared that major combat operations in Iraq were over. By mid-year, special operations forces had begun to redeploy out of Iraq, and the remaining units were engaged in the hunt, along with CIA personnel, for the "high-value targets" represented by Saddam's top government, political, and military associates. In July, Saddam's sons Qusay and Uday were located and killed in a firefight in Mosul. Five months later, "actionable intelligence" led an interagency CIA-U.S. Special Forces task force backed by troops from the 1st Brigade Combat Team of the 4th Infantry Division to Saddam Hussein. He was captured hiding in a hole in the ground about nine miles north of his ancestral home of Tikrit.[14] By that point, however, a different kind of war was emerging in Iraq.

"Black Sites" and Interrogations

The details surrounding the CIA's involvement from 2002 in secret detentions and the use of "enhanced interrogation techniques" at secret prisons or "black sites" are less than clear and remain contentious. What is clear is that the broad authorities provided to the CIA by the president on September 17, 2001, were interpreted to include the covert and prolonged detention and interrogation of al-Qaeda and other terrorists. It is also clear that Justice Department, White House, and CIA lawyers approved the program.

The detention and interrogation program grew out of the fears immediately after the 9/11 attacks that further large-scale actions by al-Qaeda were likely. It was in the initial drive to secure information about al-Qaeda's plans that CIA officer Johnny Micheal Spann was openly interviewing detainees when he was killed in November 2001 in the prisoner riot at Qala-I Jangi fortress. Within the first months of the war in Afghanistan, thousands of Taliban and al-Qaeda combatants were taken, with the majority being left to the Northern Alliance. There were still hundreds of prisoners to be sorted out as to how dangerous they might be and whether they might have useful intelligence. The possibly dangerous ended up in the hands of the U.S. military. The military prison system at Guantanamo developed out of the need to house these enemy combatants. The CIA kept a small number who appeared to offer potential intelligence value. The question then became what to do with them. Some were sent to other countries for incarceration and/or interrogation in a process generally termed *rendition*, a practice for handling terrorist suspects used long before the 9/11 attacks. Others were retained initially in secure camps in Afghanistan. Over time, potential "high-value detainees" were moved through covert sites established in several foreign countries. There is considerable media speculation about countries in Asia, the Middle East, and Eastern Europe hosting black sites, but neither the United States nor the countries that might have been involved have acknowledged the existence of covert prisons at specific locations.[15]

The first of CIA's "high-value detainees" was Abu Zubaydah, captured in a raid in Faisalabad, Pakistan, in March 2002. On September 11, 2002, Ramzi bin al-Shibh, accused of being the communications link between the 9/11 hijackers and al-Qaeda's leadership, was captured in Karachi. Then, Khalid Sheikh Mohammed was captured in Rawalpindi on March 1, 2003. Mohammed reportedly confessed to being al-Qaeda's mastermind behind the 9/11 attacks, as well as involvement in other major terrorist incidents. However, his confessions are regarded by some as suspect because they were obtained through coercion. The interrogation of Mohammed allegedly included the use of water boarding, a method that simulates drowning and is often regarded as torture, but which was one of the enhanced interrogation techniques approved for use on the high-value detainees.

President Bush acknowledged and defended the CIA detention program in a speech at the White House on September 6, 2006. (See sidebar, *President Bush's Remarks*.) He announced at the same time that 14 high-level detainees would be transferred from CIA to military custody at Guantanamo Bay.[16] The president's remarks did not end the debate over the detention program, although it shifted the focus to the nature of the interrogations and whether the methods used constituted torture. That dispute carried well into President Barack Obama's second term, and precipitated a serious break in relations between the CIA and its overseers in the Senate.

President Bush's Remarks

"In this new war, the most important source of information on where the terrorists are hiding and what they are planning is the terrorists, themselves. Captured terrorists have unique knowledge about how terrorist networks operate. They have knowledge of where their operatives are deployed, and knowledge about what plots are underway. . . . And our security depends on getting this kind of information. To win the war on terror, we must be able to detain, question, and, when appropriate, prosecute terrorists captured here in America, and on the battlefields around the world. . . . [A] small number of suspected terrorist leaders and operatives captured during the war have been held and questioned outside the United States, in a separate program operated by the Central Intelligence Agency. This group includes individuals believed to be the key architects of the September the 11th attacks. . . . These are dangerous men with unparalleled knowledge about terrorist networks and their plans for new attacks. The security of our nation and the lives of our citizens depend on our ability to learn what these terrorists know."

Source: George W. Bush, "President Discusses Creation of Military Commissions to Try Suspected Terrorists" (Washington, DC: The White House, September 6, 2006) at: http://georgewbush-whitehouse.archives.gov/news/releases/2006/09/20060906-3.html.

One of the first actions taken by President Obama in January 2009 was to issue an executive order revoking previous directives to the CIA regarding detention and interrogation of detained individuals. He ordered the CIA to close its detention facilities and not to operate such in the future. He also established that the only authorized interrogation techniques are those contained in Army Field Manual 2 22.3 (FM 2–22.3), issued by the Department of the Army on September 6, 2006. The president created a "Special Task Force on Interrogation and Transfer [Rendition] Policies," chaired by the attorney general, to review interrogation and rendition policies.[17] Just as Bush's actions in 2006 did not end the public debate over the moral, ethical, and legal issues surrounding covert rendition, detention, and interrogation, neither did Obama's actions bring closure. The Senate Select Committee on Intelligence (SSCI) launched its own investigation. The SSCI report began generating new disputes as leaks about its work made their way into the media well before the release of the report's 500-word executive summary in December 2014. The report made the determination that the CIA's harsh interrogations produced little intelligence of value and its methods exceeded legal authorities. In addition to former Bush administration officials, including former vice president Dick Cheney, two people, one who was part of the decision-making process and the other who oversaw the implementation of those decisions, former DCI George Tenet and former director of the

National Clandestine Service Jose Rodriguez Jr., respectively, have strongly defended the CIA's detention and interrogation program in terms of how it was run and the usefulness of the intelligence gained from the detainees.[18]

Emerging Wars

New War in Iraq

By the time Saddam Hussein was captured in December 2003, the Sunni/Baathist insurgency was underway. In response, additional SOF were deployed to Iraq, and assigned multiple tasks. Working in conjunction with the CIA, Army Special Forces and Navy SEALs initially focused on proactive and intelligence-driven operations to capture or kill former members of Saddam's regime and insurgents, particularly the remaining "high-value targets." Agents from the FBI's Hostage and Rescue Team (HRT) reportedly assisted in raids initiated by Army Special Forces even before the HRT unit was placed under military command in 2005.[19]

The Coalition Provisional Authority tasked the SOF units with organizing, training, equipping, and advising the multiethnic Iraqi 36th Commando Battalion, as well as a covert counterterrorism militia, the Iraqi Counter Terrorism Force. Both units were conducting combat operations by May 2004. In mid-2005, the units were incorporated into the Iraqi Special Operations Forces Brigade. In August 2004, SEALs and Special Forces ODAs provided reconnaissance and surgical strikes to support conventional forces in rooting Muqtada al Sadr's Shiite militia out of the city of Najaf. U.S. special forces units also took on training tasks with Iraqi conventional forces, and accompanied them into combat against insurgents. A squadron from the AFSOC began training the reconstituted Iraqi air force in 2004. SOF responsibilities also included training and advising specialized counterinsurgency and counterterrorism police units.[20]

By 2006, despite the success of national elections the previous year, Iraq was engulfed in the combination of a violent Shiite-Sunni civil war and a nationalist uprising against the presence of foreign troops. U.S. forces were increasingly taking losses in fighting insurgent extremist groups, including al-Qaeda in Iraq and its foreign fighters. In Afghanistan, the Taliban and al-Qaeda, working out of their "safe" areas in Pakistan, were beginning to reassert themselves in the border areas. In neither Iraq nor Afghanistan were the local forces capable of dealing with the increased violence on their own. At the same time, the covert war being waged by CIA personnel and JSOC special operations forces against terrorists in those countries and elsewhere continued as something other than a backdrop for the more conventional wars that were underway.

In an effort to counteract increasing violence (some argue, to forestall defeat), President Bush on January 10, 2007, announced a change in strategy and the dispatch of almost 30,000 additional troops to Iraq (the "Surge"). Five brigades, 20,000 troops, went to Baghdad and environs. Another 4,000 deployed to Anbar Province, al-Qaeda's home base in Iraq, to increase the pressure on the terrorists. There was also an incremental increase in special operations forces, raising the total in country to 5,000. The new strategy was designed to be more people-centric. The goal was to team with Iraqi forces in clearing and securing neighborhoods, protecting civilians, and leaving Iraqi forces in place capable of providing security in the controlled areas.[21]

By the second half of 2007, violence in Baghdad had declined almost 50 percent. When the last of the five additional combat brigades left Iraq in July 2008, the surge could be viewed at least as a tactical success. The argument exists, however, that it was not the surge per se that reduced the level of violence, but rather a combination of factors. These additional factors included operations using all available tools—including surveillance drones, signals intelligence, and human intelligence—to locate, target, and capture or kill key individuals from al-Qaeda in Iraq, the Sunni insurgents, and Shiite militias. It was such an all-source intelligence network that earlier made possible the airstrike that killed al-Qaeda in Iraq leader Abu Musab al-Zarqawi in June 2006.[22] It was also intelligence that drove the decision to launch a special operation from Iraq into Syria in October 2008. The target of the raid was Badran Turki Hishan al-Mazidih (aka Abu Ghadiyah), a facilitator for al-Qaeda for the movement of foreign fighters, weapons, and money into Iraq to support the Sunni insurgency. When intelligence confirmed al-Mazidih's presence across the border in Syria from Qaim, a special operations assault team in Black Hawk helicopters descended on a Syrian village five miles inside Syria, and in a gun battle, killed al-Mazidih and several other fighters. Syria acknowledged and protested the attack, claiming that eight civilians, including four children had been killed.[23]

Reengaging in Afghanistan

By early 2007, American intelligence and counterterrorism officials were convinced that al-Qaeda was building an operational infrastructure in the mountainous North Waziristan tribal areas of Pakistan near the Afghan border. Included in the organization's activities was the establishment of multiple training camps for Afghan, Pakistani, and foreign terrorists. In addition, the insurgent tactics being used in Iraq—suicide bombings and roadside bomb attacks—were making their way into Afghanistan.

The pace of Taliban combat operations in Helmand, Kandahar, and Oruzgan Provinces increased in 2007, especially targeting non-U.S. coalition forces (United Kingdom, Canada, and the Netherlands). Attacks included one on a firebase in Oruzgan Province. In response, U.S. conventional, coalition, and special operations forces launched offensive operations, attacking areas where there were confirmed Taliban targets. On September 3, 2008, U.S special operations forces struck back against Taliban and al-Qaeda sanctuaries in South Waziristan with a helicopter-borne assault on the village of Angoor Ada near the border with Afghanistan. Although U.S. forces in Afghanistan had shelled Taliban positions inside Pakistan previously, as well as engaged in "hot pursuit" over the border on occasion, this was the first publicly acknowledged raid of its type. Other subsequent short-term forays into the border region by special operations forces have been rumored but lack any form of official acknowledgement.[24]

An early extension of the "war on terrorism" was the decision to pursue al-Qaeda and Taliban leaders and associated militants beyond the immediate confines of the war zone. This included building closer counterterrorism collaboration with intelligence and law enforcement authorities in other countries. One approach involved efforts to improve the capability of threatened countries to resist inroads from al-Qaeda and associated militants, either overtly through economic and military aid or covertly or a combination of the two as occurred in Yemen.

The most controversial aspect of taking the fight beyond Afghanistan was probably the decision to commit armed drones to locating and targeting al-Qaeda and Taliban leaders hiding in the inaccessible corners of the Pakistani-Afghan border, predominantly in the federally administered tribal areas (FATA). The details of such supposed strikes have been shrouded in official secrecy. Nevertheless, there has been widespread reporting in U.S. media of drone attacks. For the most part, however, there has been neither confirmation nor denial from the U.S. Government of the use of armed drones. In 2009, then-CIA director Leon Panetta defended the effectiveness of missile strikes in disrupting al-Qaeda's leadership and limiting collateral damage. In an August 2011 op-ed article in the *New York Times*, former director of National Intelligence Adm. Dennis Blair argued that continued unilateral drone strikes would not result in a substantial reduction in al-Qaeda's capabilities. Then, in January 2012, President Obama pulled back the secrecy curtain a little further when he referred specifically to U.S. drone strikes in the FATA.[25]

Notes

1. William J. Clinton, *Presidential Decision Directive 39: U.S. Policy on Counterterrorism*, June 21, 1995, at: http://www.fas.org/irp/offdocs/pdd39.htm.

2. Bob Woodward, *Bush at War* (New York: Simon & Schuster, 2002), pp. 6–7; and Bob Woodward, "CIA Paid Afghans to Track bin Laden: Team of 15 Recruits Operated since 1998," *Washington Post*, December 23, 2001, A1.

3. U.S. Congress, Joint Resolution, "Authorization for the Use of Military Force," September 18, 2001, P.L. 107–40 [S.J. Res. 23].

4. George J. Tenet, with Bill Harlow, *At the Center of the Storm: My Years at the CIA* (New York: HarperCollins, 2007), pp. 170–72, 177, 187, and 207–8. See also, Bob Woodward, "CIA Told to Do 'Whatever Necessary' to Kill Bin Laden,"*Washington Post*, October 21, 2001, A1. For CIA contacts with Masood, see Steve Coll, *Ghost Wars: The Secret History of the CIA, Afghanistan, and Bin Laden, from the Soviet Invasion to September 10, 2001* (New York: Penguin, 2004), pp. 371–584; and Gary C. Schroen, *First In: An Insider's Account of How the CIA Spearheaded the War on Terror in Afghanistan* (Novato, CA: Presidio, 2005), pp. 58–64.

5. Gary Berntsen and Ralph Pezzullo, *Jawbreaker: The Attack on Bin Laden and Al Qaeda: A Personal Account by the CIA's Key Field Commander* (New York: Crown, 2005), pp. 102–242; Schroen, *First In*, pp. 73–319; Doug Stanton, *Horse Soldiers: The Extraordinary Story of a Band of U.S. Soldiers Who Rode to Victory in Afghanistan* (New York: Scribner, 2009); Tenet, *At the Center of the Storm*, pp. 127, 170–89, and 207–27; U.S. Special Operations Command (SOCOM), *History of the United States Special Operations Command*, 6th ed. (Tampa, FL: MacDill Air Force Base, 2008), pp. 91–95, at: http://www.socom.mil/Documents/history6thedition.pdf

6. Berntsen and Pezzullo, *Jawbreaker*, pp. 245–53, 262–64; SOCOM, *History of the United States Special Operations Command*, pp. 95–96; Stanton, *Horse Soldiers*, pp. 289–344; Tenet, *At the Center of the Storm*, pp. 221–24; U.S. Central Intelligence Agency, "Remembering CIA's Heroes: Johnny Micheal Spann," at: https://www.cia.gov/news-information/featured-story-archive/johnny-micheal-spann.html.

7. Peter Bergen, "The Battle for Tora Bora," *New Republic*, December 22, 2009, at: http://www.newrepublic.com/article/the-battle-tora-bora; Berntsen and Pezzullo, *Jawbreaker*, p. 212; Dalton Fury (pseudonym), *Kill Bin Laden: A Delta Force Commander's Account of the Hunt for the World's Most Wanted Man* (New York: St. Martin's Press, 2008); SOCOM, *History of the United States Special Operations Command*, pp. 96–101; Tenet, *At the Center of the Storm*, pp. 225–27; and Woodward, *Bush at War*, p. 315. For a unique perspective on the war after the fall of Kabul, see Billy Waugh with Tim Keown, *Hunting the Jackal: A Special Forces and CIA Ground Soldier's Fifty-Year Career Hunting America's Enemies* (New York: Morrow, 2004), pp. 308–34. See also, U.S. Senate, Committee on Foreign Relations, Staff Report, *Tora Bora Revisited: How We Failed to Get bin Laden and Why It Matters Today* (Washington, DC: Government Printing Office, 2009), at: http://www.gpo.gov/fdsys/pkg/CPRT-111SPRT53709/html/CPRT-111SPRT53709.htm.

8. On Operation ANACONDA, see Richard L. Kugler, *Operation Anaconda in Afghanistan: A Case Study of Adaptation in Battle*, Case Studies in Defense Transformation, No. 5 (Washington, DC: National Defense University, 2007); and Sean Naylor, *Not a Good Day to Die: The Untold Story of Operation Anaconda* (New York: Berkley Books, 2005). See also, SOCOM, *History of the United States Special Operations Command*, pp. 101–7; and Tenet, *At the Center of the Storm*, p. 219.

9. U.S. Department of State, *The United States and the Global Coalition against Terrorism, September 2001–December 2003* (Washington, DC: Office of the Historian, June 2004), at: http://2001-2009.state.gov/r/pa/ho/pubs/fs/5889.htm.

10. Ibid.

11. Ibid., entry dated November 27, 2001; and Yemen Embassy, "November 2001: An important visit by the Yemeni President to the United States," at: http://yemenembassy.org/issues/ymusrelshp/index.htm. The U.S. Ambassador to Yemen from 2001 to 2004 has published his memoirs. See Edmund J. Hull, *High-Value Target: Countering al Qaeda in Yemen* (Dulles, VA: Potomac Books Inc., 2011).

12. For U.S. interaction with the Kurds ahead of the launching of Operation IRAQI FREEDOM, see Charles H. Briscoe, et al., *All Roads Lead to Baghdad: Army Special Operations Forces in Iraq, New Chapter in America's Global War on Terrorism* (Washington, DC: Department of the Army, 2006); Tenet, *At the Center of the Storm*, pp. 386–91; Mike Tucker and Charles Faddis, *Operation Hotel California: The Clandestine War Inside Iraq* (Guildford, CT: Lyons Press, 2008); and Bob Woodward, *Plan of Attack* (New York: Simon & Schuster, 2004), pp. 108–9, 116, 139, 209, 350–51.

13. Department of State, *United States and the Global Coalition against Terrorism*.

14. CNN, "Saddam 'Caught Like a Rat' in a Hole," December 15, 2003; Gregory Fontenot, E. J. Degen, and David Tohn, *On Point: The United States Army in Operation Iraqi Freedom* (Fort Leavenworth, KS: Combat Studies Institute Press, 2004), at: http://usacac.army.mil/cac2/cgsc/carl/download/csipubs/OnPointI.pdf; Michael Smith, *Killer Elite. The Inside Story of America's Most Secret Special Operations Team* (New York: St. Martin's Griffin, 2008), pp. 239–42 and 259–63; SOCOM, *History of the United States Special Operations Command*, pp. 121–29; Tenet, *At the Center of the Storm*, pp. 391–95; and U.S. Joint Chiefs of Staff, *Operation Iraqi Freedom (OIF) History Brief*, May 14, 2003, at: http://nsarchive.files.wordpress.com/2010/10/oif-history.pdf.

15. See Jane Mayer, "The Black Sites: A Rare Look Inside the C.I.A.'s Secret Interrogation Program," *New Yorker*, 13 August 2007, at: http://www.newyorker.com/reporting/2007/08/13/070813fa_fact_mayer; and Dana Priest, "CIA Holds Terror Suspects in Secret Prisons," *Washington Post*, November 2, 2005.

16. George W. Bush, "President Discusses Creation of Military Commissions to Try Suspected Terrorists" (Washington, DC: The White House, September 6, 2006) at: http://georgewbush-whitehouse.archives.gov/news/releases/2006/09/20060906-3.html.

17. Barack Obama, "Executive Order 13591—Ensuring Lawful Interrogations," January 22, 2009, at: http://www.whitehouse.gov/the_press_office/Ensuring_Lawful_Interrogations.

18. See Jose A. Rodriguez Jr., "I Ran the CIA Interrogation Program. No Matter What the Senate Report Says, I Know It Worked," *Washington Post*, April 4, 2014; Jose A. Rodriguez Jr., with Bill Harlow, *Hard Measures: How Aggressive CIA Actions after 9/11 Saved American Lives* (New York: Simon & Schuster, 2012); Bill Sammon, "Cheney: Enhanced Interrogations 'Essential' in Saving American Lives," FoxNews.com, August 30, 2009; Tenet, *At the Center of the Storm*, pp. 239–43, 250–56; and U.S., Senate Select Committee on Intelligence, "Committee Study of the Central

Intelligence Agency's Detention and Interrogation Program: Findings and Conclusions; Executive Summary," December 3, 2014; at: http://www.intelligence.senate.gov/study2014/sscistudy1.pdf.

19. See Adam Goldman and Julie Tate, "Inside the FBI's Secret Relationship with the Military's Special Operations," *Washington Post*, April 10, 2014; and Seymour M. Hersh, "Moving Targets," *New Yorker*, December 15, 2003, at: http://www.newyorker.com/archive/2003/12/15/031215fa_fact?currentPage=all.

20. SOCOM, *History of the United States Special Operations Command*, pp. 129–34.

21. George W. Bush, "President's Address to the Nation" (Washington, DC: The White House, January 10, 2007), at: http://georgewbush-whitehouse.archives.gov/news/releases/2007/01/20070110-7.html.

22. Tom Bowman, "As the Iraq War Ends, Reassessing the U.S. Surge," *NPR*, December 16, 2011, at: http://www.npr.org/2011/12/16/143832121/as-the-iraq-war-ends-reassessing-the-u-s-surge; John F. Burns, "Al Qaeda Leader in Iraq Killed by U.S. Bombs," *New York Times*, June 9, 2006; Michael T. Flynn, Rich Juergens, and Thomas L. Cantrell, "Employing ISR: SOF Best Practices," *Joint Force Quarterly* 50 (Third Quarter 2008): 56–61; SOCOM, *History of the United States Special Operations Command*, pp. 134–35; and Bob Woodward, *The War Within: A Secret White House History, 2006–2008* (New York: Simon & Schuster, 2008), pp. 379–81.

23. Jonathan S. Landay and Nancy A. Youssef, "CIA Led Mystery Syria Raid that Killed Terrorist Leader," *McClatchy*, October 27, 2008; Eric Schmitt and Thom Shanker, "Officials Say U.S. Killed an Iraqi in Raid in Syria," *New York Times*, October 28, 2014; and Ann Scott Tyson and Ellen Knickmeyer, "U.S. Calls Raid a Warning to Syria." *Washington Post*, October 28, 2014.

24. See Spencer S. Hsu and Walter Pincus, "U.S. Warns of Stronger Al-Qaeda," *Washington Post*, July 12, 2007; Mark Mazzetti and David Rohde, "Terror Officials See Al Qaeda Chiefs Regaining Power," *New York Times*, February 19, 2007; Candace Rondeaux and Karen DeYoung, "U.S. Troops Crossed Border, Pakistan Says: 20 Locals Reported Killed in Assault," *Washington Post*, September 4, 2008; Pir Zubair Shah, Eric Schmitt, and Jane Perlez, "American Forces Attack Militants on Pakistani Soil," *New York Times*, September 4, 2008; and SOCOM, *History of the United States Special Operations Command*, pp. 117–20.

25. To view the virtual interview with the president, see "President Obama's Google+ Hangout," January 30, 2012, at: http://www.whitehouse.gov/photos-and-video/video/2012/01/30/president-obama-s-google-hangout.

CHAPTER 11

New President, Continuing Challenges

Leaving Iraq?

By the time President Barack Obama (2009–Present) took office, the framework was in place for winding down the Iraq war. In November 2008, U.S. and Iraqi officials signed a Security Agreement, similar to a Status of Forces Agreement, to go into effect on January 1, 2009. The agreement provided for the withdrawal of U.S. combat forces from Iraqi cities and towns by June 30, 2009, and the departure of U.S. troops from Iraq by December 31, 2011. In the interim, the focus was on training, equipping, and advising Iraqi Security Forces (ISF). However, targeted counterterrorism operations by a task force comprised of Joint Special Operations Command (JSOC) and Central Intelligence Agency (CIA) personnel continued.

The last American troops drove from Iraq into Kuwait on December 18, 2011. However, by September 2012, concerns about spillover from the ongoing civil war in Syria led the Iraqi government to request the deployment of a U.S. Army special operations unit to advise on counterterrorism measures. As suicide bombings and other militant attacks increased in Iraq during 2013, the Obama administration began to look for ways to aid the Maliki government without directly involving U.S. troops. In March 2014, a small U.S. special operations contingent was sent to Jordan to participate in a training exercise with counterterrorism troops from Iraq and Jordan.[1]

In June 2014, the sudden and unanticipated advance out of Syria into Iraq of the Islamist militant group variously called the Islamic State of Iraq and Syria (ISIS), Islamic State of Iraq and the Levant (ISIL), or just Islamic State (IS), combined with the virtual collapse of the Iraq military in western and northern Iraq, prompted President Obama to authorize deployment of up to

770 U.S. troops to Iraq. The initial focus was to bolster security at the Baghdad Embassy. Defense Secretary Chuck Hagel noted in early July that a small team of Special Forces advisors had established a Joint Operations Center (JOC) in Irbil, the capital of the Kurdish Regional Government. By early November, the number of U.S. forces authorized for Iraq had grown to 3,100. Their noncombat mission is to advise the Iraqi forces; support intelligence, surveillance, and reconnaissance flights; and coordinate U.S. military activities throughout Iraq, including airstrikes in Iraq and Syria by the United States and its coalition partners.[2]

Surging in Afghanistan

During the 2008 election cycle, candidate Obama had spoken of the need for additional troops and a new strategy for Afghanistan. Within a month, the new president approved adding 21,000 troops to the 47,000 already in Afghanistan. Some 8,000 Marines went to the southern province of Helmand Province where the Taliban was reestablishing a foothold. The objective was to stop the flow of Taliban and foreign fighters moving into Afghanistan from Pakistan, to maintain basic security by seizing and holding territory, and to train Afghan military units. Almost immediately, U.S. military leaders began to argue for an additional surge in U.S. troop levels. After months of discussion within the administration, President Obama announced on December 1, 2009, that the United States would deploy 30,000 more troops to Afghanistan. However, the reinforcements would begin to be withdrawn in 18 months, as responsibility for internal security was passed to Afghan forces.[3]

Much of the debate in 2009 swirled around the number of troops being sent to Afghanistan (not enough? too many?) and which strategy to pursue there (counterinsurgency versus counterterrorism). Nonetheless, other decisions were being made outside the political and media spotlight. Along with the increase in conventional forces, the president ordered a "surge" in the presence of JSOC, CIA, and other intelligence personnel and contractors in Afghanistan. Commander, International Security Assistance Force (ISAF) and Commander, U.S. Forces Afghanistan Gen. Stanley A. McChrystal used the additional resources to expand the joint task forces that combined Army Special Forces, Navy SEALs, and CIA paramilitary operatives. McChrystal had success using these kinds of task forces in Iraq for intelligence-gathering raids, on the basis of that intelligence conducting raids to kill or capture insurgents and gather more intelligence, and then going after more insurgents. He picked up the counterterrorism pace in Afghanistan, with multiple "snatch-and-grab" raids nightly on insurgents.

By late 2009, the CIA reportedly had expanded its firebases in southern and eastern Afghanistan, moving some operatives out of Kabul and the base at Bagram Airfield in order to get closer to target areas. The front-line nature of these firebases, many collocated with or near military forward operating facilities, was illustrated by the suicide attack on the CIA's Forward Operating Base Chapman, in Khost Province on December 30, 2009. Seven CIA officers and contractors, including the base chief, were killed and six others injured in the attack. According to media reports, Chapman was one of several forward bases focused on targeting for Predator/Reaper airstrikes against al-Qaeda and Taliban leaders in the Afghanistan-Pakistan border region. Because of its location, Chapman is also said to have engaged in recruiting and debriefing agents for penetration of terrorist organizations.[4]

Leaving Afghanistan?

The last of the 33,000 troops sent to Afghanistan in the surge left the country ahead of schedule on December 20, 2012. The incremental drawdown of U.S. and coalition forces then continued in line with the administration's objective of leaving only a limited number of U.S. troops in Afghanistan after the end of 2014, contingent on the signing of a status-of-forces agreement. The drawdown of conventional and special forces also had an effect on covert operations, as there was reporting by mid-2013 that the CIA had begun closing some of its covert forward operating bases.[5]

On September 30, 2014, the United States and Afghanistan signed a Bilateral Security Agreement (BSA) providing for up to 9,800 U.S. forces to continue training, advising, and assisting the Afghan security forces, as well as conducting counterterrorism operations against al-Qaeda. The nature and extent of the counterterrorism activities were not specified. A separate Afghanistan-NATO agreement allows for a contingent of 2,000–3,000 coalition troops to participate in training and advising the Afghan forces. The number and type of U.S. troops remaining in Afghanistan after 2014 will directly impact the size and nature of covert and special operations directed at al-Qaeda, its affiliates, and the Taliban in Afghanistan and Pakistan. The BSA allows for U.S. troops to have bases at nine separate locations in Afghanistan until 2016. At that time, the number of American forces will be cut in half, and they will be based only in Kabul and at Bagram air base. By the end of 2017, the U.S. force will be reduced to a military advisory component at the U.S. Embassy in Kabul.[6]

Hunting Al-Qaeda

On May 1, 2011 (Washington time), the years-long manhunt for Osama bin Laden (the CIA had formed its bin Laden unit in 1996) came to a violent end with his death in Abbottabad, Pakistan. Death came not from the sky in a drone attack, but at the hands of American special operators in a high-risk direct action ordered by President Obama and conducted under the CIA's covert action authority.

Two MH-60 Black Hawk helicopters from the U.S. Army's Special Operations Command flew out of Jalalabad Air Field in Afghanistan with 23 U.S. Navy SEALs and their interpreter. The team was transported about 120 miles inside Pakistan. Bin Laden was shot and killed in a nighttime raid on the compound where he had been living. The operation had been in the planning and rehearsal stages since March, with the president meeting regularly with his national security team to review the developing plan and to weigh the likelihood that bin Laden was at the target site in Abbottabad. One of the two Black Hawks crashed at the site and had to be destroyed. However, the arrival of one of the emergency back-up MH-47 Chinook helicopters that had flown partway and then gone to ground was sufficient extra airlift to extract the SEAL team along with bin Laden's body, which eventually was buried at sea.[7]

The unilateral attack in Abbottabad, while successful in killing Osama bin Laden, also increased tension in the often-difficult U.S.-Pakistani relations. Tension worsened in November when NATO aircraft fired on two Pakistani border posts, killing more than two dozen Pakistani soldiers. Whatever the cause of the friendly fire incident, one result appears to have been a pause for over a month in drone strikes. After the pause, the search for and targeting of al-Qaeda and Taliban leaders resumed.[8]

Even after administration officials began in 2009 to allude publicly to U.S. drone strikes and after the president referred specifically in January 2012 to drone strikes in the federally administered tribal areas (see page 188), no official confirmation of individual or collective strikes has been forthcoming. In addition, the lack of central control in these areas means there is an absence of on-scene reporters. Information comes essentially through second- or third-hand reports carried by wire services (*AP, AFP, Reuters*) or from press reporters with contacts in the affected area. This type of reporting offers little in the way of verifiable details. There are only small variances in the number of alleged strikes reported over time by two unofficial online organizations that use available information to try to chart U.S. drone activity—New America Foundation and *The Long War Journal*.[9] There is continuing debate about the effectiveness of drone strikes in terms of the number of important terrorists killed versus civilian casualties.

Spreading the Net

War in Yemen

While the pace of drone attacks began declining in Afghanistan in 2011, parallel covert and special operations activities in Yemen, directed against al-Qaeda in the Arabian Peninsula (AQAP), were on the rise. Plagued by multiple internal conflicts, Yemen under President Ali Abdullah Saleh was trending toward becoming a failed state, and there was considerable sympathy among some Yemeni tribes for al-Qaeda and its jihadist ideology. After Saleh cut off the use of armed drones in 2002, small special operations contingents remained in Yemen, although they faced restrictions on their actions. It was not until seven years later that American firepower was used again in Yemen.

On December 17, 2009, Tomahawk missiles from U.S. ships in the Arabian Gulf slammed into a desert camp where intelligence indicated al-Qaeda was preparing to send suicide bombers to attack the American Embassy in Sana. A week later, another concentration of al-Qaeda fighters was hit. Both attacks apparently killed a combination of militants and civilians. Saleh then agreed to allow U.S. warplanes access to Yemeni airspace if intelligence indicated the presence of AQAP leaders at a specific location. However, in May 2010, an airstrike killed the deputy governor of Maarib Province, who was on his way to mediate a truce with a local al-Qaeda militant. The incident provoked widespread protests, and U.S. air strikes were put on hold for almost a year.

The covert air war against AQAP resumed in May 2011 with a reported total of nine drone strikes and three air strikes (Marine Harrier jets and Tomahawk missiles) over the rest of the year. The increase in the number of strikes took place against the backdrop of increasingly violent instability in the internal situation in the country. In June, President Saleh was badly injured in an assassination attempt, and he spent the next three months receiving medical treatment in Saudi Arabia. The centerpiece of the strikes in Yemen in 2011 was the death of Anwar al-Awlaki on September 30. The decision to target the American-born al-Awlaki occasioned significant discussion within the White House, but a classified memo from the Justice Department's Office of Legal Counsel reportedly concluded that by making common cause with AQAP the jihadist cleric had surrendered his Constitutional right to due process. The drone strike that killed al-Awlaki also killed Samir Khan, an American citizen of Pakistani origin and editor of AQAP's English-language Internet magazine, *Inspire*. It is likely that Ibrahim Hassan Tali al-Asiri, AQAP's primary bomb maker, replaced al-Awlaki at the top of the U.S. government's most wanted list in Yemen.[10] (See sidebar, *Al-Asiri*.) Two weeks after Anwar al-Awlaki was killed, another drone strike mistakenly killed his 16-year-old son, Abdulrahman al-Awlaki. Thus, out of the three American citizens killed in these two drone strikes, only one of them met the criteria established for targeted killing.

Al-Asiri

"Al-Asiri is an AQAP operative and serves as the terrorist organization's primary bomb maker. Before joining AQAP, al-Asiri was part of an al-Qa'ida affiliated terrorist cell in Saudi Arabia and was involved in planned bombings of oil facilities in the Kingdom. Al-Asiri gained particular notoriety for the recruitment of his younger brother as a suicide bomber in a failed assassination attempt of Saudi Prince Muhammed bin Nayif. Although the assassination attempt failed, the brutality, novelty and sophistication of the plot is illustrative of the threat posed by al-Asiri. Al-Asiri is credited with designing the remotely detonated device, which contained one pound of explosives concealed inside his brother's body."

Source: U.S. Department of State, Office of the Spokesman, "Department of State's Terrorist Designation of Ibrahim Hassan Tali Al-Asiri" (Washington, DC: March 24, 2011), at: http://www.state.gov/r/pa/prs/ps/2011/03/158911.htm.

Salah finally ceded power to Vice President Abd Rabbuh Mansur Hadi in February 2012. The new leader inherited a Shiite al-Houthi rebellion in the north, a secessionist movement in the south, the aftermath of violent protests in Sana and across the country against Saleh's administration, and the growing threat of al-Qaeda militants. The al-Qaeda forces, consisting of a mix of Yemeni tribesmen and foreign fighters, some with experience fighting in Afghanistan, had taken advantage of the political upheaval and consolidated their control of areas in the south. The U.S. response was to institute the counterterrorism strategy employed in Iraq and Afghanistan: That is, use a limited number of U.S. personnel and drones to strike al-Qaeda elements considered to be a threat to the United States, while building up, training, and advising local Yemeni security forces in dealing with the internal insurgencies. There was a marked increase in drone and air strikes. According to the New America Foundation, strikes rose from 12 in 2011 to 56 (47 drone and 9 air) in 2012. One such strike in May 2012 killed Fahd al-Quso, who had been on the FBI's Most Wanted Terrorist list in connection with the bombing of the USS *Cole* in October 2000. The special operations troops withdrawn from Yemen at the height of the country's tumult in 2011 had returned by the spring of 2012. The special operators have both training and intelligence responsibilities, and provide Yemeni government forces with targeting data derived from satellite imagery, drone video, and intercepted communications.[11]

The incidence of drone and air strikes reportedly decreased in 2013 (25 drone and 1 air), according to the New America Foundation (*The Long War*

Journal also puts the total at 26). The most contentious of these strikes came in December when a JSOC attack apparently mistook a wedding party for an al-Qaeda convoy. Although a nonbinding vote in Yemen's parliament was nearly unanimous in its call for an end to drone strikes, the importance of the drones to the U.S.-Yemeni campaign against al-Qaeda saw President Hadi support their continued use in 2014. Through mid-November 2014, *The Long War Journal* reported 23 alleged drone strikes in Yemen, with three strikes coming on April 19–21 in support of a major government offensive in the mountains of southern Yemen. Beyond drone strikes, it was reported that U.S. assistance included pilots for the helicopters that carried Yemeni commandos to their attack on an AQAP training site. There was no indication as to whether the pilots were special forces operators or contractors.[12] In January 2015, minority Shiite al-Houthi militias seized control of Sana, displacing President Hadi's government and raising doubts about Yemen's viability as a state. How the al-Houthi takeover and the continuing violence in the country will affect the U.S. counterterrorism campaign against AQAP remains to be determined.

In or Out of Somalia?

The traumatic events of the 1993 Battle of Mogadishu (memorialized as "Black Hawk Down") cast a pall over U.S. interest in that chaotic country. However, the growing influence of al-Qaeda operatives in Somalia became a serious concern to U.S. national security policy makers in the early 2000s. By June 2006, the fundamentalist Islamic Courts Union (ICU) and its radical arm, al-Shabab, had pushed an uneasy grouping of secular Somali warlords (the Alliance for the Restoration of Peace and Counter-Terrorism) and their militias out of most of Mogadishu.

In December 2006, concerns about the nature of the ICU convinced Ethiopia, with American backing, to invade Somalia, oust the Islamists from Mogadishu, and shore up the weak UN-sponsored Transitional Federal Government. Although the Ethiopians withdrew in January 2009, al-Shabab was by then leading a full-blown insurgency. The United States used the Ethiopian action as a cover for initiating a new covert operation against al-Qaeda, this one involving special operations personnel. A task force comprised of SEALs and Army Special Forces was "temporarily" deployed to a base in Dire Dawa in eastern Ethiopia, along with AC-130 Spectre gunships. The gunships were used in several targeted attacks on presumed locations of al-Shabab leaders, but it was not until May 2008 that a major figure was struck. Intensive intelligence collection efforts led to a Tomahawk missile strike that killed one of al-Shabab's military commanders, Aden Hashi Ayro.[13]

A proposal to the new administration of Barack Obama from then-JSOC commander Adm. William McRaven to mount a full-fledged counterterrorism war in Somalia was discussed but ultimately rejected by the White House. Nonetheless, individual operations in Somalia against al-Qaeda were generally approved but still required the president's personal approval. A raid in September 2009 into territory in southern Somalia controlled by al-Shabab killed one of the most wanted Islamic militants in Africa, Saleh Ali Saleh Nabhan, who was regarded as a link between al-Shabab and al-Qaeda. Working on the basis of precise intelligence on the location of their target, Navy SEALs were transported by helicopters from a ship offshore. The special operators fired from the air on the vehicle in which Nabhan was traveling, landed, and retrieved his and other bodies.

In a non-terrorism-related action, a team of U.S. special operations forces parachuted into central Somalia in January 2012 and rescued two kidnapped international aid workers, an American woman and a Danish man. Officials said the nine gunmen holding the hostages were killed in an exchange of gunfire. This type of precision raid is only accomplished when solid intelligence is available. In October 2013, Navy SEALs raided the coastal home of an al-Shabab leader. After a substantial firefight that included the use of helicopter gunships, the SEALs withdrew having sustained no casualties but without capturing the housing compound or its owner. Almost a year later, in September 2014, a special operations airstrike using manned and unmanned aircraft achieved a different result. According to Pentagon press secretary Rear Adm. John Kirby, Hellfire missiles and precision bombs killed al-Shabab's leader Ahmed Abdi Godane and a number of the members of his entourage.[14]

Where Now?

Covert operations in general have been and will undoubtedly remain a contentious issue for the American political system and public. Presidents from the founding of this country to the present have found it necessary or at least expedient to try to conceal certain actions involving foreign and national security matters with a veil of secrecy.

In 2004, the 9/11 Commission (formally the National Commission on Terrorist Attacks Upon the United States) made a sweeping recommendation focused on one of the most controversial aspects of covert operation—paramilitary activities:

> Lead responsibility for directing and executing paramilitary operations, whether clandestine or covert, should shift to the Defense Department.

There it should be consolidated with the capabilities for training, direction, and execution of such operations already being developed in the
Special Operations Command. . . . [T]he United States cannot afford to
build two separate capabilities for carrying out secret military operations,
secretly operating standoff missiles, and secretly training foreign military
or paramilitary forces. The United States should concentrate responsibility and necessary legal authorities in one entity.[15]

This is not the first time—nor will it be the last—that such a recommendation has been made. Nonetheless, 10 years after a number of the commission's recommendations were legislatively enacted—including one that
added another layer of bureaucracy to the U.S. Intelligence Community (the
director of national intelligence)—this concept seems no more likely to be
enacted than when it was made.

One aspect of the commission's recommendations remains under discussion
on Capitol Hill, in the media, and among academics. That is, whether operational control of armed drones or what the 9/11 Commission termed *standoff*
missiles should rest with civilian or military agencies or both depending on the
circumstances. Beyond the operational control issue, however, there is the
deeper and more troubling question of whether the United States even should
be engaged in targeted strikes that amount to extrajudicial killing. Do U.S.
citizens surrender their constitutional rights when they swear allegiance to a
foreign ideology antithetical to this country? Do non-U.S. persons who want
to harm Americans have no rights? Does declaring such individuals enemy
combatants justify taking their lives without due process? The answers to these
questions are not just legal matters but require determinations of what is moral
and ethical—or, perhaps, even what is right. These are difficult decisions.[16]

Over the years since the United States created its first peacetime, civilian
intelligence agency after World War II and gave it the responsibility for conducting covert political and paramilitary actions, the executive and legislative branches of the government have incrementally worked out the means
for providing a level of accountability for presidents' secret decisions. The
system is imperfect, as such deviations as Iran-Contra have shown; but it is
backed up today by a world increasingly tied together by virtually instantaneous communications. Stated simply, it has grown harder and harder to conduct a truly covert operation. That private individuals or organizations can
follow and report on supposedly secret drone strikes illustrates this phenome-
non. There are also the "unofficial" comments that appear in the media from
unnamed officials about ostensibly covert matters. Neither the motivation
nor the accuracy of such statements is necessarily clear. A case in point is the
reporting over the last few years about supposedly covert American support to
the rebels fighting in Syria against the regime of Bashar al-Assad.

It seems as though covert has come to mean little more than "officially unacknowledged" by the U.S. government. The question of what is a covert operation has been further clouded by the growth in size and responsibilities of U.S. Special Operations Forces that accelerated under Defense Secretary Donald Rumsfeld following the 9/11 attacks. Beyond the recognized battlefields, the U.S. military has been expanding its activities in the covert war against terrorism under a Joint Unconventional Warfare Task Force Execute Order, signed in September 2009 by then-Central Command commander in chief Gen. David Petraeus. The Execute Order reflects an expansive view of the military's role in addressing the challenge of diverse militant and terrorist groups around the world.[17] The actions under the Execute Order do not require the president's approval or reports to Congress. Such activities are covered by Title 10 of the U.S. Code, rather than the Title 50 requirements under which the CIA functions. This presents the question of whether the rules mandating a presidential authorization and notice to Congress for a CIA paramilitary operation should also apply to similar covert military operations. President Obama has undertaken to provide after-the-fact notification to Congress when JSOC units engage in certain kinds of activities. Nevertheless, that is something that he is doing primarily as a courtesy and as good politics absent a requirement.

Outgoing United States Special Operations Command commander Adm. McRaven in August 2014 suggested the geographic range of unconventional activities being undertaken by his command. He noted that "U.S. Special Operations Forces are helping to fight the fast-growing Islamic State in Iraq; the al Qaeda-linked Abu Sayyaf in the Philippines; the militant group Boko Haram in Nigeria, and al Qaeda and the Taliban in the Afghanistan-Pakistan region."[18] McRaven did not include in his list the ongoing operations against AQAP in Yemen and al-Shabab in Somalia. Nor did he mention the October 2013 capture in Tripoli, Libya, of Abu Anas al-Libi, a Libyan militant indicted in 2000 for his role in the 1998 bombings of the American embassies in Kenya and Tanzania, or the daring but unsuccessful operation in the summer of 2014 to rescue photojournalist James Foley and other Americans being held in Syria by Islamic State militants.[19]

In evaluating the use of covert operations, whether it is a propaganda campaign, a paramilitary operation, or something in between, it is necessary to keep in mind that such activities represent a tool of the moment, resorted to when diplomacy is not achieving the desired effect and overt warfare is not feasible or desirable for any number of reasons. Covert operations are a tactical act of the now, and do not necessarily produce outcomes that will endure over time. In no way are covert operations a replacement for a military strategy or a political policy, although they have certainly been used as a substitute when well-articulated strategies and policies were lacking. Nevertheless, they have had their place in how American presidents have chosen to confront compelling national interests that seemingly could not be met by more traditional and open means.

Notes

1. See Tim Arango, "Syrian War's Spillover Threatens a Fragile Iraq," *New York Times*, September 24, 2012; Tim Arango and Michael S. Schmidt, "Last Convoy of American Troops Leaves Iraq," *New York Times*, December 18, 2011; Catherine Dale, *Operation Iraqi Freedom: Strategies, Approaches, Results, and Issues for Congress* (Washington, DC: Congressional Research Service, Library of Congress, April 2, 2009), pp. 3–5; and Missy Ryan, "U.S. Special Forces Sent to Train Iraqi Special Forces in Jordan," *Reuters*, March 7, 2014.

2. Rebecca Kaplan, "How Many U.S. Troops Are Currently in Iraq?" *CBS News*, July 1, 2014; Richard Sisk, "US Sends Green Berets to Northern Iraq," *Military.com*, July 3, 2014; and Justin Worland and Zeke J. Miller, "Obama Authorizes Deployment of 1,500 Troops to Iraq," *Time*, November 7, 2014.

3. Barack Obama, "Remarks by the President in Address to the Nation on the Way Forward in Afghanistan and Pakistan" (Washington, DC: The White House, December 1, 2009), at: http://www.whitehouse.gov/the-press-office/remarks-president-address-nation-way-forward-afghanistan-and-pakistan; Barbara Starr, "Obama Approves Afghanistan Troop Increase," *CNN*, February 17, 2009; and Bob Woodward, *Obama's War* (New York: Simon & Schuster, 2010).

4. Mark Mazzetti, "C.I.A. Takes On Bigger and Riskier Role on Front Lines," *New York Times*, January 1, 2010; Greg Miller, "CIA Expanding Presence in Afghanistan," *Los Angeles Times*, September 20, 2009; U.S. Central Intelligence Agency, "Statement on CIA Casualties in Afghanistan," December 31, 2009, at: https://www.cia.gov/news-information/press-releases-statements/cia-casualties-in-afghanistan.html; Joby Warrick and Pamela Constable, "CIA Base Attacked in Afghanistan Supported Airstrikes against al-Qaeda, Taliban," *Washington Post*, January 1, 2010, A01; and Woodward, *Obama's War*, p. 355.

5. Greg Miller, "CIA Closing Bases in Afghanistan as It Shifts Focus amid Military Drawdown," *Washington Post*, July 23, 2013; and Craig Whitlock, "Final 'Surge' Troops Leave Afghanistan," *Washington Post*, September 20, 2012.

6. Sudarsan Raghavan and Karen DeYoung, "U.S. and Afghanistan Sign Vital, Long-Delayed Security Pact," *Washington Post*, September 30, 2014; and Josh Smith and Slobodan Lekic, "Accord to Keep US Troops in Afghanistan Signed in Kabul," *Stars and Stripes*, September 30, 2014. See also John Kerry, "Press Statement: Signing of Bilateral Security Agreement and NATO Status of Forces Agreement" (Washington, DC: Department of State, September 30, 2014), at: http://www.state.gov/secretary/remarks/2014/09/232329.htm.

7. See Peter Baker, Helene Cooper, and Mark Mazzetti, "Bin Laden Is Dead, Obama Says," *New York Times*, May 1, 2011; Peter Bergen, "Who Really Killed bin Laden?" *CNN*, March 27, 2013; and Nicholas Schmidle, "Getting bin Laden: What Happened that Night in Abbottabad," *New Yorker*, August 8, 2011.

8. Julian E. Barnes and Adam Entous, "U.S. Erred in Deadly Attack," *Wall Street Journal*, December 22, 2011; and Salmon Masood and Eric Schmitt, "Tensions Flare Between U.S. and Pakistan after Strike," *New York Times*, November 26, 2011.

9. New America Foundation, at: http://securitydata.newamerica.net/; and *The Long War Journal*, at: http://www.longwarjournal.org/.

10. Peter Finn, "Secret U.S. Memo Sanctioned Killing of Aulaqi," *Washington Post*, September 30, 2011; Mark Mazzetti, *The Way of the Knife: The CIA, a Secret Army, and a War at the Ends of the Earth* (New York: Penguin Press, 2013), pp. 229–34, 302–10; and *Reuters*, "Yemen Strike Kills Mediator, Tribemen Hit Pipeline," May 25, 2010.

11. *CBS/AP*, "Top al Qaeda Figure Killed in Yemen Air Strike," May 6, 2012; Ken Dilanian and David S. Cloud, "U.S. Escalates Clandestine War in Yemen," *Los Angeles Times*, May 16, 2012; and New America Foundation, "Drone Wars Yemen: Analysis," at: http://natsec.newamerica.net/drones/yemen/analysis.

12. Hakim Almasmari, "Drone Strikes Must End, Yemen's Parliament Says," *CNN*, December 15, 2013; Mohammed Jamjoom and Barbara Starr, "Official: Extensive U.S. Involvement in Anti-Terror Operation in Yemen," *CNN*, April 22, 2014; *The Long War Journal*, "Charting the Data for US Airstrikes in Yemen, 2002–2014," at: http://www.longwarjournal.org/yemen-strikes.php; New America Foundation, "Drone Wars Yemen: Analysis," at: http://securitydata.newamerica.net/drones/yemen/analysis; and Robert F. Worth, "Drone Strike in Yemen Hits Wedding Convoy, Killing 11," *New York Times*, December 12, 2013.

13. Mazzetti, *The Way of the Knife*, pp. 131–43, 147–51, 242–47; and Eric Schmitt and Jeffrey Gettleman, "Qaeda Leader Reported Killed in Somalia," *New York Times*, May 2, 2008.

14. Helene Cooper, Eric Schmitt, and Jeffrey Gettleman, "Strikes Killed Militant Chief in Somalia, U.S. Reports," *New York Times*, September 6, 2014, p. A4; Karen DeYoung, "U.S. Says Raid in Somalia Killed Terrorist with Links to Al-Qaeda," *Washington Post*, September 15, 2009; David D. Kirkpatrick, Nicholas Kulish, and Eric Schmitt, "U.S. Commando Raids Hit Terror Targets in 2 Nations," *New York Times*, October 6, 2013, A1; Chris Lawrence, "U.S. Special Forces Rescue Somalia Aid Workers," *CNN*, January 26, 2012; and Mazzetti, *The Way of the Knife*, pp. 242–47.

15. National Commission on Terrorist Attacks Upon the United States, *The 9/11 Commission Report*, July 22, 2004, pp. 415–16, at: http://www.9-11commission.gov/report/911Report.pdf.

16. For a discussion of some of these issues, see John O. Brennan, "The Ethics and Efficacy of the President's Counterterrorism Strategy" (Transcript), April 30, 2012 (Woodrow Wilson International Center for Scholars), at: http://www.wilsoncenter.org/event/the-efficacy-and-ethics-us-counterterrorism-strategy.

17. Mark Mazzetti, "U.S. Is Said to Expand Secret Actions in Mideast," *New York Times*, May 24, 2010, A1.

18. Peter Bergen, "The Man Who Hunted bin Laden, Saddam and the Pirates," *CNN*, August 30, 2014.

19. David D. Kirkpatrick, Nicholas Kulish, and Eric Schmitt, "U.S. Commando Raids Hit Terror Targets in 2 Nations," *New York Times*, October 6, 2013, A1; and Adam Goldman and Karen DeYoung, "U.S. Staged Secret Operation into Syria in Failed Bid to Rescue Americans," *Washington Post*, August 20, 2014.

Selected Bibliography

Websites

Government

Foreign Relations of the United States. At: http://history.state.gov/historicaldocuments
"[T]he official documentary historical record of major U.S. foreign policy decisions and significant diplomatic activity."

Nongovernment

Federation of American Scientists Intelligence Resource Program. At: http://www.fas.org/irp/
Official and unofficial materials on intelligence policy, structure, and operations.

The Literature of Intelligence: A Bibliography of Materials, with Essays, Reviews, and Comments. At: http://intellit.muskingum.edu
Annotated listings by topics and authors of books and articles on intelligence from ancient times to the present.

Loyola University Political Science Department Strategic Intelligence Site. At: http://www.loyola.edu/departments/academics/political-science/strategic-intelligence/index.html
Useful for links to additional sites. Excellent starting point for Web searches.

Encyclopedias

O'Toole, George J. A. *The Encyclopedia of American Intelligence and Espionage: From the Revolutionary War to the Present.* New York: Facts on File, 1988.
Excellent for U.S. intelligence and the time period. Usually accurate, thoughtful selection criteria, avoids polemics.

Polmar, Norman, and Thomas B. Allen. *Spy Book: The Encyclopedia of Espionage.* 2nd ed. New York: Random House, 2004.
Most accurate and comprehensive intelligence encyclopedia available. Reliable but not perfect in all its details.

General

Ameringer, Charles D. *U.S. Foreign Intelligence: The Secret Side of American History.* Lexington, MA: Lexington Books, 1990.
Readable review of U.S. intelligence, including covert operations, through the Reagan administration.

Andrew, Christopher. *For the President's Eyes Only: Secret Intelligence and the American Presidency from Washington to Bush.* New York: HarperCollins, 1995.
Mostly how modern presidents used or misused intelligence. Strong on intelligence in presidential decision-making during Cold War.

Daugherty, William J. *Executive Secrets: Covert Action and the Presidency.* Lexington: University Press of Kentucky, 2004.
Overview of nature and use of covert action operations as tool of U.S. presidents in executing national security policy.

Kinzer, Stephen. *Overthrow: America's Century of Regime Change from Hawaii to Iraq.* New York: Times Books, 2006.
Over polemical at times, but covers the period.

Knott, Stephen F. *Secret and Sanctioned: Covert Operations and the American Presidency.* New York: Oxford University Press, 1996.
Focuses on use by U.S. presidents of covert operations during 1776–1882.

O'Toole, George J. A. *Honorable Treachery: A History of U.S. Intelligence, Espionage, and Covert Action from the American Revolution to the CIA.* New York: Atlantic Monthly Press, 1991.
Well-done history of U.S. intelligence from revolution to 1962. Reads well; presents subject matter in an informed fashion.

Prados, John. *Safe for Democracy: The Secret Wars of the CIA.* Chicago: Ivan R. Dee, Publisher, 2006.
Essentially an attack on covert operations, but provides many details.

Treverton, Gregory F. *Covert Action: The Limits of Intervention in the Postwar World.* New York: Basic Books, 1987.
Dated but still useful. Concludes that major covert actions increasingly will become public.

Revolutionary War

Allen, Thomas B. *George Washington, Spymaster: How the Americans Outspied the British and Won the Revolutionary War.* Washington, DC: National Geographic, 2004.
Well-written, interesting look at Washington as spymaster and user of intelligence.

Bakeless, John. *Turncoats, Traitors and Heroes: Espionage in the American Revolution.* New York: Da Capo Press, 2005.
Originally published in 1959 but still worth a read today.

U.S. Central Intelligence Agency. *Intelligence in the War of Independence.* Washington, DC: U.S. Central Intelligence Agency, 1976. At: https://www.cia.gov/library/

center-for-the-study-of-intelligence/csi-publications/books-and-monographs/ intelligence/index.html.
Excellent introduction to the subject. Issued as part of bicentennial.

Civil War

Allen, Thomas. *Intelligence in the Civil War*. Washington, DC: Central Intelligence Agency, 2006. At: https://www.cia.gov/library/publications/additional-publications/civil-war/index.html.
An excellent, brief introduction to the subject.

Feis, William B. *Grant's Secret Service: The Intelligence War from Belmont to Appomattox*. Lincoln: University of Nebraska Press, 2002.
Focuses on Grant's use of intelligence, first, in command in the western theater and, then, in command of the Army of the Potomac.

Fishel, Edwin C. *The Secret War for the Union: The Untold Story of Military Intelligence in the Civil War*. Boston: Houghton Mifflin, 1996.
Covers military intelligence in the eastern theater, predominantly on the Union side, through Gettysburg.

Sutherland, Daniel E. *A Savage Conflict: The Decisive Role of Guerrillas in the American Civil War*. Chapel Hill: University of North Carolina Press, 2009.
Ugly story that shows tremendous research and is well written.

Tidwell, William A., with James O. Hall and David Winfield Gaddy. *Come Retribution: The Confederate Secret Service and the Assassination of Lincoln*. Jackson: University Press of Mississippi, 1988.
Circumstantial and inferential argument for a Confederate covert action.

Spanish-American War

O'Toole, George J. A. *The Spanish War: An American Epic*. New York: Norton, 1984.
Good coverage of intelligence aspects of war, but little on covert operations.

World War I

The "Records of the Committee on Public Information" are available on the National Archives site: http://www.archives.gov/research/guide-fed-records/groups/063.html#top.

World War II

Breuer, William B. *MacArthur's Undercover War: Spies, Saboteurs, Guerrillas and Secret Missions*. Edison, NJ: Castle Books, 1995.
This is an easy read, although the language at times is over dramatic.

Brown, Anthony Cave, ed. *The Secret War Report of the OSS*. New York: Berkley, 1976.
Edited version of official report prepared immediately after the war and declassified in 1976. Dry reading, but regarded as generally accurate.

McIntosh, Elizabeth P. *Sisterhood of Spies: The Women of the OSS*. Annapolis, MD: Naval Institute Press, 1998.
  Served with OSS in the Far East. Illuminating look at women at war in the field of intelligence, without overdoing the drama.

Waller, Douglas. *Wild Bill Donovan: The Spymaster Who Created the OSS and Modern American Espionage*. New York: Free Press, 2011.
  A well-documented contribution to intelligence history.

Warner, Michael. *The Office of Strategic Services: America's First Intelligence Agency*. Washington, DC: Central Intelligence Agency, 2000. At: https://www.cia.gov/library/center-for-the-study-of-intelligence/csi-publications/books-and-monographs/oss.
  An easy-to-read presentation that provides lots of information.

Early Cold War

Darling, Arthur B. *The Central Intelligence Agency: An Instrument of Government, to 1950*. University Park: Penn State Press, 1990.
  Useful for his account of the establishment of the Office of Policy Coordination (OPC).

Grose, Peter. *Operation Rollback: America's Secret War behind the Iron Curtain*. Boston and New York: Houghton Mifflin, 2000.
  Well-researched and short (222 pages) account of sabotage, espionage, and covert action against postwar Eastern Europe and the Soviet Union.

Montague, Ludwell Lee. *General Walter Bedell Smith as Director of Central Intelligence, October 1950–February 1953*. University Park: Penn State Press, 1992.
  This is very much an inside look at Smith's transformation of the Central Intelligence Agency.

Pisani, Sallie. *The CIA and the Marshall Plan*. Lawrence: University Press of Kansas, 1991.
  The focus is on Frank Wisner's OPC.

Troy, Thomas F. *Donovan and the CIA: A History of the Establishment of the Central Intelligence Agency*. Frederick, MD: University Publications of America, 1981.
  Represents a serious, scholarly effort with the materials available at the time.

Wilford, Hugh. *The Mighty Wurlitzer: How the CIA Played America*. Cambridge, MA: Harvard University Press, 2008.
  An easy read covering the CIA's creation and funding of front organizations.

Korean War

Haas, Michael E. *In the Devil's Shadow: U.N. Special Operations during the Korean War*. Annapolis, MD: Naval Institute Press, 2000.
  Provides political-military context for on-the-ground activities.

Holober, Frank. *Raiders of the China Coast: CIA Covert Operations during the Korean War*. Annapolis, MD: Naval Institute Press, 1999.
  Operations from the islands against the mainland.

Overthrow in Iran

Koch, Scott A. *"Zendebad, Shah!" The Central Intelligence Agency and the Fall of Iranian Prime ·Minister Mohammed Mossadeq, August 1953*. Washington, DC: History Staff, Central Intelligence Agency, June 1998. At: http://www2.gwu.edu/~nsarchiv/NSAEBB/NSAEBB126/iran980600.pdf.
Essential but redactions make it difficult reading.

Roosevelt, Kermit. *Countercoup: The Struggle for the Control of Iran*. New York: McGraw-Hill, 1979.
Details the planning and execution of Operation AJAX.

Wilber, Donald. *Clandestine Service History: Overthrow of Premier Mossadeq of Iran, November 1952–August 1953*. Washington, DC: Central Intelligence Agency, March 1954. At: http://www.nytimes.com/library/world/mideast/041600iran-cia-index.html.
Written close to event by a participant.

Overthrow in Guatemala

Cullather, Nicholas. *Operation PBSUCCESS: The United States and Guatemala, 1952–1954*. Washington, DC: History Staff, Center for the Study of Intelligence, Central Intelligence Agency, 1994. At: http://www2.gwu.edu/~nsarchiv/NSAEBB/NSAEBB4/cia-guatemala5_b.html.

Indonesia

Conboy, Kenneth, and James Morrison. *Feet to the Fire: Covert Operations in Indonesia, 1957–1958*. Annapolis, MD: Naval Institute Press, 1999.
Operational details galore.

Tibet

Knaus, John Kenneth. *Orphans of the Cold War: America and the Tibetan Struggle for Survival*. New York: Public Affairs, 1999.
A well-written book that shares the author's emotional attachment to people involved in this operation.

Cuba and the Bay of Pigs

Bohning, Don. *The Castro Obsession: U.S. Covert Operations against Cuba, 1959–1965*. Washington, DC: Potomac Books, Inc., 2005.
This work provides a balanced and insightful presentation.

Pfeiffer, Jack. *Official History of the Bay of Pigs Operation*. 4 vols. At: http://www2.gwu.edu/~nsarchiv/NSAEBB/NSAEBB355/.
The fifth volume of this official history remains classified.

The Congo

Devlin, Larry. *Chief of Station, Congo: A Memoir of 1960–67.* New York: Public Affairs, 2007.

This book places the reader about as close to the world of a CIA chief of station as is likely to find its way into print.

Robarge, David. "CIA's Covert Operations in the Congo, 1960–1968: Insights from Newly Declassified Documents." *Studies in Intelligence* 58, no. 3 (September 2014): 1–9.

Provides an excellent, readable overview of CIA covert operations in the Congo.

Vietnam

Ahern, Thomas L. Jr. *Vietnam Declassified: The CIA and Counterinsurgency.* Lexington: University Press of Kentucky, 2009.

Focus is on the operations and programs to suppress the Viet Cong and win the hearts and minds of the Vietnamese masses.

Shultz, Richard H. Jr. *The Secret War against Hanoi: Kennedy and Johnson's Use of Spies, Saboteurs, and Covert Warriors in North Vietnam.* New York: HarperCollins, 1999.

Superb work covering activities of Studies and Observation Group; puts its role into broader perspective of the War.

Laos

Ahern, Thomas L. Jr. *Undercover Armies: CIA and Surrogate Warfare in Laos, 1961–1973.* Washington, DC: Center for the Study of Intelligence, Central Intelligence Agency, 2006. At: http://today.ttu.edu/wp-content/uploads/2009/03/06-undercover-armies.pdf.

Anthony, Victor B., and Richard R. Sexton. *The United States Air Force in Southeast Asia: The War in Northern Laos, 1954–1973.* Washington, DC: Center for Air Force History, United States Air Force, 1993. At: http://www.gwu.edu/~nsarchiv/NSAEBB/NSAEBB248/war_in_northern_laos.pdf.

Investigations

Johnson, Loch K. *A Season of Inquiry: The Senate Intelligence Investigation.* Lexington: University Press of Kentucky, 1985.

Professor and Church Committee staffer details the committee's inner workings and the inception of today's Congressional oversight.

U.S. Congress. Senate. Select Committee to Study Governmental Operations with Respect to Intelligence Activities [Church Committee]. *Interim Report: Alleged Assassination Plots Involving Foreign Leaders.* 94th Congress, 1st Session, S. Report No. 94-465. Washington, DC: GPO, 1975. At: http://www.intelligence.senate.gov/pdfs94th/94465.pdf.

Operations in Chile

Church Committee. Staff Report. *Covert Action in Chile: 1963–1973*. Washington, DC: GPO, 1975. At: http://www.intelligence.senate.gov/pdfs94th/94chile.pdf.

U.S. Central Intelligence Agency. *CIA Activities in Chile*. September 18, 2000. At: https://www.cia.gov/library/reports/general-reports-1/chile/index.html.

Cold War in Perspective

Gates, Robert M. *From the Shadows: The Ultimate Insider's Story of Five Presidents and How They Won the Cold War*. New York: Simon & Schuster, 1996.
Good read from former DCI (and future defense secretary). Stresses extraordinary continuity of U.S. policy from Nixon to Bush.

Special Forces

Marquis, Susan L. *Unconventional Warfare: Rebuilding U.S. Special Operations Forces*. Washington, DC: Brookings Institution, 1997.
Provides overview of the problems special forces faced by late 1970s, and tells the story of the effort to rejuvenate them in the early 1980s.

United States Special Operations Command. *United States Special Operations Command: History*. 6th ed. MacDill Air Force Base, 2008. At: http://www.socom.mil/Documents/history6thedition.pdf.

Iran-Contra

U.S. Congress. *Report of the Committees Investigating the Iran-Contra Affair, with Supplemental, Minority, and Additional Views*. S. Rept. No. 100–216, H. Rept. No. 100–433, 100th Congress, First Session. Washington, DC: Government Printing Office, 1987.

Walsh, Lawrence E. *Final Report of the Independent Counsel for Iran-Contra Matters, Vol 1: Investigations and Prosecutions*. Washington, DC: United States Court of Appeals for the District of Columbia Circuit, August 4, 1993. At: http://www.fas.org/irp/offdocs/walsh.

Woodward, Bob. *Veil: The Secret Wars of the CIA, 1981–1987*. New York: Simon & Schuster, 1987.
For anyone interested in this period, this is a must read, although it does not represent the last word on his central subject—Bill Casey.

Vying for Afghanistan

Bearden, Milt, and James Risen. *The Main Enemy: The Inside Story of the CIA's Final Showdown with the KGB*. New York: Random House, 2003.
Direct to the reader from the front lines of the Cold War.

Coll, Steve. *Ghost Wars: The Secret History of the CIA, Afghanistan, and Bin Laden, from the Soviet Invasion to September 10, 2001.* New York: Penguin, 2004.
Compelling reading, well written but not easygoing because of the massive amount of detail included.

Crile, George. *Charlie Wilson's War: The Extraordinary Story of the Largest Covert Operation in History.* New York: Atlantic Monthly, 2003.
A rollicking tale but not completely trustworthy in all its details.

Invasion of Panama

Cole, Ronald H. *Operation Just Cause: The Planning and Execution of Joint Operations in Panama, February 1988–January 1990.* Washington, DC: Joint History Office, Office of the Chairman of the Joint Chiefs of Staff, 1995. At: http:// www.dtic.mil/doctrine/doctrine/history/justcaus.pdf.

Persian Gulf War

Atkinson, Rick. *Crusade: The Untold Story of the Persian Gulf War.* Boston: Houghton Mifflin, 1993.
Covers military, diplomatic, and political aspects; Schwarzkopf dominates.

Post-9/11: General

National Commission on Terrorist Attacks Upon the United States. *The 9/11 Commission Report.* July 22, 2004.
At: http://www.9-11commission.gov/report/911Report.pdf.

Tenet, George J., with Bill Harlow. *At the Center of the Storm: My Years at the CIA.* New York: HarperCollins, 2007.
Tenet admits mistakes, his and the Agency's, but wants the world to know about the successes that were also achieved.

Post-9/11: Afghanistan

Camp, Dick. *Boots on the Ground: The Fight to Liberate Afghanistan from Al-Qaeda and the Taliban 2001–2002.* Minneapolis, MN: Zenith Press, 2011.
Provides detailed descriptions of CIA-military operations through Operation ANACONDA.

Schroen, Gary C. *First In: An Insider's Account of How the CIA Spearheaded the War on Terror in Afghanistan.* Novato, CA: Presidio, 2005; and Berntsen, Gary, and Ralph Pezzullo. *Jawbreaker: The Attack on Bin Laden and Al Qaeda: A Personal Account by the CIA's Key Field Commander.* New York: Crown, 2005.
Read together—Schroen, first; then, Berntsen and Pezzullo—these books tell the story of the post-9/11 attack on al-Qaeda and its Taliban patrons, and represent a stunningly detailed view of a major paramilitary operation.

Stanton, Doug. *Horse Soldiers: The Extraordinary Story of a Band of U.S. Soldiers Who Rode to Victory in Afghanistan.* New York: Scribner, 2009.
Tells the Special Forces side of the defeat of the Taliban in 2001, although the war had not ended at the point he decided to end his narrative.

U.S. Senate. Committee on Foreign Relations. *Tora Bora Revisited: How We Failed to Get bin Laden and Why It Matters Today.* Staff Report. Washington, DC: Government Printing Office, 2009. At: http://www.gpo.gov/fdsys/pkg/CPRT-111SPRT53709/html/CPRT-111SPRT53709.htm.

Woodward, Bob. *Bush at War.* New York: Simon & Schuster, 2002.
Going to war after the 9/11 attacks.

Post-9/11: Iraq

Tucker, Mike, and Charles Faddis. *Operation Hotel California: The Clandestine War inside Iraq.* Guildford, CT: Lyons Press, 2008.
First-hand account of working with the Kurds in preparation for Operation IRAQI FREEDOM.

United States. Department of Defense. *Conduct of the Persian Gulf Conflict: An Interim Report to Congress.* Washington, DC: July, 1991. At: http://www.dod.mil/pubs/foi/operation_and_plans/PersianGulfWar/305.pdf.

Woodward, Bob. *Plan of Attack.* New York: Simon & Schuster, 2004.
How and why President Bush decided to go to war.

Obama Administration

Mazzetti, Mark. *The Way of the Knife: The CIA, a Secret Army, and a War at the Ends of the Earth.* New York: Penguin Press, 2013.
Provides a close look at a motley crew of freelancers and contractors.

Woodward, Bob. *Obama's Wars.* New York: Simon & Schuster, 2010.
The focus is the decision on the surge in Afghanistan.

Index

About the Author

J. RANSOM CLARK, J. D., served 25 years with the Central Intelligence Agency, including assignments in Asia, Europe, Latin America, the Middle East, and Washington, D.C. After retiring from the Senior Intelligence Service, Professor Clark taught political science courses and held administrative positions at Muskingum University, New Concord, Ohio. The author of *Intelligence and National Security: A Reference Handbook* (Westport, CT: Praeger, 2007), his extensive and widely used website on intelligence—*The Literature of Intelligence: A Bibliography of Materials, with Essays, Reviews, and Comments*—is publicly available at http://intellit.muskingum.edu. Clark is a member of the Editorial Advisory Board of the *International Journal of Intelligence and CounterIntelligence*.